The Objects of Evidence

THE OBJECTS OF EVIDENCE

Anthropological Approaches to the Production of Knowledge

EDITED BY MATTHEW ENGELKE

WILEY-BLACKWELL
A John Wiley & Sons, Ltd., Publication

Royal Anthropological Institute

This edition first published 2009
Originally published as Volume 14, Special Issue April 2008, of *The Journal of the Royal Anthropological Society*
© 2009 Royal Anthropological Institute of Great Britain & Ireland

Blackwell Publishing was acquired by John Wiley & Sons in February 2007. Blackwell's publishing program has been merged with Wiley's global Scientific, Technical, and Medical business to form Wiley-Blackwell.

Registered Office
John Wiley & Sons Ltd, The Atrium, Southern Gate, Chichester, West Sussex, PO19 8SQ, United Kingdom

Editorial Offices
350 Main Street, Malden, MA 02148–5020, USA
9600 Garsington Road, Oxford, OX4 2DQ, UK
The Atrium, Southern Gate, Chichester, West Sussex, PO19 8SQ, UK

For details of our global editorial offices, for customer services, and for information about how to apply for permission to reuse the copyright material in this book please see our website at www.wiley.com/wiley-blackwell.

The right of Matthew Engelke to be identified as the author of the editorial material in this work has been asserted in accordance with the Copyright, Designs and Patents Act 1988.

Library of Congress Cataloging-in-Publication Data

Engelke, Matthew Eric.
  The objects of evidence : anthropological approaches to the production of
knowledge / edited by Matthew Engelke.
        p. cm.
  "Originally published as Volume 14, Special Issue April 2008, of The Journal of the Royal
Anthropological Society"—T.p. verso.
  Includes bibliographical references and index.
  ISBN 978-1-4051-9296-5 (pbk. : alk. paper)
  1. Anthropology—Research.   2. Evidence.   I. Journal of the Royal
Anthropological Institute. II. Title.

  GN42.E56 2009
  301.072—dc22

                                                                2008052042

A catalogue record for this book is available from the British Library.

Set in 10/12pt Minion by SNP Best-set Typesetter Ltd., Hong Kong

01   2009

Contents

Notes on editor and contributors

Matthew Engelke is a lecturer in anthropology at the London School of Economics and Political Science. He is a specialist on Zimbabwe and the anthropology of religion, and has developed interests more recently on religion and public culture in England. His book, *A Problem of Presence: Beyond Scripture in an African Church* (University of California Press, 2007), won the 2008 Clifford Geertz Prize. He is the co-editor (with Matt Tomlinson) of *The Limits of Meaning: Case Studies in the Anthropology of Christianity* (Berghahn Books, 2006) and the editor of the Prickly Paradigm Press.

Rita Astuti is a Reader in Anthropology at the London School of Economics and Political Science. She has conducted fieldwork among the Vezo of Madagascar and her writings have focused on issues of gender, ethnic identity, and kinship. In her more recent work, she has combined anthropological and psychological methods to explore how Vezo children construct the adult understanding of the social and supernatural world. She is the author of *People of the sea* (Cambridge University Press, 1995) and *Constraints on conceptual development* (with G. Solomon & S. Carey, Blackwell, 2004).

Maurice Bloch is emeritus Professor of Anthropology at the London School of Economics and Political Science. He is the author of many books, including, most recently, *Essays on cultural transmission* (Berg, 2005).

Sharad Chari is a human geographer at the London School of Economics and Political Science, affiliated to Development Studies at the University of KwaZulu-Natal, South Africa. Author of *Fraternal capital: peasantworkers, self-made men, and globalization in provincial India* (Stanford University Press, 2004), Chari now researches the remains of Apartheid in Durban.

Stefan Ecks is Lecturer in Social Anthropology and Co-Director of the Anthropology of Health & Illness Programme at the University of Edinburgh. He graduated with a PhD in Anthropology from the London School of Economics and taught at the South Asia Institute, University of Heidelberg. He has carried out ethnographic fieldwork in India since 1999, focusing on postcolonial concepts of body, health, and medicine. His current work looks at emerging forms of pharmaceutical uses, evidence-based medicine, and global corporate citizenship in India. From 2006 to 2009, he is Co-Investigator in the ESRC/DFID-funded project Tracing Pharmaceuticals in South Asia that studies the trajectories of key drugs through production, distribution, prescription and consumption in India and Nepal.

Anthony Good is Professor of Social Anthropology in Practice at Edinburgh University, and Head of its School of Social and Political Science. His field research in South India focused on kinship, and on the ceremonial economy of a Hindu temple. He has worked as a consultant for the Department for International Development, and has acted as expert witness in numerous asylum appeals by Sri Lankan Tamils.

Martin Holbraad works at the Anthropology Department of University College London. He has conducted fieldwork on Afro-Cuban religion in Havana since 1998. His is co-editor (with Amiria Henare and Sari Wastell) of *Thinking through things: theorising artefacts ethnographically* (Routledge, 2007) and his monograph on Cuban divination and anthropological truth is in preparation.

Webb Keane is Professor in the Department of Anthropology at the University of Michigan. He is the author of *Signs of recognition: powers and hazards of representation in an Indonesian society* (University of California Press, 1997) and *Christian moderns: freedom and fetish in the mission encounter* (University of California Press, 2007), as well as numerous articles on social and cultural theory.

Nicola Knight is a lecturer in research methods at the Institute of Cognitive and Evolutionary Anthropology and a researcher at the Centre for Anthropology and Mind, University of Oxford. He has worked on Yukatek children's attributions of beliefs to humans and supernatural entities, on cultural and socioeconomic status effects on categorization, and on problems relating to the epistemology of anthropology – in particular on the way anthropologists make and support claims about cognition. Currently, he is researching the psychological foundations of moral and broadly normative judgement and justification.

Christopher Pinney is Professor of Anthropology and Visual Culture at University College London, and Visiting Crowe Chair in Art History at Northwestern University. His most recent book is *Photos of the gods* (Reaktion, 2004) and he delivered the Panizzi Lectures at the British Library in 2006.

Charles Stafford is Professor of Anthropology at the London School of Economics and Political Science. He is the author of *Separation and reunion in modern China* (Cambridge University Press, 2000) and the editor of *Living with separation in China* (RoutledgeCurzon, 2003). He is also co-editor (with Rita Astuti & Jonathan Parry) of *Questions of anthropology* (Berg, 2007).

Foreword

The subject of anthropology has always been of wide scope, and at times its various specialisms have seemed to drift very far apart. The twenty-first century, however, has seen a return to older questions which demand engagement across the spectrum of the sub-disciplines. These questions are once again engaging evolutionary arguments for human universals as against the autonomy of culture and historical agency. They are beginning to bridge the gulf between the traditional sciences and humanities in their attempts to accommodate, for example, 'biology' and 'culture', or 'cognition' with the materiality of our existence and impact on the world. Methods too are coming increasingly under scrutiny. How far can the socio-cultural anthropologists' ambition of gaining important new knowledge of the human condition through *personal engagement* in intensive fieldwork remain valid in a world dominated by mass data, statistical trends, and narrowly-defined objectives not only in the biological but also in the social sciences?

The Royal Anthropological Institute of Great Britain and Ireland, since its foundation over more than a century and a half ago, has supported efforts both at specialization, and at inclusive coverage, of the field. From its London base, it has also endeavoured to reflect the changing emphases of debate within anthropology on a broadly international platform. Recent initiatives have been taken to promote and support publications which are designed to further the new generation of conversations across the different sub-fields, and among these was the launching of a new series of annual Special Issues of the *Journal* of the RAI in 2006. The present volume first appeared in this series, and we are pleased that it will now reach a wider audience in a self-standing book format.

The topic of 'evidence' touches all disciplines, not only those of academia but those of the practical world such as medicine, the operations of the law, as well as those of political struggle, or the worlds of 'belief' and the imagination. It also touches on raw issues such as how people in everyday life – perhaps very widely across the world – place faith in what they feel themselves to know, through the senses, or through what they have been told. Anthropology is faced on at least two levels with such issues: initially, the question has to relate to the distinctive method of personal fieldwork, the source of so much 'ethnographic knowledge' of human life in society, in its greatest diversity. How can observations gained from 'inter-subjective' encounters be taken as serious evidence? And evidence for what?, apart from the theories or preoccupations of the observer who happened to be there at a particular moment in history, and in his or her own lifetime. Can such observations carry real integrity when faced with the statistical surveys on which so many practical decisions are made, for example in medicine or in applied social projects of economic development or humanitarian assistance? Can such observations, rendered into a formal defence of 'cultural difference', hold up in courts of law, where anthropologists may be invited to act as expert witnesses in matters such as asylum cases or even criminal trials? How can the weak or suffering deploy accounts of their own lives as 'evidence' in their political campaigns?

The second level on which anthropologists have approached the issue of evidence in relation to the production of knowledge is the more abstract one of how we know anything anyway. Here, the slippery nature of language becomes an issue. Do people always speak the truth; can you trust any verbal account of an event, or do you need to be there yourself, to have seen it with your own eyes? How far do the very grammatical structures of language, or even of numerical or other logical sign-systems, shape what we know to be true? While the faculty of sight might seem a bottom-line guarantee of 'evidence' – when compared to hearsay – there are traps here too. The camera was once thought not to lie, but we are now wiser. Because religious visions may be 'seen', what does this necessarily imply about their standing as evidence for the gods?

All these issues are brought into play in the chapters of this volume, and bring together matters of common concern to a wide range of anthropologists and indeed both natural and social scientists. Students, not only in anthropology but also in fields such as the law, medicine, or politics, will also find much here to reflect on. 'Evidence' at first might seem a rather obvious, concrete thing – as for example an axe dug up in archaeology. But even in that discipline, as Collingwood pointed out so long ago (see Engelke's leading chapter), objects in themselves are not evidence. They become evidence in the context of an enquiry, as items which might help to answer a set of working questions already set up about the site and its significance. Not all contexts where the notion of 'evidence' crops up are quite the same as archaeology. But quite generally, where we do employ the concept, 'evidence' never stands just on its own; it has a *relational* quality, whether to previous understandings which as a consequence need revising, or to some schema of similarity or difference against which we use it in our 'production of knowledge'. Evidence acquires its dynamic from being *used*, especially perhaps in the context of argument. This volume is a rich mine of anthropological reflection not only on the theme of 'evidence' but also on the nature of argument, doubt, and the sources of certainty in social life. I am delighted to have the pleasure of recommending it both to students and to 'general readers', a species I believe to be still alive and well.

Wendy James
Chair, RAI Publications Committee

Preface

The contributors in this book participated in a workshop called 'The Objects of Evidence' held at the London School of Economics and Political Science in October 2005. We came together for the day to explore the variety of ways in which anthropologists use the concept of evidence in their work, both explicitly and implicitly. The initial impetus for the gathering came from something of the epistemological culture shock I experienced upon arrival at the LSE three years earlier; having been trained in the United States, I was struck by the different kinds of questions asked of me and my work in the United Kingdom. While the differences between American cultural and British social anthropology are real and worth exploring, I did not want to frame the workshop or this volume explicitly in relation to them. In one sense this volume is concerned with transatlantic discussions and differences, but as I came to realize, the more general questions behind my acculturation in London had to do, at least in part, with conceptions of evidence – of how anthropologists construct the objects of their knowledge. As this book attests, these are questions that can be fruitfully explored from a number of perspectives and starting-points, including, for instance, developments in cognitive anthropology, the concern with a return to grand theory, the provenance and focus of subfields such as the anthropology of religion, or the intersections between academic research and expert evidence in courts of law. Via these and other avenues, the contributors expose and explore some of the key conceptions of evidence within socio-cultural anthropology. Indeed, taken as a whole, the diversity and range of approaches to questions of evidence contained herein are, we think, fitting for a book such as this.

Funding for the workshop was provided by the LSE's Department of Anthropology and the Suntory and Toyota Centres for Economics and Related Disciplines (STICERD). In addition to the contributors here, Catherine Alexander, Laura Bear, Simon Coleman, and Eleonora Montuschi served as the workshop discussants. Along with the handful of LSE and University College London staff and students in attendance, they greatly enriched the conversation and direction of the event and resulting volume.

Matthew Engelke
November 2008

1

The objects of evidence

MATTHEW ENGELKE *London School of Economics and Political Science*

For anyone interested in exploring the concept of evidence, *Questions of evidence: proof, practice, and persuasion across the disciplines* (Chandler, Davidson & Harootunian 1994a) is a good place to start. Thirteen major scholars from a range of disciplines discuss how it has been understood within their respective fields, including history, art history, history of science, philosophy, biology, law, and literature. The underlying strength of the volume is its emphasis on the historicity and disciplinary specificity of evidentiary protocols. In every chapter readers can follow vibrant debates on episte-mology, played out most immediately in a series of commentaries and responses that accompany the main pieces, but which connect to wider conversations within the academy. Yet what ought to strike any anthropologist who reads the volume is that none of the thirteen main essays is by an anthropologist.[1] Whether or not this was a product of timing and chance, as with many edited collections, it is relatively difficult to find social and cultural anthropologists writing about the concept of evidence in an explicit or sustained manner.[2]

To say that anthropologists are not interested in evidence is a step too far. In fact anthropologists regularly refer to evidence in their writings. Pick up any journal, skim the articles, and you can find the word being used. Or take a look at what many Ph.D. students are obliged to: the Wenner-Gren Foundation's application forms for pre-doctoral field research. Question 3 asks: 'What evidence will you need to collect to answer your research question? How will you go about collecting this evidence?' (Answer in one page.) So there is plenty of evidence that we are users of evidence. What does not really exist, however, is an explicit set of discussions on the concept of evidence – or how it is used in practice – within the discipline. In a way, we can read the history of anthropological thought as a series of debates over questions of evidence, from Franz Boas and Bronislaw Malinowski's early critiques of the social evolutionists, to more recent debates, such as that between Marshall Sahlins and Gananath Obeyesekere, or, in a wider arena, David Stoll's critique of Rigoberta Menchu's *testimonio* and the responses it sparked within the anthropological community. In each of these cases disagreements over interpretation, argumentation, and the provenance of anthropology hinge, at least in part, on the constitution of evidence. Anthropologists deploy the concept of evidence and often contest the ways in which others 'misconstruct' or 'misuse' it, in their view. But rarely do they define what they mean by it in any depth.

In this chapter I suggest that socio-cultural anthropologists need to develop more sustained discussions on the concept of evidence. I do this in part by bringing a recent spate of articles (Csordas 2004; Hastrup 2004; Mosse 2006; see also Carrithers 1990) that tackle evidence head-on into conversation with the chapters included here. One of my primary aims is to underscore the fact that evidence has to be seen as both an epistemological and a methodological concern. It is often the latter we turn to first in our thoughts, and that which colleagues in other disciplines remark upon as what makes anthropology unusual or, even, problematic. How can such an intersubjective exercise as fieldwork produce evidence? Of course questions of method are important. But for any human science 'method does not make the object' (Fabian 1994: 87-88). For that we need epistemology. What I want to present here, then, is something of the 'epistemological unconscious' (Steinmetz 2005) that shapes the objects of evidence in and for anthropology.

In the broadest terms there are at least three reasons why social and cultural anthropologists should devote more attention to the concept of evidence. Perhaps above all, reflection on the concept of evidence should prompt us to consider the standards of judgement to which we hold our own and others' work. Why do we consider an ethnography good or bad? What makes an argument compelling or unconvincing? We all have standards. But how are they set? As George Marcus has argued, there is a sense in which anthropologists refuse to address these questions head on: students are often trained and socialized according to the rather vague benchmark of 'you only know a good ethnography when you read one' (1986: 266). Marcus made this observation more than two decades ago now, but the kind of Malinowskian ethnographer's magic it captures is still very much in play. More recently Kirsten Hastrup (2004) has raised a similar point by relating standards of judgement to questions of evidence. How, she asks, do anthropologists 'become convinced of "being right"' (2004: 458)? And how do we convince others that we are so? How can we turn fieldwork experience – a highly personal, temporally bound, and intersubjective method for collecting data – into objects of evidence? What justifies our convictions or conclusions, and how can they be marshalled in and through ethnography? By asking these questions, we gain important insights into the processes of judgement that shape our professional debates. And evidence surely ought to precede any sound judgement.

Devoting more attention to the concept of evidence might also help us to understand some of the intellectual divides within the discipline. There are plenty of these. They are often not as real as they are made to sound, but they do exist, gaining occasional airing in blunt and polemical tones (see, e.g., Bloch 2005; Leach 1961; Needham 1974; Sahlins 2002; Sperber 1985; Wolf 1980). Some of us feel an affinity for the humanities and arts, others for the natural sciences. Some of us deride the concept of culture. Some of us are wary of words such as 'power' and 'resistance'. Some of us claim X's understanding of culture (or power or resistance) is flawed, and that Y uses it more effectively. There are some anthropologists who think studying 'at home' is poor practice. Others moan about postmodernism, and still others that little of value has been published after 1980. Again: in practice these derisions, concerns, critiques, and moaning are not as divisive or debilitating as they appear. And for every anthropologist who cares enough to align him- or herself 'with' something and 'against' something else, there will be several more who feel no such compulsion, who see value in different takes – occupying what Bruce Knauft (2006) has recently referred to as 'the middle'. It is, moreover, not necessarily a bad thing to have disagreements, even heated ones. But whether productive or not, it is notable that arguments over evidence are rarely set out within disciplinary debates. Socio-cultural anthropology does not have a well-developed language of evidence with which to thrash out its differences. Taken together, the chapters in this book explore how and whether such a language might be useful for understanding the differences in outlook and practice that characterize the field.

Whether, indeed. This second argument raises the important question of whether there are good historical reasons for an underdeveloped language of evidence within socio-cultural anthropology. As I discuss later, Martin Holbraad's chapter in this book raises this question in relation to what he sees as a misguided reading of evidence as a quest for 'indubitability'. More generally the absence might be attributed to anthropology's tradition of participant observation, into which any kind of positive knowledge does not easily fit (cf. Hastrup 2004). It may also have to do with the material and sensual nature of our data; we may be increasingly familiar with archives, for instance, but the roots of anthropology are grounded in social experience, not documents. However, even with these points in mind there is much to be gained through more explicit considerations of evidence, as my third argument further suggests.

Finally, then, reflection on the concept of evidence might give us a language with which to engage colleagues in other human sciences, the humanities, and the natural sciences, as well as actors and interest groups in the wider world. In experimental psychology, for example, as the chapter here by Charles Stafford shows, the nature of evidence is a central and fairly explicit concern. Experimental psychologists have a language of evidence in a way we do not, and the scale of their research has an important effect on the scope of their field. If we want to engage with the work that grows out of that discipline (or any other), it makes sense for us to consider where our own approaches might fit in. Likewise, take just one example from what I have called the wider world. As an increasing number of anthropologists are documenting (e.g. Drexler 2006; Gregory 2006; Skidmore 2003; cf. Chari, this volume), human rights and social justice activists are thinking long and hard about the nature and social effects of the evidence presented in their work. The sophistication with which these presentations are being made ought to prompt some thinking of our own, not least for how we might define the connections between scholarship and politics (cf. Wilson 2004). A truly public anthropology ought to have a language of evidence at its disposal, a way of presenting its findings in a manner that speaks across the academic divide.

The primary aim in this volume is to reflect on how evidence works in and for the discipline of anthropology in its generation of knowledge. It is in this sense that the volume is concerned with evidence as a problem of epistemology as much as, if not more than, a problem of method. A conscious effort was made to gather colleagues working within Anglo-American traditions on a wide range of topics, in a number of specializations, and from different theoretical points of view. Thus Maurice Bloch, who has recently (2005) been calling for a return to grand theory in anthropology, presents on what he understands as the crucial link between evidence and sight as the bedrock of truth. Christopher Pinney also addresses the link between vision and evidence, but with a concern to show how truths are manufactured and contested. Anthony Good, reflecting on his work as an expert witness and researcher in legal anthropology, assesses the nature and impact of cultural evidence in courts of law. Sharad Chari, a geographer with extensive fieldwork experience in both India and South Africa, focuses on the ways in which activists in Durban document their lives to present evidence of discrimination, reflecting in the process on the forms and formation of political evidence. Stefan Ecks compares the prescription of antidepressants by general practitioners and psychiatrists in Kolkata (Calcutta), and relates these to the rise of evidence-based medicine and the burgeoning field of medical anthropology. Martin Holbraad, a Caribbeanist with training in analytic philosophy, ruminates on the similarities and differences between questions of evidence for practitioners of Santería in Cuba and those of the anthropological community. Webb Keane, extending his innovative work on semiotics, turns attention to questions of the materiality of evidence within the anthropology of religion. Charles Stafford explores the differences between objects of study in experimental psychology and anthropology, and how each field's understanding of evidence can shed light on the other's. And Nicola Knight and Rita Astuti offer a challenging reading of the ways in which anthropologists marshal evidence to make collective ascriptions, arguing that cognitive anthropology and the cognitive sciences more generally provide useful insights into the potential pitfalls of such ascriptions. Taken together, the chapters here are testament to the fact that questions of evidence are animating ones deserving of more considered attention. Indeed, they pick up on what seems to be a growing recognition within the discipline that our conceptions of evidence have not received their due (Csordas 2004; Hastrup 2004; Lau, High & Chua in press).

The remainder of this introduction is divided into two main parts, throughout each of which I offer support for the three claims made above. In the first part I review some key definitions of evidence and relate them to the agendas and concerns of anthropology. In the second part I sketch four themes that recur in this volume's chapters which I hope will prompt further discussion and debate: *scale* (how anthropologists circumscribe their objects of study); *quantity and quality* (how 'much' and what 'kind' of evidence is needed to substantiate a claim); *certainty* (the extent to which evidence can settle any claim); and *intention* (how evidence is produced and whether it has an agency of its own – how and whether it 'presents' itself to us). These are not the only themes that can be raised in relation to the chapters, of course; each is but one point of entry that might help us understand the diversity of anthropological modes of reasoning.

Defining evidence

In the *Oxford English Dictionary* the first definition of evidence is 'the quality or condition of being evident; clearness, evidentness'. As Bloch and Pinney highlight (this volume), this quality is often linked to the sense of sight. To be 'in evidence', the *OED* states, is to be 'actually present, prominent, conspicuous'. What needs to be stressed, however, is that in any professional or academic inquiry the primary definition of evidence is insufficient. Indeed, for an anthropologist (among others) the quality or condition of being evident exists more as a desire than an actual state of affairs. We want our work to make the objects of anthropology evident – even those amongst us who would (rightly, in my view) reject the idea that those objects could ever be *fully* evident. But the body of work that achieves this goal is small to non-existent. Is there any approach to the understanding of kinship, or ritual, or violence, or exchange which can claim, on the basis of the evidence it presents, to be settled? This is not the way evidence works in anthropology or the human sciences. It is only when we get to a secondary *OED* definition of evidence that we find something akin to what we need. We need evidence first as a tool, not as a quality or condition. In anthropology evidence is always also an argument. 'Evidence has to be evidence of or for something, and that something is an hypothesis in the broadest sense' (Csordas 2004: 475). Thus, in what the *OED* links to the word's legal uses, evidence is defined as 'information, whether in the form of personal testimony, the language of documents, or the production of material objects, that is given in a legal investigation to establish the fact or point in question'. From the *OED* definition based on the word's legal uses, we are given a crucial point. Evidence exists in relation to questions (cf. Daston 1994).

Questions are what lead from evidence-as-tool to evidence as the quality or condition of being evident. R.G. Collingwood's short essay 'Historical evidence' (1946) helped make this correlation especially clear, and is itself the best exception to the neglect of the topic in the modern disciplines (Chandler, Davidson & Harootunian 1994*b*). Collingwood argues that history, like any profession, has to establish and work by a set of evidentiary protocols. Evidence, in other words, has a disciplinary specificity. Collingwood says that history 'is a science whose business is to study events not accessible to our observation, and to study these events inferentially, arguing to them from something else which is accessible to our observation, and which the historian calls "evidence" for the event in which he is interested' (1946: 251-2). History cannot be produced if this understanding is abandoned or abused.

It is necessary to read Collingwood's essay on two levels. At its core, it offers the crucial insights that evidence has disciplinary specificity and that, because of this, 'nothing is evidence except in relation to some definite question' (Collingwood 1946: 281). In the process of making these points, however, Collingwood engages in what has come to be seen as heavy-handed boundary-drawing (Chandler *et al.* 1994*b*: 2). By setting out what history is, Collingwood sets out what it is not. Like Malinowski's introduction to *Argonauts of the Western Pacific* (1984 [1922]), 'Historical evidence' creates the template for the methodology of a profession; like Malinowski's introduction, it is a template that has been both enacted and recalibrated. In the end, however, as Chandler *et al.* (1994*b*: 2) suggest, Collingwood's understanding of disciplinary specificity is too specific. The lesson is that in attending to the disciplinary specificity of evidentiary protocols, we need to be aware that evidence is defined not only by questions but also by competing pressures and regimes.

Disagreements within a profession often hinge on what counts as evidence, and for what claims. Take the following brief example from a review by Richard Wilk (1998) of Jonathan Friedman's *Cultural identity and global process* (1994). This example allows us to expand on the points I made earlier about standards of judgement and anthropology's divides. Wilk 'found the book a stimulating read, full of original ideas that point the way toward the next generation of global anthropology' (1998: 288). Yet he is also of the opinion that the global (or what Friedman calls 'global systemic processes' [1994: 1]) is 'difficult territory for anthropology' (an opinion Friedman would surely support) and that some of the leading scholars working on it seem to have a hard time connecting 'highly abstract processes and the tiny fragments of evidence we control' (1998: 287).

> In global anthropology richness and creativity of ideas and diversity of theoretical connections are not complemented by much empirical evidence. In Friedman's book (as in others of the genre) the author's veracity rests on clever argument, dazzling and sophisticated references and connections, and striking examples which appeal to our own experience, all of which are provided in abundance. But

the theoretical richness raises the question of what kinds of comparative, historical, or ethnographic evidence a truly global anthropology will need to call upon if alternative propositions are to be evaluated (1998: 287-8).

It is not the place here to assess Friedman's work in light of Wilk's comments, and still less the merits of global anthropology or global systemic processes (even as I have made the case that anthropologists need to be more in touch with their procedures of judgement). Rather the point is to highlight how the objects of anthropology are settled and unsettled through appeals to specific notions of evidence. What counts as empirical evidence or ethnographic evidence? Are these constant, or can a case be made for their variability depending on the context or subject under discussion? These are the types of questions that reveal disciplinary fault-lines and barricades. In Wilk's case they do not appear as deep or heavily fortified as for Collingwood in his day, but they are there none the less. Wilk is basing his cautions over global anthropology on his understanding of anthropological evidence. At the time, at least – 1998 – he had yet to be convinced that global anthropology could produce the necessary evidence at all – something that would bridge the divide between grand ideas and actual observations. The problem for Wilk seems to be that global systemic processes are not necessarily something that can be observed anthropologically: namely that global systemic processes cannot be fashioned into anthropological evidence.

As I mentioned in passing, Knight and Astuti (this volume) warn us that ascription is a dangerous act. But my assumption is that we can ascribe to Friedman some respect for the importance of evidence. The essays in *Cultural identity and global process* do not appear to be written with a wanton disregard for any sense of evidence. Friedman refers in most chapters to the ethnographic record, developing extended discussions in some cases, such as that in chapter 9 on Congolese *sapeurs*. On face value we have to accept that one person's 'dazzling and sophisticated references' (so described) might be another's appeal to the record – to the evidence accrued. It is true that scholars sometimes throw caution to the wind, or go out on a speculative limb without the safety of evidence behind them: think of some of Edmund Leach's more provocative essays. Friedman's book is not written in this vein. There is no point at which he claims to be making arguments or connections without the backing of evidence, and in the absence of such a claim, I believe we have to accept that some evidentiary protocol is in place. The problem, of course, is that because such protocols are often left implicit, it becomes difficult to have a discussion about the nature of the evidence being deployed.

To extend this point let me turn to a piece in which some anthropologists might expect the concept of evidence to come in for some scrutiny: James Clifford's introduction to *Writing culture*, 'Partial truths' (1986). This is one of those essays that elicit strong reactions. It is a good example of scholarship that has been used to draw the kind of 'for' and 'against' lines in disciplinary debates to which I alluded above. But it remains an important piece to read because of the attention it draws to anthropology's rhetorics of authority. In picking apart these rhetorics, a number of concepts come in for criticism – most notably 'truth', which is Clifford's main concern, but also 'fact' and, even, to an extent, the notions of 'certainty' and 'reality'. Reading the chapter in light of the issues raised in this volume, however, what seems notable is the extent to which 'evidence' escaped interrogation during the crisis of representation. Where there is concern with facts and truth, evidence cannot be far behind. As several of the authors here suggest (Bloch; Ecks; Good; Holbraad; Pinney), 'evidence' is often linked to questions about truth, and, given such, the relationships that obtain – whether in places, like Cuba and Madagascar, or projects, like experimental psychology or semiotics – need to be investigated.

The word 'evidence' appears only once in Clifford's essay, when he cites a book by Richard Price as 'evidence of the fact that acute political and epistemological self-consciousness need not lead to ethnographic self-absorption' (1986: 7). Here it functions as an unproblematic concept. Yet later on in the essay, questions of evidence are implicit in the argumentation, as when Clifford notes that 'to recognize the poetic dimensions of ethnography does not require that one give up facts and accurate accounting' (1986: 25-6). If one is not giving up on facts and accurate accounting – and one should not, *as Clifford clearly suggests* – neither is one giving up, and neither can one do without, some understanding of evidence. It is what we do with facts – not only what questions we ask of them, but how we justify them to be 'facts' in the first place – that makes ethnography important. Anthropology ought to produce an excess of details, to borrow an image from Veena Das (1998: 179). But that excess has to settle around an argument, or, at least, a set of questions, in order to be legible as anthropology. It can only do this properly when the facts or details are marshalled as evidence of or for something.

Having considered Clifford's work briefly, let me present an unjustifiable caricature of what the crisis of representation was about in order again to drive home the points about why evidence is worthy of more detailed investigation. The crisis of representation is often understood as an attack on anthropology's status as a 'hard' science – as a discipline that can speak truths. More bluntly, the crisis of representation was used to draw the battle-lines between anthropologists who thought they had more in common with literature professors from those who thought they had more in common with biology professors (those who thought they had most in common with other social scientists existed somewhere akin to Knauft's [2006] 'middle' – neglected).

In this light, however, evidence comes partly unhooked from terms such as truth and fact. A literature professor may not emphasize a language of truth and facts, but she might still well employ a language of evidence. My point here is to suggest that the concept of evidence can mediate the unproductive and even misleading bifurcation of anthropology into 'scientific' and 'poetic' camps. Clifford himself is careful not to reproduce this bifurcation in his essay, despite the fact that it is often read as an attempt to shore up the differences. Reading his essay with an interest in evidence, I argue, can help disambiguate its reception. Clifford's work, and much of the 'postmodern' work with which it is associated, has never abandoned a notion of reality and never operated without a standard of judgement set by some evidentiary protocol. How one evaluates that protocol is a different matter. But there are, I would venture, few anthropologists who will say that all interpretations are equally valuable – equally *valid*, perhaps, but that is not the same thing. It is worth noting that Clifford titled his essay 'Partial truths' and not 'No truths'. To borrow a line from the law professor Mark Kelman, inasmuch as we make a commitment to evidence – to the very possibility that it can exist, somehow, somewhere, for somebody – '[w]e are all ... in that sense, closet positivists' (1994: 188).[3]

The concern with truths has become an important entry point into questions of evidence within the emerging body of anthropological literature. As Hastrup (2004) argues, for instance, anthropology cannot trade in the kind of positive knowledge with which 'the truth' is so often associated. Anthropological evidence 'cannot be empirical knowledge in conventional positivist terms' (2004: 461) because of the irreducibly social nature of our objects. Jonathan Spencer also captures this point: 'Because ethnographic experience is so specific as to be unrepeatable – a fact which in itself removes ethnographic evidence from most understandings of scientific data – generalisation is peculiarly problematic' (1989: 152). So just as we study 'social facts', we might be said to produce 'social evidence'. This does not mean that evidence has to be agreed upon as such by the community from which it is drawn; to make an argument about the function or meaning of a ritual or kinship relation does not require group consensus by a congregation or family. What it does mean is that we have to accept that our arguments and interpretations about social life cannot be validated by an externally objective source. As Hastrup puts it, 'our relation to the object is already instilled as part of the object when we begin to understand it' and so '"evidence" cannot be disengaged from the objective of the investigation' (2004: 468).

In his recent Malinowski lecture, David Mosse (2006) explains how he found this out the hard way. Mosse's (2005) study of an irrigation project in western India run by the United Kingdom's Department for International Development (DFID) was fought tooth and nail by many of the colleagues with whom he had worked. They did not recognize themselves in his academic writing, still less their work, and disagreed with many of his conclusions. In part they simply did not understand on the basis of what evidence he came to his findings. They felt poorly judged and personally criticized (see Mosse 2006: 942) and that 'the ethnography dismissed empirical evidence' (2006: 943) – such as improved seed technology – in favour of a highly subjective personal take caught up in a curious concern for meaning.

While we do not all have 'the natives' knocking at the doors of colleagues in our departments to refute the findings in our book manuscripts (see Mosse 2006: 947), Mosse's experience with the DFID is part of an increasingly common dynamic within the discipline. To paraphrase Caroline Brettell (1993), they are reading what we are writing. We are used to facing objections from our colleagues, and many of us do share what we write with those written about, often with an eye to incorporating their comments and, even, engaging in debates with them. But as Mosse's experience makes clear, there is something especially troubling, emotionally and epistemologically, when the objections that come from our fieldwork informants, interlocutors, colleagues, and friends are as strenuous as the ones he faced. Because we are caught with them in the social evidence we produce, it can be particularly unsettling to be challenged in this way. Not many anthropologists would be glad to know that the people they studied – people with whom they forge close ties and often friendships – do not recognize themselves in ethnographic registers. We might be willing to accept misrecognition at the level of genre and style ('I don't understand that academic jargon'), but misrecognition of being ('That is not me!') cuts closer to the bone.

Mosse stood his ground, more or less. He did not simply amend his work because some former DFID colleagues felt he got it (and them) wrong. He tells us how he took their arguments seriously, and that the objections threw him into some moments of self-doubt. But in the end he was not convinced by them, not least because of what he came to see as his erstwhile colleagues' Janus-faced approach to the issue of evidence. On one hand, it seems, they demanded 'hard evidence' from Mosse to back his conclusions. How, for example (see Mosse 2006: 943), could Mosse reasonably conclude, as they understood it, that 'success' in the development project was not measured by the encouraging 'scientific data' but rather the extent to which they could justify a particular model of development practice as authoritative? On the other hand, they wanted to amend his conclusions on the basis of what they saw as the larger truth of their work; they were people with good intentions and that was what should be conveyed. 'Indeed', Mosse notes, 'my colleagues' positivism concealed an essentially relational epistemology which rejected the notion of "evidence" as external to the situation' (2006: 944-5). There was no such thing as just the facts. In an important sense, facts and evidence were thought to be matters of group consensus and moral visions.

The development workers' objections, and his counter-objections, left Mosse with a nagging problem: '[H]ow was I to defend the "rightness" of my ethnography against those who could say "you are wrong, I was there", or "what evidence do you have to back this statement" or even, "come on, we know you!"' (2006: 949). How could Mosse both recognize that anthropological evidence is relational – at best a partial truth – and, at the same time, insist on standing his ground? The irony did not escape him (see Mosse 2006: 954 n.26). Just as the development workers were closet relativists – hiding behind a faith in the really real – Mosse had been acting as something of what I referred to above as a closet positivist. Mosse's experience shows that, however much we accept the situated nature of our knowledge, when push comes to shove – as it almost did in Mosse's case – it dawns on us that we *do* think we can be right, and that we can be so on the basis of our professional credentials in accordance with the evidence we understand ourselves to possess. This state of things is in fact a healthy one. Keeping the subjective and objective in a dance with one another is the best way to prevent professional scleroses. It allows us to keep positivism and postmodernism in the safe confines of rhetoric, since neither is really real.

One way in which anthropologists become convinced of getting it right – and perhaps the most powerful – is through the recognition of patterns in the social life they observe. To conclude this section, then, let me offer a few remarks on what this means.

Claude Lévi-Strauss once admitted experiencing discomfort over how, when taken in isolation, the things humans do 'are, or seem, arbitrary, meaningless, absurd' (1978: 11). Whether or not one finds comfort in the meaningfulness offered by structuralism, the recognition of order through the discernment of patterns has often served as the discipline's epistemological security blanket. In the absence of something that is equally accessible to others in a professional community – our colleagues cannot independently confirm our observations – the emergence of patterns in ethnographic writing (both intra- and intertextually) speak for themselves, as it were, and can be circulated as reasonably stable pieces of evidence. If you are like me, you get very excited when (a) in fieldwork you observe similar actions, reactions, or events in different settings, or when people who have no direct connection to one another reinforce your understanding of them through what they say and do, and/or (b) these fieldwork experiences resonate, in both expected and unexpected ways, with what you read about in other ethnographies, all the more so if you work with, say, the Yoruba and the other ethnographies are about Gê-speaking peoples or Japanese businessmen. Of course for many anthropologists making the leap from (a) to (b) – from culturally specific patterns to cross-cultural or even universal ones – is considered misguided or unjustifiable. But at some level the pattern argument has to hold. We could never package and transport our intersubjective experiences without it. While we may not be able to point to evidence as a clearly bound object, then, we do something similar by tracing its outlines in the flow of social life (Carrithers 1990; Csordas 2004: cf. also Mosse 2006: 949).

Of course, the anthropological interest in patterns is not new: most famously expressed by Ruth Benedict (1934), it was also set out by E.E. Evans-Pritchard (1962). But within this classic work, questions of evidence and of its emergence through patterns remain largely implicit. Franz Boas did remark in his Introduction to Benedict's *Patterns of culture* that 'the old method of constructing a history of human culture based on bits of evidence, torn out of their natural contacts, and collected from all times and all parts of the world, has lost much of its hold' (1934: xix), but Benedict does not advance her teacher's historical particularism through a language of evidence within the text itself. It is relatively recent that the pattern argument has been set out with the concept of evidence in mind, most fully in an essay by Michael Carrithers (1990; see also 1992, chap. 8).

Carrithers frames his concern with evidence around the question of whether anthropology is an art or a science. Written as it was in the late 1980s, the concern is given life by leading figures of that day: Clifford Geertz and James Clifford, who are cast as proponents of 'art', and Dan Sperber, who is similarly recruited for 'science'. The details of Carrithers's take on their respective works (Clifford 1988a; Geertz 1988; Sperber 1985) are not of central importance here. Suffice it to say that he sees value in both the interpretivism of the artistic approach and the positivism of a scientific approach, while cautioning, sensibly, against any 'absolutist view' (see Carrithers 1990: 265) (a view he attributes to each of the three men, although I think unfairly). Despite offering serious criticisms of the hermeneutic approach, in the end he presents a vision of anthropology that has more in common with Geertz and Clifford than it does with Sperber (cf. Brady 1990: 273). He does not accept that anthropology can produce anything close to a positive knowledge. (Following Ian Hacking [1983], he argues that no discipline could produce this, as all are 'human activity and as such ... not so alienated from the world as to produce an absolute truth, absolute facts, or absolute confidence' [Carrithers 1990: 264].) At the same time, he does not want to surrender the possibility that anthropology is a 'serious activity' (Carrithers 1990: 263). Like Collingwood he argues that disciplines have their own evidential protocols and canons. Carrithers believes that anthropology can make a durable contribution to our understanding of the social on the basis of the evidence it presents, an understanding that might be taken up by others and used for profit. His final point is important: 'We may ask [of ethnography] not certainty but reliability' (1990: 272). Ethnography would in this sense be like the best kind of scholarship, since certainty is not the concern of either the human or natural sciences as properly practised. The problem is how reliability can be gauged. This is where patterns come in.

Carrithers argues that for something to be a pattern is has to be recognizable as such at the intersubjective level. It has to be consensible, which he defines as 'the ability of people to perceive things in common, to agree upon and to share perceptions' (Carrithers 1990: 266). It does not mean that everyone who has observed something actually does see the pattern in question; the requirement here is simply that the pattern is publicly intelligible. To illustrate this argument, Carrithers presents short extracts from the ethnographic record, including an episode in the work of Raymond Firth (see Carrithers 1990: 266-72). In this episode, Firth's friend, Pa Rangifuri, who is a chief's son, is described by Firth as *teke*, a Tikopia word which can mean 'unwilling (to do something)', 'angry', or 'objecting (even violently)':

> When we got to his house we found him highly agitated. He and I greeted each other with the usual pressing of noses, as publicly recognized friends, but for him that was an unusually perfunctory gesture, and he paid me little attention. He was uttering brief incoherent statements: 'I'm going off to see' ... 'They said their axe should cut first' ... 'But was it for a dirge, no! It was for a dance!' Men were trying to soothe him down by respectful gestures, and to enquire the reason for his agitation. Tears were streaming down his cheeks, his voice was high and broken, his body quivering from time to time (Firth in Carrithers 1990: 266).

Even without knowing much about the Tikopia, Carrithers notes, it is possible for readers of this passage to understand that Pa Rangifuri was upset. It is worth noting, too, that we do not need the whole passage to understand this. Some anthropologists (e.g. Sperber 1985) might question Firth's use of a phrase like 'highly agitated' or his claim that Pa Rungifiri's nose rub was perfunctory. But we recognize the upset through the most 'stripped-down' elements of Firth's account, the fact that tears were streaming down Pa Rangifuri's cheeks and that his body was quivering from time to time. In the most general and basic sense, then, what this ethnographic extract provides us, according to Carrithers, is an intelligible (because discernible) pattern of human behaviour, what he calls a 'human pattern'. 'Pa Rangifuri's tears, the incoherence of his words, and his general demeanour are distinct, vivid, and discriminable from other patterns such as, say, "riotous jollity"' (Carrithers 1990: 266). As such, Firth's ethnography can be evidential.

But what is Firth's ethnography evidence for? It is not enough for a reader of anthropology to say, 'Well, tears, shaking: sounds like he's upset, so ... he must be upset'. If anthropology teaches us one thing it is that we cannot make such assumptions. Indeed, anthropology is often at its best precisely when it can challenge our common-sense understandings of emotions, or relatedness, or the dynamics of political power. Firth's work becomes evidential not out of what we might call this 'first-level' recognition of pattern, which is fairly superficial. (*News flash: 'Anthropologist provides evidence that Tikopians cry'*.) Rather, Carrithers claims, it becomes evidential through its confirmation as a human pattern within 'the dense and interwoven specificity' (Carrithers 1990: 269) of Firth's ethnographic *oeuvre*. When human patterns emerge out of ethnographic ones, confirmed as such by a community of critical readers, and in a sense independent of the intentions of an author, they gain shape as ethnographic evidence. Exactly what the incident Firth described can be used as evidence for is still open to question. But that is precisely what makes it evidential in Carrithers's opinion. 'The episode as told has robustness and independence from its use by Firth. It could be used by someone else to illustrate fraternal rivalry, generational conflict, an anxiety to pacify chiefs, or the very peculiar position of axes among the Tikopia at the time' (Carrithers 1990: 271). It is this robustness and independence that confirms its reliability. It becomes what Webb Keane (2005) has referred to in an essay on anthropology's epistemologies as a 'portable objectification'. As Keane suggests, we cannot do without these objectifications, a fact which tells us something important about the peculiar nature of our brand of 'positivism'. As I have argued, this is a positivism that should not and cannot insist on absolutes. It is, rather, a positivism that allows us to sense (and positivism, after all, is about the ability to *sense*) that we can 'get it right'. As Carrithers (1990: 272) might put it, it is about shifting our concerns from the ontological and epistemological to the practical.

There are several problems with the pattern argument. Let me mention three. The first is perhaps not so much a problem as a depressing conclusion (or at least what some might see as depressing): that, in our practicality, we are nothing more than the academy's *bricoleurs*. Second, as I suggested above, and as Roger Keesing has pointed out, we cannot assume 'the cross-cultural transparency and translatability of patterns' (1990: 274). It is in this second sense that any anthropology with universalist aspirations faces significant and perhaps insurmountable problems. Patterns are not always as evident or concrete as we might hope. And neither can we be sure that they are ever fully revealed. (There can be patterns within patterns.) Finally, consider, as it were, the metaphysical mechanics of the pattern argument. As anthropologists we substitute the unrepeatable nature of our fieldwork experiences (our versions of experiments) with the appeal to patterns. This is a strange surrendering of our subjectivity; it carries the danger of making us over into something like spirit mediums. But in this we find a key stream of our 'epistemological unconscious'.

Four key themes raised in this volume
It would be possible and no doubt profitable to frame the chapters in this collection strictly in relation to the discussions thus far. Some version of the pattern argument, for example, is inherent to the structure of Bloch's provocative chapter. Turning to a wide variety of sources – from the theological and philosophical literature to the Zafimaniry's own observations – the evidentiary force of Bloch's argument rests on the appeal he makes to recurrent patterns of the link between the senses and truth. Likewise, the very nature of his 'pattern recognition' raises questions similar to those Wilk asks of Friedman about the provenance of our discipline. Can ethnography and philosophy produce commensurable sources of evidence? Is this a mix of empirical observation with dazzling and sophisticated references? These are some of the connected questions which can be raised in relation to the following. Rather than restricting the focus to them, however, I want to use the first main section as a point of departure for considering others themes and issues: scale; quantity and quality; certainty; and intention. Each is helpful for understanding methodological and epistemological aspects of the objects of evidence.

Scale
Of all the issues questions of evidence raise, scale is perhaps the most important. What are anthropology's objects of evidence? What 'size' are they? These are not only some of the most important questions of evidence we face, but also the most vexing (Strathern 1996).[4] Scale is a bugbear in our efforts to come up with evidentiary protocols. As the brief discussion of Friedman and Wilk makes clear, the scale of our work, conditioned by the shape and size of our evidence-catching nets, helps fuel disciplinary debates about not only what we can properly investigate, but also how. Likewise, when our work is read by outsiders (and some colleagues), the oddity of anthropology is often traced to the penchant we have for using a vignette or anecdote about what we observed one Tuesday morning in an open-air market outside Timbuktu eighteen years ago to explain the workings of political power in Mali, or African economies, or globalization. The vignette and the anecdote have been powerful vehicles of both communication and confirmation within the discipline. They are some of the most useful tools in our chest of rhetoric, an indication of our faith in metonymy to explain the human condition.

All of the chapters here raise issues of scale, from Bloch's foray into grand theory, which sweeps across the spatial and philosophical maps of history, to Good's comments on cultural evidence, which reveal the difficulties anthropologists have in mapping their ethnographic knowledge into the much roomier certainties prompted by courts of law. But I want to focus on the chapters by Stafford, Chari, and Knight and Astuti to develop the issue.

Stafford points out in his chapter on numeracy that the default assumption within anthropology is that we examine human relations in 'very fine, even "microscopic", detail' (p. 122). It is this microscopic focus, which emerges out of intersubjective relations, that can make anthropological evidence dubious in the eyes of some other academics. Yet in a sense Stafford argues that the scale of our work is not really the problem; compared with some experimental psychologists, who examine such things as infant staring times, the objects of anthropology seem huge indeed. There is, moreover, what many outsiders might consider a strange twist in our approach: ethnographies are particularist but in that particularity are supposed to take everything into account. For an anthropologist – particularly one who works in an 'exotic' locale (be that Kansas or the Kalahari) – everything is potential evidence (cf. Csordas 2004).

Thanks to 'collaboration' between an experimental psychologist and an anthropologist among the Pirahã, in the Amazon, Stafford is able to examine questions of scale in relation to the two disciplines in some depth. This collaboration, between the experimental psychologist Peter Gordon and the linguistic anthropologist Daniel Everett, was far from a match made in heaven: it turns out that Everett, the long-standing expert on the Pirahã, had neither much interest nor time for Gordon when he set up his experiments to test Pirahã numeracy in the village. As Stafford relates, in the results that Gordon published almost no mention is made of the cultural and linguistic specificities of his case study: he abstracts Pirahã understandings of numeracy into a universalist frame, treating the data as so much experimental evidence that can be fed into a larger hypothesis-testing machine. What is interesting is that when Gordon did try to include some 'cultural' analysis in a paper, it was dismissed by a peer reviewer as an attempt to smuggle mere anecdotes into a scientific journal. For evolutionary psychologists working on numeracy, it seems it simply cannot matter that an anthropologist such as Everett spent twenty years working with the Pirahã, or that culture more generally has a place in the halls of science. Everett, in turn, argued, in classic anthropological fashion, that if Gordon wanted to understand Pirahã numeracy, he needed to collect 'evidence about "everything"' (Stafford, p. 127, this volume).

Stafford's chapter raises the important issue of how the scale of a discipline has a direct but often overlooked effect on how practitioners make judgements about the validity of others' claims. Stafford is prompting us to consider these effects. He wants us to realize not only what we so easily can – that there are dangers in the abstracting reductionism and eurocentrism of experimental methods – but equally that our traditional focus on 'everything' leaves us in something of a muddle. 'By holding that all things are interconnected', Stafford argues, 'we tend to make falsification of our claims (e.g. via experimentation) more or less impossible' (p. 132).

Knight and Astuti's chapter, coming from a similarly appreciative view of what the cognitive sciences and psychology can teach us, also raise issues of scale. Their focus here is on how anthropologists ascribe certain properties and dispositions to social groups. Ascription, they stress, is not a problem in itself for anthropology. Indeed, it is on the basis of ascription, and the intuitive judgements that anthropologists are able to make through the in-depth nature of their personal engagements, that we produce much valuable evidence. The problem, they argue, is that anthropologists do not always pay enough attention to the different kinds of ascription they make. It is one thing to say, on the basis of repeated observations, that the Dobuans are bad sailors; it is another to say that the Vezo think bodily properties are socially transmitted. This second kind of ascription, which has to do with questions of cognition, is, they point out, much harder to scale properly. When it comes to cognitive processes, anthropologists have to tread cautiously in claiming to have evidence on a large scale.

It is, of course, standard practice for anthropologists to avoid generalizations of most sorts, especially when it comes to what 'the natives' in question believe or think. There are not many anthropologists who would claim, after having worked in, say, a Zulu village for eighteen months, that 'the Zulu believe ...'. As other of the chapters in this volume attest (Holbraad; Keane) – adding voice to a long-standing debate – 'belief' is a particularly explosive word when employed analytically. It is one of the most difficult attributions for us to scale. For Knight and Astuti, however, the general awareness that exists within anthropology about the dangers of collective ascription is unsatisfactory. They are not satisfied with the caveats and qualifications one often finds ('most Zulu believe ...' or 'many Zulu say ...' [thus shifting the object from inner thought to outer expression]), and still less with the penchant for peppering ethnography with reference to the 'contests' and 'negotiations' in play. These are for them vague hedgings that downplay or ignore some of the important insights cognitive studies have produced on the constitution and social transmission of knowledge: namely that knowledge is not evenly distributed within any 'cultural group'. Perhaps the most valuable fruits of research along these lines have come from anthropologists working on children and learning (but see also the classic work on knowledge by Frederik Barth, discussed by Keane in his chapter), research which is forcing us to recognize the need to disaggregate our objects of investigation along the lines not only of gender, power, and other important concepts, but also of cognitive development in relation to age.

Sharad Chari raises questions of scale and the problems it creates for ethnography from a different perspective. In one section of his chapter, he focuses on life histories, both offering an investigation of their qualities as objects of evidence and presenting details from several he collected in the field. The range of Chari's work gives us an excellent sense of how life histories serve as evidence in a variety of ways, and according to a range of protocols (personal, social, and professional). In his research in Durban, Chari has been struck by the extent to which political and social activists use their life histories as a way of mobilizing evidence of discrimination (both during and after apartheid) and for, in some cases, claims to specific entitlements such as land. The activists he knows invest their life histories with a faith in what I mentioned at the outset of this section as the power of metonymy – that is, the power of part for whole representations.

Like ethnographers, it seems, these activist-residents are self-conscious about the extent to which their personal stories and experiences can serve as evidence of or for something greater. In an effort to bolster their objectivity, the residents turn to a host of objects – from deeds and other official documents, to newspaper clippings, photos, and other externally validating things. Chari's chapter suggests that life histories and other forms of activists' self-presentation that he describes can be valuable precisely because of their unstable nature as social scientific objects. While they may not be as paradigmatic as their authors (and sometimes anthropologists) can imply, these formations of political evidence are valuable precisely because they do not resolve the tension between subject and object.

Quantity and quality

This second theme I want to raise is closely related to the first. As Stafford's concern with scale suggests, for example, anthropologists face a peculiar burden of balancing the quality and quantity of their evidence. When everything is potential evidence, how do you make it legible as such? In one sense you cannot have too much evidence for something, but you do not *necessarily* need 'a lot' of evidence – however one wants to quantify it – to have a compelling argument. This point is also made by Holbraad in the discussion of his friend Jorge, a Santería follower in Cuba. In a different way, Chari's observations in Durban suggest that people (from activists in Durban to the ethnographers studying them) often have the impulse to horde as much 'stuff' ('data') as they can in the (vain) attempt to be exhaustive. This is an impulse that tends to kick in for anthropologists about half-way through a field trip, an impulse I have felt and which has been confirmed to me by several Ph.D. students in the last few years: how do we know when we have enough? Should we try to stay a few months longer? Surely that could make all the difference.

In many cases, we learn from Ecks's chapter, medical doctors seem to suffer not from the lack of evidence, but from too much of it. Issues of quantity and quality stand at the heart of his chapter. He relates these issues to both his field research in Kolkata and the intersections between 'evidence-based medicine' (EBM) and medical anthropology.[5] For doctors in Kolkata, quantity and quality are defined in large part by specialization. Ecks found that when it comes to making sense of depression, general practitioners (GPs) are more willing to take 'social factors' (living in a slum, for example, with no chance of escape) as evidence for a rise in rates of depression, a rise in which many GPs are convinced. Psychiatrists, on the other hand, while willing to accept that life in a slum is difficult, are less willing to accept social factors as evidence, in large part because they do not have 'proper' studies that transform their anecdotal experiences into reliable evidence of a causal link.

Ecks notes that most anthropologists reading an account by GPs in Kolkata citing the link between depression and social factors would accept it as reliable evidence 'without blinking an eye' (p. 76). As with activists in Durban, there seems to be an affinity between the folk-level evidentiary protocols of Indian GPs and our profession. But Kolkatan GPs are not in the majority view when it comes to the medical profession, in India or elsewhere. Or, at least, their understandings of evidence are not the dominant model. That honour belongs to EBM, a movement within medical science that is shifting the sources of knowledge and the justification for action from practitioners to 'the literature', a kind of quasi-object that some hope in the future will be available to all doctors on their hospital rounds as internet downloads.

Proponents of evidence-based medicine argue that it helps preserve and promote best practice by shifting the profession away from 'ego-based' and 'eminence-based' medicine, a state of affairs in which the good and great might act on their own authority, rather than the findings of science. Critics of evidence-based medicine caution that the utopian vision of doctors with instant on-line access to the gargantuan EBM database robs practitioners of alternatives and concomitantly of agency. It is important not to overstate the pro and con positions; Ecks does not suggest that opponents of EBM want doctors to throw away their books, refuse to read some percentage of the 5,000 articles published every day, and work on impulse and intuition. Especially when viewed in light of his thought-provoking section on developing an 'evidence-based medical anthropology', however, Ecks brings to the surface important issues about the disciplinary pressures and regimes to which I referred in the previous section in the discussion of Collingwood. The vibrancy and potentials of any discipline or profession can often hang in a delicate balancing act between rigorous quality controls of what counts as 'good' evidence and a recognition that these controls must remain flexible lest they blinker a professional vision.

Certainty

In the previous section I highlighted the point that anthropology can be reliable but not certain. In this it is like any proper science. Certainty is one of the issues that recurs in discussions of evidence, although there are not many professional communities that will insist on its delivery. Evidence-based medicine, for example, is not about certainty, but about a kind of 'certain reliability' amassed in a shelf-load of studies. Even in many religious worldviews certainty is not the point, or at least it is a certainty conditioned by the productivity of doubt. So why does this issue resurface?

Holbraad's chapter on Santería in Cuba can be read as an answer to this question, or, at least, an exploration of it. He begins the chapter with a discussion of his friend Jorge, a Santería follower who accumulates 'proof' of the gods, a process that Holbraad likens to the anthropologist's accumulation of social facts, which are subsequently turned into ethnographic evidence. In each he sees a metaphysical longing for certainty at work and, on the basis of this claim, tries to show how the Santería follower and the anthropologist are versions of one another – how 'proof' (*prueba*) in Santería functions like 'evidence' in anthropology, and vice versa. Picking up on a point by Lakatos, Holbraad suggests that the concern with evidence looks more theological than scientific and that, as a result, we might well consider abandoning any 'faith' in evidence as that which confirms or produces knowledge (cf. Miyazaki [2004] on anthropological investments in hope as a method).

Holbraad's argument is an exercise in figure-ground reversal of the kind we find in the works of Roy Wagner, Marilyn Strathern, and Eduardo Viveiros de Castro. It is, in part, an effort to dislodge anthropology from the 'art or science?' discussion altogether. Holbraad is not convinced we need gather 'evidence' in the pursuit of reliability – much less certainty. It might be more productive to align ourselves closer to philosophy, a discipline committed to 'conceptual analysis'. Holbraad is well aware this is a contentious claim, and it is not the only strand in his chapter, but as I suggested near the outset of this introduction, it raises an important point we ought to consider.

Keane's chapter, like Holbraad's, raises important issues about how certainty is a concern not only among religious subjects but the anthropologists who study them. He does not call for an end to evidence, and he limits his discussion to the anthropology of religion (a discussion which includes an insightful set of remarks on the difficulty of bounding such a sub-field in the first place). In Keane's analysis certainty manifests itself in part through the prism of belief, a cognitive state that is often contrasted with certainty. What we cannot be certain of – what we cannot know, prove, see, or point to – gets cast as belief. We know about horses; we believe in unicorns. Keane challenges this contrast because of the burdensome work it makes the concept of evidence perform, work that 'may obscure certain dimensions of that which we want to understand' (p. 105). Turning instead to the materiality of religious phenomena, and in particular the materiality of religious language, he gives a detailed explanation of how these semiotic forms can stand as evidence of something as seemingly immaterial as belief. Far from being concerned with the airy realm of the ideal, semiotics (especially after Peirce) is well grounded, so to speak. 'Semiotic practices can therefore both furnish evidence of something that is not directly found in experience, and, as components of experience, give rise to new inferences and serve as evidence in new ways' (Keane, p. 119, this volume).

Finally, Good's chapter makes clear the problems in entertaining Holbraad's call for 'conceptual analysis' for anthropologists who act in the courts as expert witnesses. In the courts there is no room for this. Good's chapter thus serves as a useful complement to the more analytical interventions on the problem of certainty by Holbraad and Keane (although there is a practicality in the latter's argument, too), giving us a sense of how in legal contexts anthropologists might well employ a strategic certainty, or at least be pressured to. Anthropology, Good notes, tries to preserve ambiguity and complexity. The results of this can be disastrous in the legal system, as the case of the Mashpee Indians on Cape Cod makes clear. In the 1970s, the Mashpee were pushing to be recognized as a tribe and thus gain certain rights to the land. In the Mashpee trial, as Clifford (1988b) shows, the anthropologists (and historians) who acted as expert witnesses on behalf of the Mashpee were unable to give the kind of confident answers the judicial system seeks. The existence of the Mashpee tribe boiled down to a series of yes and no answers. As Good tells us, however, legal analysis will always 'prune away "extraneous" details' (p. 47). 'Experts are therefore under pressure to profess greater certainty than they really feel' (p. 45).

Intention

This is an appropriate theme with which to end, if only because it is a main concern of the first two chapters – Bloch's more explicitly, but no less so in Pinney's. Intention has already surfaced in several of the discussions, both in the preceding section and in the sketches offered as to what we can expect from this volume. In a classic sense – and certainly when it comes to the word's legal uses – human intention ought to be absent from evidence. The historian of science Lorraine Daston (1994: 244) clarifies this point. A bloody knife might serve as evidence in a murder trial, but if we learn the knife was planted by someone, it is no longer evidence (at least of the murder). As Daston also tells us, the concern with human intentions corrupting scientific experiments led to 'methodological precautions' such as double-blind trials. For anthropology, as we have discussed, pattern recognition has served as a similar kind of methodological precaution. When found in patterns, the evidence we offer can be trusted as reliable (if not certain). In a sense this means it has to have an agency of its own.

Bloch's short chapter builds a case for the important link between sight and truth, a link he then relates to the concept of evidence. 'I saw it with my own eyes' becomes the tell-all phrase. What is interesting about this phrase is the appeal to objectivity that stands behind it. Prompted in part by his conversations with the Zafimaniry (after administering the 'false belief task' to them), and in part by his knowledge of the ethnographic record, Bloch suggests that we (i.e. humans) privilege seeing over hearing as a window onto the truth because the former is not mediated by language. The Zafimaniry he spoke with all agreed that language is what allows humans to be deceptive and lie, an observation that Bloch ties to larger currents of human thought. This makes any description of social experience suspect. There is, then, an experiential side to generating evidence in which 'being there' and 'seeing it for yourself' becomes the *sine qua non* of authority and, in a sense, certainty. This is not so different from the logic of anthropology! (Compare it as well with Schaffer [1994] on 'self-evidence' and

Scott [1994] on the evidence of experience.) So, what we say is subjective, while what we see is objective. As Bloch argues, sight is 'verification which avoids the treacherousness of language used in social life' (p. 25). What we see, in other words, is not, like language, 'vitiated by Machiavellian social intentionality' (p. 25).

Bloch's chapter can be read alongside Pinney's, which takes up the interrelated themes of intentionality and certainty in a more restricted frame, but with equal analytical rigour. Pinney's focus is not human nature but colonial India. In the chapter he traces the rise of photography in the second half of the nineteenth century as the ultimate visual medium; whereas lithographs depended on the skills of the lithographer, there was a sense in which the photographic image was not so much representation as presence. 'Its *positivity*', he writes, drawing from the semiotics of Peirce, 'lay in its indexicality' (p. 32, original emphasis). Throughout much of the nineteenth century, then, Pinney says that photography was perceived as the 'cure' for the weaknesses of other kinds of visual representation.

For the colonial state, however, photography as cure slipped all too quickly into photography as 'poison', as those critical of the state used its positivity to their own advantage. The key example on this point is drawn from the historical records of the massacre at Amritsar in 1919, in which hundreds of people were killed by the authorities. After the massacre, the photographer Narayan Vinayak Virkar took a series of photographs where the massacre took place, including a bullet-riddled wall against which locals stand, pointing to the bullet holes ringed in white chalk. Virkar's documentation of the Amritsar massacre showed what photography could do: serve as 'eyewitness' (Pinney, this volume). It was direct evidence, stripped of human intention and free, in a sense, from the subjectivity of its producer. Not long after, 'images in India were at war' (p. 37), a state of affairs, Pinney goes on to suggest, that threw the innocence of photography's positivity into doubt. In this chapter of the history of seeing, intention makes a rude return. As evidence, the photograph is neither certain nor free from the interpretative frame in which it is offered.

Because all anthropologists have to grapple with questions of evidence in their research and writing, it behooves us to take them seriously. Evidence is a concept not far from the heart of our discipline's internal debates over epistemology and the nature of anthropological knowledge. As such, evidence cannot be separated from our concerns with truth, certainty, and reliability; facts, social and otherwise; the dynamics of objectivity and subjectivity; intention and agency; and, most generally, in Hastrup's succinct phrase, getting it right. The chapters here do not provide one answer to how we get it right, and still less an exhaustive list. What they offer are several productive avenues into understanding the techniques of persuasion, illumination, and objectification that stand behind our contributions to the human sciences.

NOTES

I would like to thank Dominic Boyer, Stefan Ecks, Richard Handler, Eleonora Montuschi, and John Tresch for helpful comments and advice on this chapter, as well as one of the reviewers for the RAI Publications Committee and Richard Fardon, who served as the Committee's liaison.

[1] The only anthropologist in the volume is Jean Comaroff, who provides a commentary on Ian Hacking's article on multiple personalities and questions of evidence in psychology.

[2] The partial exception here is work in legal anthropology (e.g. Jeffrey 2006; Just 1986). In most of this literature, however, evidence is presented as an ethnographic object rather than an epistemological tool. It is important to note as well that the situation is somewhat different in anthropology's other sub-disciplines, even linguistic anthropology, which is probably the most relevant sub-discipline for the chapters here. For some important discussions on the role of evidence in linguistic analysis, see Chafe & Nichols (1986) and Hill & Irvine (1993).

[3] Within Anglo-American anthropology, and especially the dominant tradition of American cultural anthropology, strong versions of positivism – those which proffer universal laws of history, or causation, for instance – have been consistently eclipsed (Fabian 1994; Keane 2005; cf. Bowman 1998). In George Steinmetz's estimation, anthropology's 'nonpositivist' commitment 'represents something of an extreme in the epistemological space of all the human sciences' (2005: 9). I would not dispute this argument. But in my reading, Kelman's idea of closet positivism is not incompatible with anthropology's nonpositivism. What it captures is the hesitancy or even embarrassment that accompanies any 'clarity of vision' (Kelman 1994: 188) we might express – and often feel we have – when advancing a point of analysis or interpretation, even as and when that vision is explicitly recognized as momentary and partial.

[4] Not everyone may be comfortable with such a materializing metaphor as 'scale'; in reading an earlier draft of this chapter, Dominic Boyer suggested we might also talk about the 'tuning' of our ears, for instance, since 'anthropological evidence is almost all absorbed from words and images'. This is an important point, and one that was explored in a workshop at the London School of Economics and Political Science in March 2008 on 'The Pitch of Ethnography' co-organized by Rita Astuti, Olivia Harris, Michael Lambek, Charles Stafford, and myself.

[5] This hyper-explicit shift to the value of evidence is happening in other fields, too, such as the move to evidence-based policy (Riles 2006; Strathern 2006) and evidence-based crime prevention (Sherman 2006). In some of my most recent research, I have even come across literature on evidence-based spiritual healthcare (South Yorkshire NHS Trust 2003).

REFERENCES

BENEDICT, R. 1934. *Patterns of culture*. Boston: Houghton Mifflin.

BLOCH, M. 2005. Where did anthropology go? Or the need for human nature. In *Essays on cultural transmission*, M. Bloch, 1-20. Oxford: Berg.

BOAS, F. 1934. Introduction. In *Patterns of culture*, R. Benedict, xix-xxi. Boston: Houghton Mifflin.

BOWMAN, G. 1998. Radical empiricism: anthropological fieldwork after psychoanalysis and the *Année Sociologique*. *Anthropological Journal of European Cultures* **6: 2**, 79-107.

BRADY, I. 1990. Comment on Carrithers. *Current Anthropology* **31**, 273-4.

BRETTELL, C. (ed.) 1993. *When they read what we write*. London: Bergin & Garvey.

CARRITHERS, M. 1990. Is anthropology art or science? *Current Anthropology* **31**, 261-82.

——— 1992. *Why humans have cultures: explaining anthropology and social diversity*. Oxford: University Press.

CHAFE, W. & J. NICHOLS (eds) 1986. *Evidentiality: the linguistic coding of epistemology*. Norwood, N.J.: Ablex.

CHANDLER, J., A. DAVIDSON & H. HAROOTUNIAN (eds) 1994a. *Questions of evidence: proof, practice, and persuasion across the disciplines*. Chicago: University Press.

———, ——— & ——— 1994b. Editors' introduction. In *Questions of evidence: proof, practice, and persuasion across the disciplines* (eds) J. Chandler, A. Davidson & H. Harootunian, 1-8. Chicago: University Press.

CHUA, L., C. HIGH & T. LAU (eds) in press. *How do we know? Evidence, ethnography, and the making of anthropological knowledge*. Newcastle: Cambridge Scholars Publishing.

CLIFFORD, J. 1986. Introduction: partial truths. In *Writing culture: the poetics and politics of ethnography* (eds) J. Clifford & G. Marcus, 1-26. Berkeley: University of California Press.

——— 1988a. *The predicament of culture: twentieth-century ethnography, literature, and art*. Cambridge, Mass.: Harvard University Press.

——— 1988b. Identity in Mashpee. In *The predicament of culture: twentieth-century ethnography, literature, and art*, J. Clifford, 277-346. Cambridge, Mass.: Harvard University Press.

COLLINGWOOD, R.G. 1946. Historical evidence. In *The idea of history*, R.G. Collingwood, 249-82. (Revised edition), Oxford: University Press.

CSORDAS, T. 2004. Evidence of and for what? *Anthropological Theory* **4**, 473-80.

DAS, V. 1998. Wittgenstein and anthropology. *Annual Review of Anthropology* **27**, 171-95.

DASTON, L. 1994. Marvelous facts and miraculous evidence in early modern Europe. In *Questions of evidence: proof, practice, and persuasion across the disciplines* (eds) J. Chandler, A. Davidson & H. Harootunian, 243-74. Chicago: University Press.

DREXLER, E. 2006. History and liability in Aceh, Indonesia: single bad guys and convergent narratives. *American Ethnologist* **33**, 313-26.

EVANS-PRITCHARD, E.E. 1962. *Essays in social anthropology*. London: Faber.

FABIAN, J. 1994. Ethnographic objectivity revisited: from rigor to vigor. In *Rethinking objectivity* (ed.) A. Megill, 81-108. Durham, N.C.: Duke University Press.

Friedman, J. 1994. *Cultural identity and global process*. London: Sage.

Geertz, C. 1988. *Works and lives: the anthropologist as author*. Palo Alto, Calif.: Stanford University Press.

Gregory, S. 2006. Transnational storytelling: Human rights, WITNESS, and video advocacy. *American Anthropologist* **108**, 195-204.

Hacking, I. 1983. *Representing and intervening: introductory topics in the philosophy of natural science*. Cambridge: University Press.

Hastrup, K. 2004. Getting it right: knowledge and evidence in anthropology. *Anthropological Theory* **4**, 455-72.

Hill, J. & J. Irvine (eds) 1993. *Responsibility and evidence in oral discourse*. Cambridge: University Press.

Jeffrey, L. 2006. Historical narrative and legal evidence: judging Chagossians' High Court testimonies. *Political and Legal Anthropology Review* **29**, 228-53.

Just, P. 1986. Let the evidence fit the crime: evidence, law, and 'sociological truth' among the Dou Donggo. *American Ethnologist* **13**, 43-61.

Keane, W. 2005. Estrangement, intimacy, and the objects of anthropology: reflections on a genealogy. In *The politics of method in the human sciences: positivism and its epistemological others* (ed.) G. Steinmetz, 59-88. Durham, N.C.: Duke University Press.

Keesing, R. 1990. Comment on Carrithers. *Current Anthropology* **31**, 274-5.

Kelman, M. 1994. Reasonable evidence of reasonableness. In *Questions of evidence: proof practice, and persuasion across the disciplines* (eds) J. Chandler, A. Davidson, and H. Harootunian, 169-88. Chicago: University Press.

Knauft, B. 2006. Anthropology in the middle. *Anthropological Theory* **6**, 407-29.

Leach, E. 1961. *Rethinking anthropology*. London: Athlone Press.

Lévi-Strauss, C. 1978. *Myth and meaning*. London: Routledge & Kegan Paul.

Malinowski, B. 1984 [1922]. *Argonauts of the Western Pacific: an account of native enterprise and adventure in the archipelagoes of Melanesian New Guinea*. Prospect Heights, Ill: Waveland Press.

Marcus, G. 1986. Afterword: ethnographic writing and anthropological careers. In *Writing culture: the poetics and politics of ethnography* (eds) J. Clifford & G. Marcus, 262-6. Berkeley: University of California Press.

Miyazaki, H. 2004. *The method of hope: anthropology, philosophy, and Fijian knowledge*. Stanford: University Press.

Mosse, D. 2005. *Cultivating development: an ethnography of aid policy and practice*. London: Pluto Press.

——— 2006. Anti-social anthropology? Objectivity, objection, and the ethnography of public policy and professional communities. *Journal of the Royal Anthropological Institute* (N.S.) **12**, 935-56.

Needham, R. 1974. *Remarks and inventions: skeptical essays about kinship*. London: Tavistock.

Riles, A. 2006. Introduction: in response. In *Documents: artifacts of modern knowledge* (ed.) A. Riles, 1-38. Ann Arbor: University of Michigan Press.

Sahlins, M. 2002. *Waiting for Foucault, still*. (Prickly Paradigm 1). Chicago: Prickly Paradigm Press.

Schaffer, S. 1994. Self-evidence. In *Questions of evidence: proof, practice, and persuasion across the disciplines* (eds) J. Chandler, A. Davidson & H. Harootunian, 56-91. Chicago: University Press.

Scott, J. 1994. The evidence of experience. In *Questions of evidence: proof, practice, and persuasion across the disciplines* (eds) J. Chandler, A. Davidson & H. Harootunian, 363-87. Chicago: University Press.

Sherman, L. (ed.) 2006. *Evidence-based crime prevention*. London: Routledge.

Skidmore, M. 2003. Darker than midnight: fear, vulnerability, and terror making in urban Burma (Myanmar). *American Ethnologist* **30**, 5-21.

South Yorkshire NHS Trust 2003. Caring for the spirit: A strategy for the chaplaincy and spiritual healthcare workforce (available on-line: *http://nhs-chaplaincy-collaboratives.com/resources/caringforthespirit0311.pdf*, accessed 7 January 2008).

Spencer, J. 1989. Anthropology as a kind of writing. *Man* (N.S.) **24**, 145-64.

Sperber, D. 1985. *On anthropological knowledge: three essays*. Cambridge: University Press.

Steinmetz, G. 2005. Positivism and its others in the social sciences. In *The politics of method in the human sciences: positivism and its epistemological others* (ed.) G. Steinmetz, 1-58. Durham, N.C.: Duke University Press.

Strathern, M. 1996. *The relation: issues in complexity and scale*. Cambridge: Prickly Pear Press.

——— 2006. A community of critics? Thoughts on new knowledge. *Journal of the Royal Anthropological Institute* (N.S.) **12**, 191-209.

Wilk, R. 1998. A global anthropology? *Current Anthropology* **39**, 287-88.

Wilson, R. 2004. The trouble with truth: anthropology's epistemological hypochondria. *Anthropology Today* **20**: 5, 14-17.

Wolf, E. 1980. They divide and subdivide and call it anthropology. *New York Times*, 30 Nov., E9.

2

Truth and sight: generalizing without universalizing

MAURICE BLOCH *London School of Economics and Political Science*

The English word 'evidence' is based on the Latin verb *videre*: to see. Familiar phrases such as 'seeing is believing' or the assurance that something must be true because 'I saw it with my own eyes' are everywhere. Such observations and many others all bear witness to a well-established European connection between seeing and truth which, as the *Shorter Oxford Dictionary* tells us, is so often associated with evidence.

Such a link seems very ancient. Thus Thucydides says that, in contrast to that based on hearsay, the only true history is that based on the authority of sight (*autopsia*): 'of the two ways of knowing, through the eye and the ear, only the former gives us a true picture', because accounts based on memory distort and lie.[1] St Paul, for his part, in a famous Platonic mood, makes the same equation when he tells us of the dark glass which, by interfering with our sight, keeps us from the full truth. The idea that seeing is a guarantee of truth continues in less ancient times. Thus, the greater truthfulness of what is *seen* over what is reported through language is a major theme in the writings of Augustine (Stock 1996), and Bacon, Hume, Condillac (Roos 1999), and the empiricist/sensationalist philosophers generally all make the point. This type of argument is found, with modifications, in Kant. In a completely different way, writers such as Broca, after having noted the prominence of the lower brain in non-human primates, especially the olfactory bulb, see evolution as the progress of the development of 'higher' senses, above all sight, over 'lower' senses, especially smell (Dias 2004).

But what do such recurrences of an association between truth and sight mean for the anthropologist? Are they more than a manifestation of a particular turn of our own culture, which, once again, we might naïvely take to be universal? Such a classic form of professional scepticism does not, at first, seem to be borne out by a cursory inspection of the ethnographic record. In an article to which I return below, Stephen Tyler (1984) informs us that the association of truth and sight recurs in all Indo-European languages, including Hittite, and also in many other language families. Ranging even more widely, the comparative linguist Viberg (2001) sees the association as extremely common in all languages. Certainly, a random trawl through ethnographic sources comes up with many examples from all over the world. Thus Strathern (1975) and Robbins (2001) tell us that the New Guinea Islanders they studied are obsessed with the unreliability of language and, by contrast, stress the truth of knowledge obtained through sight. Taylor confirms that the Amazonian Achuars are similar.[2] Izard also tells me that much the same is true of the Mossi of Burkina Faso.[3] According to Pinney (this volume), Indian nationalists, the British colonial administration, and the old lady in the film convinced that photographs show gods who are real are all influenced in their attitude to photography by the belief that what the lens sees is so.

There are some dissenting voices, however, that give examples where sight is not linked to the notion of truth. A number of anthropologists provide ethnographic cases which purport to show that, among this or that group, another sense, usually hearing, is valued above vision (Feld 1982; Gell 1995; Tyler 1984).[4] The question of the relative significance of the different senses has also come up in the scholarly tradition. Some, especially those eighteenth-century philosophers who engaged with Molineux's problem (would a man, blind from birth, who had then been cured recognize through sight those objects which he had only felt before his cure?), most notably Diderot in the *Lettre sur les aveugles*, tangled endlessly with the question of the relation and hierarchy of touch and sight.

The presence of possible exceptions, based on a few exotic ethnographies, which are then used as negative evidence against an assumed universality, is a familiar form of argument in anthropology. Such rhetoric was the cause of the popularity of work such as that of Margaret Mead. Indeed, it might seem that the only defence against such negative argument is either to challenge the reliability of the supposed exception, as was famously done by Derek Freeman (1983), or to broaden and weaken the claim to universality. Thus, we might modify the proposition that sight is always associated with truth to one that merely claims an association between truth and knowledge through the senses in general. However, even such a less specific claim would also be vulnerable in a different and more fundamental sense, in much the way that all generalizations in kinship theory have been attacked (Bloch & Sperber 2002; Needham 1971) by pointing out the obvious fact that the details of every ethnographic case are different. Lumping these cases together would thus be a case of begging the question, an example of mere reductionism, where it seems that a universal category is created when in fact the cases only have in common what the definition created by the observer has arbitrarily decided is significant.

These are familiar ways in which generalizing claims in anthropology have been attacked, and they are not without basis. Such destructive tactics have been effective to such an extent that many in the discipline have abandoned all attempts at grand theory and shudder at any claims that anything non-particularistic could exist in cultural phenomena. However, the problem with such timid nihilism is that the prominence of recurrences in the ethnographic record, such as the association of truth and sight, can only be ignored through acts of blatant theoretical bad faith. But, given the soundness of the objections, we are left with the question of what are we to do about them.

In this short chapter I propose to give an example of precisely how we might attempt to generalize about a phenomenon such as the non-universal but frequent recurrence of the association between truth and sight without ignoring the important anti-universalist points referred to above. In doing this, I hope to give one example of how anthropology, in the original sense of the term, is still a possible enterprise, in spite of the criticisms such an approach has had to face in the last thirty years. But, before engaging in grand theorizing, I invite the reader to take a detour via an ethnographic case.

Zafimaniry theory

During a recent period of research in the remote Zafimaniry village in Madagascar where I have been working for so long, I tried out a new research strategy, new for a social anthropologist at least, in order to understand what might be called 'Zafimaniry ethno-psychology'. This consisted in demonstrating in front of my fellow villagers a well-known psychological experiment concerned with the cognitive development of children. This was in order to hear how the adults interpreted what they saw their children doing, as they observed the tasks they were asked to do. In other words, I put ordinary people, who had never heard the word 'psychology' and who, for the most part, could neither read nor write, in the position in which professional psychologists normally place themselves.

The experiment referred to is called the 'false belief task'. It has been considered in cognitive psychology as being of great significance since it seems to reveal a critical moment in the development of the child's cognitive development. The false belief task, in the version I used, consists in asking a child where a person who saw an object placed under one hat will look for it when they return after a spell outside the house, during which period the subject has seen the object being switched to another hiding place by the experimenter. Adults and children over the age of 6 normally say that the person will look for the object under the hat where the person saw it placed before they left the house, but where they therefore know it is not anymore. This is taken to mean that they understand that the person who left the house holds a false belief. Young children, by contrast, say that the person returning will look for the object at the place where it actually is. In most of the psychological literature at least, this is usually taken to mean that the young child has not yet understood that other people act in terms of what they *believe* the world to be; a notion that is obviously necessary for someone to realize that others could hold false beliefs about the world. Such a difference between the older children who rightly predict that the person will look where they *believe* the object is and the younger ones who predict the person will look for the object where it actually *is* is striking and thought-provoking. It raises much broader questions, concerned not only with child development, but also with what our understanding of others and their minds requires in order to act competently in the social world.

It is precisely because this experiment raises such fundamental questions and because reflecting on its significance leads to such fundamental reflection about the human mind and the nature of human sociability that it seemed interesting to see how the Malagasy villagers would rise to the challenge. I thus used the Zafimaniry witnesses of the experiment and their surprise at the difference between the responses of the younger and older children to trigger wide-ranging discussions on, among other things, the nature of thought and language, child development, and the cognitive differences between humans and other animals. These discussions took the form of animated conversations in which all sorts of ideas were aired. Certain of the musings of the villagers were expressed with a good deal of hesitation and others were much contested. Some propositions, however, came loud and clear and were acknowledged as obviously right by everybody present. It is only these that I consider here.

Among these broadly agreed propositions was the idea that thought is, at bottom, a matter of organizing action so that it achieves desired ends. In the villagers' view two things follow from this pragmatic way of understanding mind. First, non-human animals are as capable of thought as humans, since pigs, for example, will think of turning up during the preparation of food in order to eat what peelings might be available, and since fleas will think of hiding in the seams of clothing in order not to be caught. Secondly, and this follows inevitably from the previous point, the villagers were quite clear that thought is independent of language, since they well know that animals strategize their actions but do not talk.[5]

However, my informants did not undervalue language for all that. They were adamant that language was a key factor in the superiority of humans over animals. Their affirmation in this matter led me to ask them what language was for, if it was not, as they asserted, necessary for thought. The answer that was invariably given is that language enables humans to lie. According to Zafimaniry theory, speech, and lying, which speech renders possible, is an extra technique, not available to animals but available to humans, that enables older children and adults to obtain by means of deceit what they have desired in their thoughts. Furthermore, and in response to the experiment, the villagers also argued that this refined technology for Machiavellian gratification, not possible for animals, is also not available to very young humans, since infants obviously do not know how to speak. Language is something that develops as human children mature and learn. Such reasoning was the basis of the villagers' interpretation of the false belief task in terms of lying. It explains why young children, like animals, cannot lie because they do not yet have language, or, at least, sufficient control over language. Infants fail the false belief task because they have not yet reached the developmental stage when they so control language that they are able to lie. This is an ability that requires, in the first place, an understanding that others can hold false beliefs, since otherwise there would not be any point in lying.[6]

The villagers also made clear that such ideas about language, motivation, and thought have important further implications. The first concerns their description of the experience of the social. The second concerns the experiential side of evidence. I take these two in turn.

In the discussions that followed the observation of the false belief task, the social was described as a dangerous and exciting matter. It involves living among chattering individuals who, like you, are seeking to further their own ends by fair means or foul, and who therefore use all the tools available as speaking human adults. This makes normal life risky because it involves being among people endowed with, and indeed continually using, their capacity for lying. At every step, therefore, there is a danger that one acts in terms of a world that is false. This feeling is often expressed in the fear that those who falsely profess to love you might, really, be trying to poison you.

Secondly, since it is assumed that pragmatic deceit is the default form of social life, this makes claiming truthfulness for what one is saying no trivial matter; therefore doing so must be clearly distinguished from the everyday. This leads to a continual emphasis in discourse which makes clear that normal interchange is not strongly claiming that what one is proposing is true, so that, when one will actually want to claim truthfulness for one's declaration, these instances will really stand out from normal dialogue. This attitude has the effect that, for example, when one is asking for information, the most common answer is a semi-indignant *asa*: 'search me', followed for greater emphasis by *tsy fantatro*: 'I don't know', and then the information requested is offered. Similarly, this information, when it is finally volunteered, is either preceded or followed by the word *angamba*, meaning 'perhaps'.

All this tentativeness can thus then contrast with those moments when one *does* want to be believed categorically. I may want to say, 'There really *is* a mad dog in the village!' To do this one can either follow the assertion by the word *marina*, usually and appropriately translated as: 'It's true', or, for even greater claim to truth, say, '*Hita maso!*', lit. 'It was seen by my own eyes!'

The Zafimaniry, and all the Malagasy I know, are thus yet another example of the many people around the world who associate statements claiming the authority of sensations, and especially sight, as being powerful evidence of truthfulness. But their discussions following their observations of the false belief task take us even further. They willingly explained why sight is so important: this is because it is verification which avoids the treacherousness of language used in social life, since social life is a matter of dealing with speaking individuals who can hide the truth in order to further their own ends and trick you. The Zafimaniry thus, continually, implicitly and explicitly, operate a strong contrast between information obtained through ordinary speech, which they rhetorically mark as uncertain, and which they associate with lying, and information obtained through the sense of sight.

But why do they use knowledge through the senses, and sight in particular,[7] to contrast with the treachery of the social? The answer is implicit in all their discussion of language. What they seem to be saying is that: via language, truth is vitiated by Machiavellian social intentionality. Sight, on the other hand, as it is thought about in Zafimaniry theory – if one can call ideas that are usually only implicit 'theory' – does not involve the dangerous imagined intentionality projected by the source of knowledge. What one sees has no intention to represent itself, falsely or otherwise; one may mistake what one sees but that's your fault, not, as in the case of linguistic dialogue, the result of the intention of the schemers with whom one is in a relationship.

Machiavellian intelligence

The question which the above suggests, however, is the following. Even if my interpretation of what the Zafimaniry told me in response to their witnessing the false belief task is accurate, why should that tell us anything about human beings in general, the definitional aim of anthropological theory? Is the above simply one more local theory, to be added to the stamp collection of local representations which anthropology sometime seems to see as its only purpose?

As a first step in arguing against such a typically frequent pessimistic conclusion, we should, first of all, remind ourselves of the problem of recurrence which such insistence on the uniqueness of each case creates for a culturalist approach. If we take the particularistic stance, this becomes incomprehensible. Indeed, the similarity of discourses in the different ethnographic cases to which I refer is even greater than suggested at first. It is not only that we find, again and again, an association between sight and truth, we also find this associated with the distrust of what one might call 'hearsay evidence', for the reason that this may be vitiated by the treacherous intentionality which characterizes ordinary social life. In other words lying is linked, as it is so clearly for the Zafimaniry, to what the philosophers call theory of mind, the continual reading of intentionality which human communication uniquely implies and which ultimately makes deceit easily possible. Furthermore, this potential treacherousness is most often seen as the product of the capacity for language that makes lying possible.

Thus, we cannot ignore the fact that so many people, in different cultures all around the world, are saying similar things again and again. Such recurrences are a challenge that anthropology should not dodge by finding occasional counter-examples.

Then, there is another type of recurrence. What ordinary people argue, according to ethnographic reports, such as the one I briefly supplied above for the Zafimaniry, is interestingly very close to a set of very differently styled propositions that are not the product of ethnographic interpretation but are typical of the theories of some evolutionary scientists reflecting on human sociability and language.

Evolutionary theory has again and again stressed the problem caused by the potential which theory of mind, human intentionality, and human language creates by making deceit so easy. There is no place here to discuss this massive literature which stresses the point that the supremely well-adapted tool for human sociability – language – creates at the same time and by its very nature, a major problem for individual members of a community in that it places them at risk of being misled. Scholars of many different kinds see the awareness and significance of this fact as central. This fundamental point is found in the work of many anthropologists (e.g. Bateson 1951; Cosmides & Tooby 1992; Knight 1998; Rappaport 1979; Sperber 2001), leading biologists and theoreticians of evolution (e.g. Dawkins & Krebs 1978; Krebs & Dawkins 1984; Maynard Smith & Harper 1995; Waddington 1960), and linguists (Dessalles 2000; Lyons 1977), to name only a few. The views expressed are varied, but, like the Zafimaniry, all these writers are agreed that the complexity created by our ability to read other minds – that which makes language use possible (Sperber & Wilson 1995) – exposes older children and adult members of the species to a risk which exists only to a limited extent for other animals, if at all: that of being misled by conspecifics and thereby acting against one's own interest.

We might conclude from this massive scholarly endorsement of Zafimaniry theory that, in this matter, there is little to be said other than that the villagers are right. But, if this is so, it raises a fascinating question. How can this agreement have come about given the totally different circumstances and contexts in which scholars and, in the case of the Zafimaniry, unschooled shifting cultivators live?

The answer must be that there is something in the human condition that is accessible to the understanding of different members of the human species irrespective of history, living in however different circumstances around the globe, which produces cognate representations. In this case, it means that the experience and the awareness of the experience of social life and its dangers, of human intentionality and of the reading of human intentionality, is, in this most fundamental aspect, universal. To assume this implies that the representations people have are *about* this something – the dangers of living among communicative intentional beings – and that this same thing exists independently of the representations people have of it. And, indeed, it is extraordinarily difficult to imagine a human group unconcerned with deceit and lying. Of course, this does not mean that the representations of the dangers of language, deceit, and lying are determined by what they are about. It would be as wrong to forget the specificities of each case as to forget the recurrences. Inevitably cultural, historical, and personal circumstances will lead to variation in styles, directions, and contents. How far purely intellectual speculation on this matter is pushed also varies. For example, scientists are professionally trained to push their reflection, and some groups of people, amongst whom I would include the Zafimaniry, seem to have developed a greater aesthetic orientation towards theoretical speculation than others. There is room for much variation. It is possible that the kind of speculation I have been talking about is totally absent in some cases. This, however, would not invalidate the argument I am developing, simply because these exceptions would not remove the existence of frequent recurrences. But, in spite of variation, all this theorizing, when it occurs, is about the universal awareness of the same thing. And this awareness of this thing is sufficiently constraining to the images that can be produced to cope with it that frequent similarities in representations will occur. This is what explains the recurrences. But because the process of representation is also affected by other important factors – cultural, historical, and so on – we will *only* have family likenesses among the representations of this same awareness.

The commonality of these representations has a further cultural implication that, this time, has a practical side to it. The awareness of the potential treacherousness of the social and of the tool which language offers for deceit is recognized in all the ethnographic cases cited not just as a subject of speculation but also as a major political problem and a threat to in-group sociability. As a result, various practices and institutions are developed explicitly in order to cope with this threat, of which legal devices, such as those discussed by Good in this volume, are the most obvious example. And, in parallel, the specificity of the threat of deceit that exists in language leads to the development and the valuing of devices and ideas for guaranteeing truthful knowledge that is not caught in the web of human intentionality and speech.

This is the explanation for the recurrence that this chapter seeks to explain: the association of truth and the senses and, more particularly, sight. With the type of psychology that the awareness of deceit creates, the idea that what is seen is more truthful than what is reported in speech seems an obvious way to go in order to bypass human intentionality and deceit. Again we have a weak form of determinism. The total causal path is the following. The reality of the human social and the potential of human language lead necessarily to an awareness of the dangers of deceit and lying. This universal awareness strongly influences the representations we find of the social, of language and of deceit, hence the recurrences. These types of representations regularly, but not necessarily always, predispose to the association linking truth and sight. It is thus not surprising that this particular path is so often chosen, though, of course, there might well be cases where it is refused.

And we can go even further in the line of weak determinism that has guided me throughout this chapter. Another case of recurrence which the ethnographic record throws up can be seen to have the same root. This is the similarity displayed by techniques of divination found in so many places around the world. These techniques commonly aim to produce truthful propositions that, unlike other forms of telling, do not involve language and its inevitable corollary, human intentionality. The famous techniques of Azande divination are of this type, as are such practices as tea leaf reading, astrology, and many others. The point about all these is that they use devices which produce truthful answers that are the fruit of a form of causation, such as physiological configuration, in the case of the reading of entrails, or physics, in the case of throwing stones in the air, that is not social. (This, of course, creates the well-known problem that the answers must then be interpreted and translated by humans who reintroduce intentionality and hence fallibility.) Such divination techniques seem to tell the truth through what can be *seen* in states of affairs not brought about by the intentionality of human minds, and thus implicitly recognize the dangers of the social and of human language with its potential for lies.

This seems to be, in part, what Holbraad (this volume) seems to be arguing for Cuban divination, which, like Azande divination, is also taken by its practitioners as truth-telling by definition. According to Holbraad, divination is ontologically creative, a process that seems somewhat mysterious if ontology is taken to mean an exhaustive account of the world as it is. If that is so, it is difficult to understand how it could be added to. However, the sheer demonstration of an effect that seems purely the product of the naïve laws of physics that, as we know (Spelke, Phillips & Woodward 1995), we innately recognize as necessarily true seems a more convincing explanation of the feeling of ontological certainty than Holbraad is describing. The revelation of divination would thus seem to be, for the practitioners, a peep at the world as it appears to the senses, in contrast to the treacherous representations peddled by others.

Interestingly the truth-telling powers of divination seem to have a similar basis to the naïve attitudes to photography discussed by Pinney, where, at first, all sorts of people were convinced that cameras told the truth because they were machines: in other words, because human intentionality was not involved in their powers of representation.

Here again the line of causation, from the shadowy awareness of the nature of the social and of the implications of the human mind to actual practices, seems a tempting and, therefore, frequently followed path. But, for all that, it is not a necessary path, nor is it a rigidly mapped-out one. Thus, if divination techniques are commonly similar, they are also each and every one different, and there may well be societies where such techniques are totally absent. This variation and occasional absence, however, would not contradict the kind of argument I have been developing here. As so many anthropologists rightly, if somewhat trivially, insist, the social world we live in is the product of dialogue, of discourse, of culture, and so on. But this does not mean that these dialogues, discourses, and cultures are not *about* something which people, thankfully to a certain extent, apprehend, and this something, as the psychologist James Gibson stressed, itself suggests non-random affordances that are, again and again, represented.

But there is more to this question than simply the constraints that come from what the representations concern. The ability to read each other's minds and the dangers this creates is a fundamental matter for the adaptation of *Homo sapiens*. This ability necessarily evokes the ideas about the dangers about deceit that concern my Malagasy informants and evolutionary psychologists. However, unlike theory of mind itself, which can operate below the level of consciousness, and usually does, knowledge about deceit and lying needs to be, and evidently is, available to consciousness, if only so that it can be guarded against. This is clearly of crucial importance for all who live in a human-type society, and therefore it is quite likely that, as the evolutionary psychologists argue, we are probably innately predisposed to detect cheaters. But even if this is so, such ability cannot be just automatic since it requires consequent conscious protective actions which, I would argue, are likely to be organized in dedicated institutions. These include, among others, the ones mentioned above: certain divination techniques and legal systems.

This long and tentative line of causation is the story that can explain the familiar mix of recurrences and variations that I have been concerned with throughout this chapter. The universal consciousness of the presence of lying and deceit in society logically implies the possibility that people can hold false beliefs. This awareness can be, and often is, used as a handle for creating, in varying degrees of elaboration, a representation of the mechanisms of the nature of mind, a representation that is constrained both by what mind is like and by our social need to be on guard against lying. Peeping at the mind by using the handle of mistaken knowledge is what the inventors of the false belief task intended to do, and it is also what the Zafimaniry and the people from the other ethnographic cases evoked seem to be doing when, for example, in observing the experiment, and also in many other moments of their lives, they try to explain the difference between the younger and the older children. Knowledge of lying and deceit is thus only a handle, however it is *only* a handle, hence the relative variation, but it is a good handle that we may be predisposed to use, hence the recurrences and the profundity of the reflection.

And this sort of weak determination works the other way, too. The consciousness of the problem of deceit, so often carrying with it an associated and over-determined theory of mind, leads to recurrences in institutional means to enforce the truth and also to imaginative speculation about what might establish truth. These speculations, in turn, lead to recurrent rhetorical formulations such as: 'It's true, I saw it with my own eyes!', or in Malagasy, considerably more elegantly, 'Hita maso!'

NOTES

Although this is a short chapter, it has often involved me in reaching out beyond my usual competence. As a result I have had to rely on the help of many fellow scholars. I wish to acknowledge the following for their generous help either in reading an earlier draft or suggesting relevant leads to the literature: Rita Astuti, Nelia Dias, Matthew Engelke, Michel Izard, Eva Keller, Gerard Lenclud, Gloria Orrigi, Nathaniel Roberts, Åakon Viberg.

[1] I am grateful to Gerard Lenclud for drawing my attention to this quotation.

[2] Pers. comm., 2005.

[3] Pers. comm., 2005.

[4] I have to admit a certain scepticism as to how far the particular claims of Gell and Feld are based on a general ranking of hearing over sight within these cultures and not simply on certain contextually specific evaluations: for example, hunting in dense forests or the typical New Guinea association of unseen birds with ancestors. In any case, it is not clear how far these authors intend to push their argument. Such hesitation, on the other hand, does not apply to the most categorical of the anthropologists. Stephen Tyler, in an article already referred to, and which ironically supplies us with a great number of examples of the coupling of truth and sight, nevertheless concludes that 'the hegemony of the visual is not universal' and that empiricism as a folk theory is a peculiarity of certain grammars. The counter-example he gives to set against the mass of the *visualists*, whom he dismisses, are the speakers of Dravidian languages. His evidence is based on a form of primitive Whorfian examination of Dravidian verbs for knowing, which are taken to offer an easy window to thought. But even if we accept his epistemology, there are serious reasons to doubt what he says about this particular example. Thus, in a personal communication, Nathaniel Roberts tells me that in Tamil, the most spoken Dravidian language, the word most used for 'to know' is *theriyum* (root form: *theri*), for which the standard modern Tamil dictionary in the first place defines: '(1) be visible; be seen; (2) (of eyes) see; to perform the function of seeing'.

[5] This work is ongoing, but for a somewhat fuller discussion of this material, see Bloch (2006).

[6] This point requires further elaboration not possible here.

[7] It is probably because language is associated with hearing that sight is usually favoured over hearing, the only other serious contender among the senses as the source of complex wide-ranging information.

REFERENCES

BATESON, G. 1951. Conventions of communication: where validity depends upon belief. In *Communication: the social matrix of psychiatry* (eds) J. Ruesch & G. Bateson, 212-27. New York: Norton.

BLOCH, M. 2006. *L'anthropologie cognitive à l'epreuve du terrain*. Paris: Fayard.

———— & D. SPERBER 2002. Kinship and evolved psychological dispositions: the mother's brother controversy reconsidered. *Current Anthropology* **43**, 723-48.

COSMIDES, L. & J. TOOBY 1992. Cognitive adapatation for social exchange. In *The adapted mind: evolutionary psychology and the generation of culture* (eds) J.H. Barklow, L. Cosmides & J. Tooby, 163-228. Oxford: University Press.

DAWKINS, R. & J.R. KREBS 1978. Animal signals: information or manipulation? In *Behavioural ecology: an evolutionary approach* (eds) J.R. Krebs & N.B. Davies, 282-309. Oxford: Blackwell.

DESSALLES, J.-L. 2000. *Aux origines du langage: une histoire naturelle de la parole*. Paris: Hermes.

DIAS, N. 2004. *La mesure des sens: les anthropologies et le corps humain au XIXème siècle*. Paris: Aubier.

FELD, S. 1982. *Sound and sentiment: birds, weeping and song in Kaluli expression*. Philadelphia: University of Pennsylvania Press.

FREEMAN, D. 1983. *Margaret Mead and Samoa: the making and unmaking of an anthropological myth*. Cambridge, Mass.: Harvard University Press.

GELL, A. 1995. The language of the forest: landscape and phonological iconism in Umeda. In *The anthropology of landscape: perspectives on place and space* (eds) E. Hirsch & M. O'Hanlon, 232-54. Oxford: University Press.

KNIGHT, C. 1998. Ritual/speech coevolution: a solution to the problem of deception. In *Approaches to the evolution of language* (eds) J. Hurford, M. Studdert-Kennedy & C. Knight, 68-91. Cambridge: University Press.

KREBS, J.R. & R. DAWKINS 1984. Animal signals: mind reading and manipulation. In *Behavioural ecology: an evolutionary approach* (eds) J.R. Krebs & N.B. Davies, 380-405. (Second edition). Oxford: Blackwell.

LYONS, J. 1977. *Semantics*, vol. 2. Cambridge: University Press.

MAYNARD SMITH, J. & D.G.C. HARPER 1995. Animal signals: models and terminology. *Journal of Theoretical Biology* **177**, 305-11.

NEEDHAM, R. 1971. Remarks on the analysis of kinship and marriage. In *Rethinking kinship and marriage* (ed.) R. Needham, 1-34. London: Tavistock.

RAPPAPORT, R.A. 1979. *Ecology, meaning, and religion*. Berkeley: North Atlantic Books.

ROBBINS, J. 2001. God is nothing but talk: modernity, language, and prayer in a Papua New Guinea Society. *American Anthropologist* **103**, 901-12.

ROOS, S. 1999. Consciousness and the linguistic in Condillac. *MLN* **114**, 667-90.

SPELKE, E., A. PHILLIPS & A.L. WOODWARD 1995. Infants' knowledge of object motion and human action. In *Causal cognition: a multidisciplinary debate* (eds) D. Sperber & A.J. Premack, 44-78. London: Oxford University Press.

SPERBER, D. 2001. An evolutionary perspective on testimony and argumentation. *Philosophical Topics* **29**, 401-13.

———— & D. WILSON 1995. *Relevance: communication and cognition*. Oxford: Blackwell.

STOCK, B. 1996. *Augustine the reader*. Cambridge, Mass.: Harvard University Press.

STRATHERN, A. 1975. Veiled speech in Mount Hagen. In *Political language and oratory in traditional societies* (ed.) M. Bloch, 185-203. London: Academic Press.

TYLER, S.A. 1984. The vision quest in the West, or what the mind's eye sees. *Journal of Anthropological Research* **40**, 23-40.

VIBERG, Å. 2001. The verbs of perception. In *Language typology and language universals: an international handbook* (eds) M. Haspelmath, E. König, W. Oesterreicher & W. Raible, 123-63. Berlin: De Gruyter.

WADDINGTON, C. 1960. *The ethical animal*. London: Allen & Unwin.

3

The prosthetic eye: photography as cure and poison

CHRISTOPHER PINNEY *University College London/Northwestern University*

> Then, straight away, he plays his trump card. He offers to show his victim the Colonel's photograph. There's no resisting this. As the light, by now, is poor, the kind soul bends down to see better, and that seals his doom.
>
> Eugene Ionesco, *The Colonel's Photograph*

In a recent book, Kajri Jain (2007: 4-5) describes with great insight an encounter between the film-maker Anand Patwardhan and a Rajput woman named Godavari. Patwardhan, a rationalist activist, interrogates Godavari's faith in a photograph showing the immolation of a young Rajasthani woman named Rup Kanwar in 1987. The picture shows Rup Kanwar consumed by flames on her husband's pyre while a mother goddess hovers above, emitting the beam of fire which has ignited the pyre and whose presence authorizes this as divinely sanctioned orthodoxy rather than patriarchal coercion (here my reading of this part of the image differs from Jain).

The film-maker insists that this is surely a fake and demands that Godavari looks at it carefully in order to understand this. She counters that that's the way it is in the *photo*, and that the photo can depict gods who are invisible to quotidian vision ('Others can't see him, but he'll definitely come in the photo'). Even the photographer would not have seen it when he took the photograph, she continues, before adding what Jain terms a 'lethal twist': 'If you couldn't see the god [in the photo], how would people know she was burned, that it was god's rays?'

The image here serves simultaneously as two irreconcilable forms of evidence – evidence of an *event* and evidence of a *mentalité*.[1] It is both evidence of something which happened and evidence of someone's theory about what has happened. It also establishes a framework within which I will consider certain 'moments' in struggles over witnessing and evidence in India.

Punjab 1919-22

The history of British colonial engagement with photography in India can be seen to have a symmetrical form. From the announcement of photography in 1839 until (very roughly) the beginning of the twentieth century, photography was perceived as a cure. It was seen as a solution to the weaknesses and corruptions of earlier technologies of representation. Its *positivity* lay in its indexicality, in a Peircean sense. For the semiotician and logician Charles Sanders Peirce, an index was distinguished from other kinds of signs by its physical relationship of causal contiguity with its referent. Just as smoke indexes fire, so photography indexes the play of light on objects in front of the camera's lens. As the twentieth century progressed, however, it was increasingly viewed as a curse. Deployed by agents other than the colonial state, it revealed its dangerous ability to store juridical evidence. This new and threatening mobility reflected the changing technomaterial (Kittler 1999) nature of photography: it could access new kinds of spaces with a greater speed. However, the *negativity* which now attended its practice, like its former positivity, was due in equal part to its indexicality.

Pre-photographic representations always depended on the trustworthiness of the author/artist, and many early volumes of lithographs included assurances of the closeness of fit between the image and the reality.[2] Here what mattered was what Pagden terms 'autopicism', the authority of the eyewitness; and as he shows in his discussion of the debate between Las Casas and Oviedo, the claims to authority can be hard to establish (Pagden 1993: 51ff.). Oviedo, the writer of romances, claimed an experiential authority: 'I know that my writings will not vanish, for they have passed through the doorway of truth, which is so difficult and heavy that it will sustain and prolong my vigils' (cited by Pagden 1993: 67). Las Casas, in *A short account of the destruction of the Indies*, continually emphasized his own eye-witnessing as a proto-ethnographer of Spanish Imperial barbarities: 'I myself witnessed the grilling of four or five local leaders', 'I saw all these things for myself and many others beside' (1992 [1542]: 15-16).

Nearly all early travel literature is riven by an anxiety that the author's account might not be believed. Richard Walter's account of Anson's *Voyage round the world*, first published in 1748, is typical in its earnest desire to persuade the reader that its authority is entirely uncompromised by the defects that afflict competing authors. Walter notes in his preface that his own account is distinguished by the superfluity of grand views and maps but that

> besides the number and choice of these marine drawings and descriptions, there is another very essential circumstance belonging to them, which much enhances their value; and that is, the great accuracy they were drawn with ... they were not copied from the works of others, or composed at home from imperfect accounts, given by incurious and unskilful observers as hath frequently been the case in these matters ... The greatest part of them were drawn on the spot with the utmost exactness, by the direction, and under the eye of Mr. *Anson* himself. (1974 [1748]: lvi)

Introducing his *Scenery, costume and architecture, chiefly on the western side of India* (1830), Capt. Robert Melville Grindlay felt it necessary to assure the reader/viewer that 'the author pledges himself to the fidelity of the representations'. A few years later a warning was issued in G.F. White's *Views in India, chiefly among the Himalaya mountains* (1836), which included engravings by Turner based on White's sketches, that 'in order to render them valuable as works of art, truth of representation should not be sacrificed to mere embellishment'. Subsequently the illustrations to Hooker's *Himalayan journals* (1854) were to be roundly condemned by W.T. Blandford in 1871 because they did 'not convey by any means a correct impression; like most lithographs of foreign scenes printed in England the characteristic features are lost ... everything is

Europeanised' (*Journal of the Asiatic Society of Bengal*, 1871: 393 – all quotes in this paragraph cited by Wadell 1889: ix).

Clearly intervention continued to be possible during the creation and printing of photographic negatives, but it was an intervention of a different order. Photography required no additional autoptic testimony for eyewitnessing was the ontological condition of the very existence of the photograph. Photographs were widely seen to provide what the Rev. Joseph Mullins, in an address to the Photographic Society of Bengal, described as 'stern fidelity' (*Journal of the Photographic Society of Bengal*, 1857: 2, cited by Falconer 1990: 270).

This stern fidelity would later come to be understood in Peircean terms as related to the photograph's 'indexicality', the relationship of causal contiguity between image and referent. Early anthropological enthusiasm for the camera was (obviously) not able to draw on Peirce's theoretical articulations, but it was precisely photography's quality of indexicality and its superiority over other more equivocal signs which gave it such importance in the colonial imagination.

In 1855, the *Journal of the Photographic Society of Bombay* reported the interest of the East India Company's Court of Directors in obtaining 'Photographic *Fac Similes* of the Caves and Temples of Western India' prepared by one Captain Biggs. Biggs's photographic documentation was in competition with a pre-existing scheme to record cave paintings with oil paintings. The journal had no doubt about which media were likely to prove the most useful:

> [H]owever perfect, and beautiful these paintings may be in themselves, it will still remain a question ... how far they are to be relied upon as accurate, and how much of the details are to be set down to that peculiar species of 'license' which 'Poets and Painters' are proverbially partial to. Even with the works of eminent Masters, [only] four out of ten may be regarded as more than a fair average of degree of accuracy attained, and by a parity of reasoning, we may safely anticipate the same degree of uncertainty with respect to the labour of those who are now engaged upon the caves. Should Captain Biggs prove successful ... Photography will have accomplished a stupendous undertaking, and the Court of Directors will be placed in possession of a series of Photographic views, from which Oil Paintings of any size might be made, which shall combine the truth and faithfulness of the 'PENCIL OF THE SUN' with the grace and beauty of the 'PAINTER'S BRUSH'. (1855, II: 17-18)

In a similar vein, Captain Henry Dixon, in his 1860 publication *Orissa, its temples and rock-cut caves, illustrated by a series of photographs*, observes – with reference to a plate showing the 'Singh Darwaza, or Lion's Gate of the Great Temple, Bhubeneswar, in Orissa' – that '[i]n this picture the wall is shown to great perfection. Nothing but photography could give the minutiae of the laterite or iron conglomeration stone, so much used in this district' (1860: n.p.).

By the end of the nineteenth century, however, this excitement about the new technology's fidelity was fading. Other technologies such as dactylography (fingerprinting) enthused colonial technocrats, and legal precedent undermined the status of the photograph as legal evidence. The momentum still retained by state deployments of photography as a dimension of carceral power seemed to throw up as many problems as it solved (see, for example, the controversy about the photography of those awaiting trial in 1911 [National Archives 1911; 1912], where the anxiety arose that criminal procedure and identification might be corrupted by the circulation of photographic images). In addition, photography was no longer a means of surveillance controlled only by the colonial state. It had very quickly been embraced by elite Indians for portraiture purposes (with numerous Indian-run studios active from the early 1860s onwards), but in the early part of the twentieth century it was an increasingly mobile technology, more easily able to document increasingly chaotic public spaces in which colonial hegemony appeared increasingly fragile. It is two examples of this – both occurring within a few years of each other in Amritsar – which I will now discuss.

The Jallianwallabagh (Amritsar) massacre on 13 April 1919 might be seen as the colonial state's response to a growing Hindu-Muslim-Sikh unity among anti-Rowlatt[3] demonstrators in the Punjab (Sarkar 1989 [1983]: 190ff.) and was to kick-start a resurgence in anti-colonial struggle. A peaceful crowd, mostly villagers, who had arrived for a fair were fired on without warning on the orders of General Dyer. The official death toll – widely considered an under-estimation – was 379. As Sumit Sarkar notes: 'Dyer's only regrets before the Hunter Commission were that his ammunition ran out, and that the narrow lanes had prevented him bringing in an armoured car – for it was no longer a question of merely dispersing the crowd, but one of "producing a moral effect"' (Sarkar 1989 [1983]: 191).

Soon after this, a committed young photographer, Narayan Vinayak Virkar, arrived to photograph the evidence of this atrocity. Born in Ratnagiri, Maharashtra, in 1890, Virkar studied photography in Lahore with the Vedic scholar Shreepad Damodar Satavalekar. He then moved to Bombay, where he worked initially as an X-ray photographer on the hospital ship *Madras* before opening his own studio on Girgaum Road (Bombay).[4]

Right from the beginning of his career Virkar was intimately involved in documenting the nationalist struggle. The Amritsar images – to be detailed shortly – are atypical when set against the body of his output. For the most part he wielded his camera not as a documentary tool but rather as a medium for the production of authority. His numerous portraits of nationalist leaders (such as Bal Gangadhar Tilak, Chittaranjan Das, Subhash Chandra Bose, and M.K. Gandhi) place them in the opulence and comfort of a bourgeois European photographic studio. Subhash Chandra Bose sits garlanded in an ornate chair with his left hand resting on a pile of books that lie upon a carpet-draped table. On the floor is another richly patterned carpet and at the back a European-style painted backdrop with a vase of flowers in front of a window. This is the sort of appropriation of the photographic studio as a place of European power that Michael Aird (1993) has documented in the case of Aboriginal Queensland, and Santu Mofokeng (1998) for Black South Africa. The efficacy of this strategy is even more apparent when one is confronted with the lustrous beauty and overwhelming size of the vintage prints (largely still retained by his grandson Rajendra in the Girgaum Road studio). Most of the Virkar images currently in circulation are very poor copies emanating from the Nehru Memorial Library in Delhi and do scant justice to his superb technical accomplishments.

Virkar's Amritsar images, by contrast, document the scene of a crime. Their task is not to produce likenesses that can jostle against Europeans inhabiting similar likenesses in the imperial portrait gallery. It is, rather, to witness and preserve an event, although, rather like Boyle's vacuum pump,[5] it is an event whose meaning requires mediation by other eyewitnesses.

Here we see how photography differed radically from earlier technologies. In a lithograph depicting the Apparition at Knock, County Mayo, Ireland, the artist assures the viewer that the image was 'taken on the spot' and has been 'submitted to, and approved of by the several persons who saw the above'. Lacking indexicality, the image requires authentication from elsewhere.

In Virkar's photographs, however, eyewitnessing is necessary only to attribute evidential significance to this opaque element in the image – no further eyewitnessing is necessary to establish the veracity of the image itself. Virkar's images document the bullet-pocked wall against which so many hundreds of villagers died. Bullet holes are ringed with white chalk and various crouching figures point to these, serving as internal verifiers of a quasi-object (the hole in the wall which is also the evidence of an atrocity). The walls are also covered in graffiti (predominantly Urdu but with some Devanagri) (Fig. 1).

In 1922 Amritsar was once again a flash-point. In this year, however, cameras were there to record events as they unfolded. One of the cameras belonged to an American cinematographer named A.L. Varges. An official report written by V.W. Smith, Superintendent of Police CID Punjab, on 10 September (National Archives 1922) described how Varges had photographed an Akali protest procession *en route* for the Guru-ka-Bagh, a shrine 20 kilometres from Amritsar. Four waves of protesters attempted to access a disputed piece of land and were beaten back by *lathi*-wielding police, all this being filmed and photographed by Varges (Fig. 2). 'Eventually 23 of the Akalis were taken off on stretchers, the remaining two, who were more obstinate, were treated more roughly by the Police ... meanwhile the cinematograph operator and other photographers and Press representatives were all busy', Smith noted in his report. Following this, the protesters (now numbering 12,000) met in Jallianwallabagh and were addressed by

Figure 1. Survivors of the Jallianwallabagh (Amritsar) massacre direct the viewer's gaze to evidence of Dyer's atrocity. Nehru Memorial Library, Delhi 1056. Photograph by N.V. Virkar, 1919.

Figure 2. One of the sensational photographs of the Guru-ka-Bagh incident in Amritsar in 1922, documenting police brutality. Nehru Memorial Library, Delhi 23088. Photograph possibly by Ariel Varges, 1922.

Pandit Mohan Malaviya, who declared that 'it was the duty of every Indian to express hatred and contempt for the actions of the Government and to raise a unanimous voice of protest and demand a change of policing'.

Sumit Sarkar and Ranajit Guha have both documented the important role of rumour in circulating evidence among rural populations during the colonial period. In Smith's report the actions of the Akalis are attributed to the circulation of rumours about the appearance of the Guru Nanak's hawk and horse. It was reported that his horse had appeared at Pathankot, and subsequently Anandpur, and that his miraculous hawk was hovering over the Golden Temple. However, Smith notes that 'it has now been established' that this hawk was 'a species of a common variety of Kingfisher (*Haleyon Smyrnensis*)'. In contestation of the evidence of these divine signs (which appeared to be motivating Akalis), he suggested that 'this banal explanation of the current superstition might be given due publicity'.

Smith here pitted European taxonomy (founded on description) against a messianic world-view in a familiar colonial reflex. However, his antagonism to Varges's descriptive photographic images shows how quickly this duality could be disrupted. Appended to Smith's report is 'Notes in the Intelligence Bureau' directing that it be shown to H.E. (the Governor in Council), whose handwritten response records that '[h]e does not feel happy about the activities of the cinema operator and the possible ill-effect of these films in fostering anti-British feeling in the United States', and then instructs the Home Department to ascertain whether there was any way of stopping Varges from shooting more film.

Later investigation within the Home Department revealed that Varges's activities had been facilitated by a member of the General Staff who had introduced him to Rushbrook Williams, a professor of history turned civil servant and adviser on media relations, who had then introduced him to local officials. At this stage they had no idea that he might have any intention of taking photographs and shooting film 'of an objectionable character'. The Governor in Council issued instructions that Varges's whereabouts be identified, that the films should not be shown in India, and if possible they should be prevented from being exhibited anywhere else. Rushbrook Williams was deputed to liaise with Varges and request him to 'exercise caution that none are exhibited which are likely to cause misunderstanding' (National Archives 1922).

By this stage any researcher sitting in the National Archives in Delhi and retracing this immense flow of official paperwork in pursuit of Varges would be aware that a profound anxiety is at large. Partly this is simply bureaucratic buck-passing: no one, for understandable reasons, wants to be shown to have been sufficiently gullible to have let this foreigner in with his threatening equipment. But the anxiety also marks the deep and destabilizing realization that control of the technology of photography and its evidentiary protocols had now slipped from the hand of the state. Photography's 'penetrating certainty', which earlier colonial figures had extolled, had been desirable to the extent that it was a certainty that the state could own. In these obscure and strangely introverted set of files is dramatized the passing of carceral surveillance. From this point on the archive documents a state which perceives itself increasingly vulnerable to the evidential scrutiny of others.

From Guru-ka-Bagh in 1922 onwards, images in India were at war, to invoke Serge Gruzinski (2001). Colin Powell's presentation of satellite imagery of putative WMD sites before the UN in 2002 and snapshots of the Bush civilizational process being enacted at Abu Ghraib are later renditions of a struggle between competing indexicalities which is already apparent in 1920s India. Official response to Varges initiated a notion of the 'embedded' photojournalist whose resonance in the early twenty-first century will be obvious. Indeed in the different British and US engagements with photographs (as 'poison' to the British after 1922 and 'cure' to the Americans), one can also see prefigured the invisibility of the Malayan insurgency and the photojournalistic scrutiny of Vietnam.

The Guru-ka-Bagh episode initiated an official discussion about whether unsanctioned filming of public places could be controlled. In December 1922 the Secretary of State for India concluded that section 144 of the Criminal Procedures Code could be used to 'prevent the photography or filing of objectionable subjects' and asked for further clarification of this possibility by the Legislative Department. They replied that section 144 probably did not apply, but even if it did, 'it would be quite useless. In practice a film would be taken long before an order preventing it had been received'. The solution proposed was more pragmatic:

[I]f a photographer were attempting to take pictures with a view to the production of incidents with objectionable features, such as for example the forcible dispersal of the Akalis at Guru-ka-Bagh, it would always be possible for the police by executive action 'to move him on', since a film is not obtained with the same speed and ease as an ordinary photograph. (National Archives 1923)

Here we see a subconscious official desire to relocate the damaging evidence, which films such as Varges's embodied, from the referent to the representation. With films such as Varges's, 'a certain amount of preparation is required and probably some stage management' (National Archives 1923). The cause of the poison lies not so much in the events themselves – disseminated through the indexical medium of (cine-) photography – as in the artifice and manipulation of the photographer. This became a common refrain in 1920s and 1930s colonial India.

One year later, in 1923, Varges applied to the Viceroy for permission to film M.K. Gandhi in jail in Poona. In his request he noted that he had been unable to convince the authorities in Poona of the 'advantage of modern methods of publicity' despite the fact that his work 'will do a lot for steadying confidence in India' (National Archives 1923). In response, S.P. O'Donnell, Private Secretary to the Governor-General, noted that: 'I am not surprised that the Bombay Government were not impressed with the advantages of the modern method of publicity suggested by Captain Varges, and were not disposed to accept a proposal which is repugnant to every canon of administrative propriety and even decency'. W.M.H. Hailey, commenting on the request, simply wrote: 'The proposal seems to me to be simply disgusting'.

In the course of interacting with Varges and his products, the colonial state provisionally abandons its concern for the image for an ostensible concern with the caption. Post-structuralists of various hues might be tempted to see in this proof of Walter Benjamin's declaration in the 1930s that in future 'the caption [will become] the most important part of the shot' (cited by Evans & Hall 1999: 7). However, I propose a different interpretation – namely that this was a disingenuous attempt at further buck-passing. Having failed to prevent these images being taken, and then having failed to prevent the images leaving the country, various vulnerable middling officials look to the caption as a final redemptive alibi.

Rushbrook Williams, in a document dated 18 September 1922, laid emphasis on the importance of captions in framing the kind of work that photojournalists such as Varges produced: 'It is noticeable that the captions employed, *which are so important from the propaganda point of view*, are [illegible: conducted?] in the most moderate terms' (emphasis added). This is certainly an argument that the image is less important than the caption, *à la* Benjamin, but my suggestion is that we should understand this as an attempt to displace responsibility by Rushbrook Williams rather than self-evident proof of the indeterminacy of the image.

So the colonial state then pursued the caption as a means of redeeming the image. Among others, J.E. Ferard, Secretary of the Judicial and Public Department, communicated with film distributors such as Louis F. Behr of the Gaumont Company in London, who agreed to interpolate colonially dictated captions and inter-titles. Among the various new inter-titles that Behr agreed to interpolate into Varges's Guru-ka-Bagh newsreel were:

> 6. A rough military formation was adopted. Pools of water can be seen, the result either of rain or irrigation. But rainfall is scanty in the Punjab and millions of acres are irrigated from canals from the 'five rivers'.
> 7. The police were prepared to resist the would-be trespassers.
> 8. Their persistence day after day and increasing numbers necessitated more vigorous methods, a persistence worthy of a better object.
> 9. The police use force against the trespassers, causing it may be in some cases serious injuries, but the ease with which the 'non-violent' Akali falls is evident ...

In this manner language was used in an attempt to re-engineer and defuse the indexical potency of the image. Pools of water become signs of a beneficent colonial administration's irrigation policies, and Akalis bearing the blows of colonial *lathis* fall too easily.

1920s film and censorship

The *Report of the Indian Cinematograph Committee 1927-1928* notes in its very first sentence that 'the great potentialities of the cinematograph for good and for evil are generally recognized'. In the Varges case the colonial state devoted its energy to attempt-ing to stop images *leaving* the country. In the activities of regional censorship boards we can trace a systematic attempt to control the *inflow* of equally threatening images. The detailed records of the censorship boards preserve episodes of otherwise extinct movies for they document in detailed prose the sections of films which were to be deleted. Most of these deletions were required lest the scenes within them destroy the moral authority of white colonizers.

Through this extreme chiaroscuro, we see perfectly delineated anxieties on the part of the colonial authorities about what others might think of them. The following are typical of the regional censor boards' adjudications in the 1920s:

- *Earth's curse or passion and love*, 18 January 1922: 'Passed with endorsement [...] b) that part in Act III in which a wild orgy takes place after the bicycle races (42 feet); c) that part of the scene in Act IV which shows Lil rising out of an Indian Juggler's basket quite naked to the waist, and thereafter dancing a serpentine dance naked to the waist ...' (Bombay Censor Board).
- *Temptations of Paris*, 6 June 1928: '[Omit] (a) scenes in the Moulin Rouge. Omit the scene showing two drunk men dancing with a lot of girls' (Bengal Board of Film Regulation).
- *Temptress*, 8 August 1928: '(1) [Omit] from the sub-title "Spring and nights of Paris throb with love and desire" substitute "Spring and the nights of Paris". (2) Omit scenes of revelry showing semi-nude woman being carried ... Omit all the close-ups of the dinner scene where the busts of ladies are discernible. Omit all scenes showing the manipulation of feet and legs under the dinner table' (Bengal Board of Film Regulation).

The colonial state of course surveilled mass-produced images resulting from earlier technologies (Pinney 2004). However, its concerns with these other technologies were focused on the twin threat of 'sedition' and images which were perceived to pose a threat to 'communal' relations. The problem with 'seditious' and 'communal' political imagery was that it was deemed to excite the imagination and provoke future action. Hence chromolithographic images depicting monstrous forms decapitating cows which were proscribed on the grounds that viewers of the image might mistake the monster *analogically* for a Muslim (and thus *imaginatively* act out their response violently) were controlled precisely because of their ability to provoke such actions. There is never any sense that the problem with these images is one of evidential mis-identification in the sense that the viewers of these images would behold them and see indexical *evidence* of Muslims decapitating cattle.

In the dealings of the regional film censorship boards, by contrast, it is quite clear that a perception of what might be termed *performative indexicality* was present. Film boards also had concerns about an imaginative agency (e.g. in relation to the question of whether seeing people with guns – which so preoccupies the 1928 Cinematographic Committee Report – would encourage people to use guns). But in relation to sex and alcohol their concerns were other: what would Indians think if they saw 'Westerners' engaging in modes of behaviour that so flagrantly negated Indian moral orthodoxy? The question here of whether *all* 'Westerners' engaged in such behaviour (i.e. whether the filmic representation was to be taken as sociologically representative) was irrel-evant. All that mattered was *those people on the screen* had *performatively indexed* this behaviour. Film became an index of the actions of those whom the film documented.

A notion of the performative index was quite explicitly theorized in the summary comments of T. Rangachari, the chair of the 1927-8 Cinematographic Committee, in response to oral evidence by a Mr Tipnis on 13 February 1928. Tipnis described a film titled *The answer of the sea*, which narrated a tale of sea nymphs in which 'dozens of girls absolutely and almost naked appear on the surface of the water swimming with their buttocks exposed and in some places their fronts exposed also. As a fairy tale it has no lesson to convey. It is designed to be a feast for the eyes ...' After listening to this, Rangachari concluded that:

> I think I must add that after seeing [*The answer of the sea*] there is no doubt in my mind that the fact (*it is not a question of representation or misrepresentation of western life on the screen in this case*) that so many western girls are available for exposing their bodies in this manner is bound to create a deservedly bad impression about western morals in this country. (Indian Cinematographic Committee 1928: 45, underlining in original, emphasis added)

The camera and the eye

As a coda to the above we might consider two recent controversies involving Indians and eyewitnessing. The first of these concerns Rakesh Sharma, the film-maker responsible for *Final solution*, a film documenting riots in Gujarat in February and March 2002 which (in his own words) 'graphically documents the changing face of right-wing politics in India through a study of the 2002 genocide of Moslems in Gujarat'. *Final solution* was banned in India by order of the Censor Board, a decision which was overturned in October 2004 following a 'Pirate and Circulate' campaign. This involved the distribution of free copies of VCDs (CDs formatted for video) to anyone prepared to make at least five further copies for further distribution. This campaign resulted in the circulation of over 10,000 copies of the film, a dissemination which undermined the Censor Board's attempt to control the circulation of the film's evidence.

In early 2005, Rakesh Sharma participated in a US screening tour and, following a showing of the film at the New School, on 12 May, found himself in an analogous conflict with the New York Police Department (NYPD). To cite from his website,[6] he was subject to 'harassment by NYPD on May 13 while I was taking some candid shots with my tourist-grade Sony palmcorder (PDX 10P). For nearly 3 hours, I was "detained" for no apparent reason, physically and verbally assaulted by a plainclothes detective and harassed and questioned by several others'.

The NYPD considered his photography of the MetLife Building suspicious, leading Sharma to ask: 'Do visitors to New York need police permission to click photographs and take random, candid shots on the streets of Manhattan? If not, was I deliberately misinformed and misled by one of NYPD detectives?' The issues that the Guru-ka-Bagh incident raised are evidently alive and well.

The second controversy concerns another film, but this time a commercial Bombay-produced 'supernatural', Shripal Morakhia's *Naina*. Starring Urmila Matondkar, the story is best summed up via the précis in the publicity material for the film:

> A day of solar eclipse, a young girl of five loses her eyesight and her parents in a freak accident in London. Twenty years later she is bestowed with the gift of sight. Thanks to the marvels of modern science, a cornea implant brings her vision back. Her period of darkness is over ... or is it?[7]

Naina is plagued with ghosts – the material residue of the corneas through which she now filters the world. One review proclaims that the film is 'imaginative and pulse-pounding', leaving the viewer 'frightened, terrified, and petrified ... the film delivers the goods'.[8]

The All-India Ophthalmological Society agreed that the film was likely to terrify its audience. They attempted to persuade the Delhi High Court to ban the film on the grounds that it would deter prospective donors who feared that their eyes would 'live on after they are dead'.[9] It was claimed that India required between 40,000 and 50,000 corneal donations per year but currently there are only 15,000. Dinoo Gandhi of the National Association for the Blind argued that 'a film portraying corneal donations in a negative light is bound to have a detrimental effect'. Annie Singh, Executive Director of Lucknow Eye Bank, was reported by the *Times of India* as saying: 'You and I might laugh, but people actually refuse to donate eyes because they think they will be born blind in their next lives ... It is a fact that Indians are a superstitious lot, one major reason why the corneal transplant programme is so slow in taking off. This view was shared by Tanuja Joshi, President of the Eye Bank Association of India, who observed: 'We fear that the film will be harmful both to the donor and the recipient. Especially the recipient[s], most of whom are from the lower economic strata. Incidentally, they are the ones who are most likely to watch the film, as are people from rural areas'.[10] Ophthalmologist Navin Sakhuja, meanwhile, told Reuters that the movie could precipitate a 'fear psychosis among cornea recipients'.[11]

This anxious response (by professionals, hypothesizing a response by the masses) draws our attention to radically different models of eyewitnessing, and of the relationship of the body to evidence. Here the body is not a conduit for the transmission of evidence (in the idiom of the translucent camera lens), but becomes a densely opaque enfleshed circuit in which the brain is bombarded with evidence of a self-corporeality.

However, the putative response to *Naina* resonates with what in the nineteenth century appeared to be photography's privileged relationship with the corporeality of the eye. In 1856 Norman Chevers produced a memorable account of how the photographic prosthesis could be turned back onto the body:

> [W]e have yet to judge the effect which would be produced upon the conscience of [an Indian suspect], obstinate in the denial of guilt, by placing before him, in the stereoscope, the actual scene of his atrocity – the familiar walls, the charpoy, the ghastly faces – as they last appeared to his reeling vision – the sight which haunted his brain every hour since the act was done – while he believed to certainty, that its reality could never come before his eyes again. (Chevers 1870 [1856]: 121)

A few years later, in 1863, the *Journal of the Photographic Society of Bengal* excerpted a remarkable letter from the London *Photographic News*. This was written by W. H. Warner, a Metropolitan Police photographer describing his correspondence with a Detective Thomson in charge in the case of the murder of one Emma Jackson in St Giles, London. Warner had written to inform Thomson that 'if the eyes of a murdered person be photographed within a certain time after death, upon the retina will be found depicted the last thing that appeared before them, and that in the present case the features of the murderer would most probably be found thereon'. Warner also related how four years earlier he had taken a negative of the eye of a calf a few hours after death, and how 'upon microscopic examination of the same, [he] found depicted thereon the lines of the pavement on the slaughterhouse floor'. Thomson replied that the victim had been dead for forty hours before he saw her corpse, and that, following a conversation with 'an eminent occultist', he was aware that 'unless the eyes were photographed within 24 hours after death, no result could be obtained, the object transfixed thereon vanishing in the same manner as an undeveloped negative photograph exposed to light'.

Warner, nevertheless, was keen to restate the importance of photographing the retina, of placing the camera's negative parallel to the fast-decaying negative of the eye: 'The subject is of too great importance and interest to be passed heedlessly by, because if the fact were known through the length and breadth of the land, it would in my estimation, tend materially to decrease that most horrible of all crimes, – *Murder*' (Warner 1863: 39).

Conclusion

In this discussion I have considered how photography's endless technological transformations increased the mobility of its prosthesis. Photography as 'cure' and photography as 'poison' are seemingly opposed, but I would claim complementary dimensions of photography's particular relation to evidence. The daguerreotype and the calotype – with their descriptive intensity – appeared to supersede the deficiencies of earlier systems. But in due course – as we have examined in some detail – the possibilities of photography would make the colonial state extremely anxious. However, photography's qualities as cure and poison stemmed from the same source. The 'data ratios' that photography generated reflected a supple and changing technology. In the mid-nineteenth century these data ratios could only be produced by bulky and expensive equipment which required immense logistical support and were moderated within what we might think of as a 'colonial habitus'. The supple nature of photographic technology entailed a progressive miniaturization of equipment and mobility of the photographer which permitted an increasing dislocation from that habitus. As the twentieth century progressed, photography was increasingly viewed as a curse. Deployed by agents other than the colonial state, it revealed its dangerous ability to store juridical evidence. Its *negativity* was now seen to lie in the *self-same* indexicality which had earlier underwritten it as a cure. However, as indicated by *Naina* and the suggestions of Chevers and Warner, alongside this story of mobility and de-corporealization (the protean and seemingly infinite prosthesis of photography), a contrasting narrative of embodiment has endured in which the human eye, trapped ineluctably in an enfleshed body, becomes the original camera.

NOTES

[1] For a parallel argument see Cañizares-Esguerra (2001), who argues that indigenous American historical records were most commonly treated by Europeans up until the eighteenth century as historical records, and afterwards as evidence only of a 'native mind'.

[2] The question of authority and veracity had been resolved in medieval Europe through the attachment of elaborate wax seals to documents. These were indexical impressions from a master seal frequently attached to vellum tags.

[3] The Rowlatt Act, passed in March 1919, indefinitely extended emergency measures allowing imprisonment without trial.

[4] This paraphrased from Dwivedi (2004: 40). Virkar subsequently also opened a studio in Nasik.

[5] See Latour (1993) and Shapin & Schaffer (1989).

[6] *http://www.rakeshfilm.com/NYPD/index.htm*, accessed 31 December 2007.

[7] *http://www.indianproductiondesigner.com/naina.htm* (accessed 31 December 2007). The film shares the same premise as the Pang brothers' earlier *The eye (Jian gui)* (2002).

[8] *http://movies.indiainfo.com/reviews/2005/naina.html* (accessed 31 December 2007).

[9] *http://news.bbc.co.uk/2/hi/south_asia/4566753.stm* (accessed 31 December 2007).

[10] *http://timesofindia.indiatimes.com/articleshow/1120605.cms* (accessed 31 December 2007).

[11] See note 9 above.

REFERENCES

Archival sources

NATIONAL ARCHIVES OF INDIA 1911. Police – August, Part A, 107-8. Procedure to be observed in photographing accused persons either before trial or after conviction, discharge or acquittal.

———— 1912. Police – July, Part A, 81-91. Orders regarding the photographing of under-trial prisoners.

———— 1922. Amritsar and Guru-ka-Bagh. Summary of Intelligence for the 10th September '22. (Memo by V.W. Smith.) Home Political, 949.

———— 1923. Exhibition in America of objectionable cinematograph film of the Guru-Ka-Bagh incident taken by Captain A.L. Varges. Question of controlling or preventing the photographing or filming of objectionable incidents and of preventing the exhibition of objectionable films. Home Political. F.71

Printed sources

AIRD, M. 1993. *Portraits of our ancestors*. Brisbane: Queensland Museum.

CAÑIZARES-ESGUERRA, J. 2001. *How to write the history of the New World*. Stanford: University Press.

CHEVERS, N. 1870 [1856]. *Manual of medical jurisprudence for India including the outline of a history of crime against the person in India*. Calcutta.

DIXON, H. 1860. *Orissa, its temples and rock-cut caves, illustrated by a series of photographs*. Crystal Palace: Printed by the Crystal Palace Printing and Publishing Company Ltd.

DWIVEDI, S. 2004. In pursuit of history. *Harmony*, August, 40-50.

EVANS, J. & S. HALL (eds) 1999. *Visual culture: the reader*. London: Sage.

FALCONER, J. 1990. Photography in nineteenth-century India. In *The Raj: India and the British 1600-1947* (ed.) C.A. Bayly, 264-77. London: National Portrait Gallery.

GRUZINSKI, S. 2001. *Images at war: Mexico from Columbus to Blade Runner (1492-2019)*. Durham, N.C.: Duke University Press.

INDIAN CINEMATOGRAPHIC COMMITTEE 1928. *Indian Cinematic Committee 1927-28, vol. V: Oral evidence of witnesses examined in camera with the written statement of Mr Tipnis; the memorandum of the Government of Burma and the Chairman's inspection notes on cinemas visited*. Calcutta: Government of India Central Publication Board.

JAIN, K. 2007. *Gods in the bazaar: the economies of Indian 'calendar art'*. Durham, N.C.: Duke University Press.

KITTLER, F. 1999. *Film, gramophone, typewriter*. Stanford: University Press.

LAS CASAS, B. de 1992 [1542]. *A short account of the destruction of the Indies* (trans. N. Griffin). Harmondsworth: Penguin.

LATOUR, B. 1993. *We have never been modern* (trans. C. Porter). London: Prentice-Hall.

MOFOKENG, S. 1998. The black photo album. In *Anthology of African and Indian Ocean photography*, 68-75. Paris: Revue Noire Paris.

PAGDEN, A. 1993. *European encounters with the New World*. Yale: University Press.

PINNEY, C. 2004. *Photos of the gods: the printed image and political struggle in India*. London: Reaktion.

SARKAR, S. 1989 [1983]. *Modern India 1885-1947*. London: Macmillan.

SHAPIN, S. & S. SCHAFFER 1989. *Leviathan and the air pump*. Princeton: University Press.

WADELL, L.A. 1889. *Among the Himalayas*. London: Constable.

WALTER, R. 1974 [1748]. *Anson's voyage round the world in the years 1740-44*. New York: Dover.

WARNER, W.H. 1863. Photography and murder. *Journal of the Photographic Society of Bengal* II: 5, July, 39.

4

Cultural evidence in courts of law

ANTHONY GOOD *University of Edinburgh*

The word 'culture' occurs nowhere in either the *1951 United Nations Convention Relating to the Status of Refugees* or the UNHCR's interpretative *Handbook* (UNHCR 1992). None the less, in Article 1A(2) of the Convention, which defines a refugee as someone suffering from a 'well-founded fear of being persecuted *for reasons of race, religion, nationality, membership of a particular social group or political opinion*' (my italics), clear reference is made to matters which seem central to that refugee's 'culture'. It is therefore not surprising that British anthropologists are so often approached by solicitors seeking expert evidence which they hope will support the case that their client does indeed have a well-founded fear of persecution. After all, everyone knows that anthropologists are experts on culture ...

The mantle of 'culture expert' sits uneasily upon the hapless anthropologist's shoulders, however, for a variety of epistemological, moral, ethical, and professional reasons. This chapter – prompted by my own experience of playing such a role in asylum appeals – concerns the problems arising when culture is teleologized in courts of law, transformed from a conceptual tool of anthropological analysis into 'objective evidence', or asserted as the direct cause of persecution or delinquency. The issues are complex, and their treatment is necessarily partial. For example, there is no space here to examine the crucial differences in how lawyers and social scientists are trained to think and reason (see Clifford 1988; Good 2004*a*; 2004*b*; 2006; Kandel 1992; MacCormick 1994).

The discussion starts by explaining the role of expert witnesses, and the kinds of evidence they can and cannot provide. It addresses the widespread use, especially in the United States, of the 'cultural defense' in cases involving immigrant or minority defendants. It summarizes anthropological approaches to the notion of culture; the ongoing debate between rights-based and culture-based approaches to international law; and the impact upon anthropology of current notions of legal and cultural pluralism. It concludes by briefly addressing the treatment of anthropological evidence in English courts, with special reference to asylum appeals.

The admissibility of expert evidence

The role of expert witness as it now exists in common law systems is the product of a centuries-old struggle for hegemony between the judiciary and the scientific and technical professions – above all, the medical profession – over who has the definitive last word (see Good 2004*a* and 2006 for more complete discussions of this history).

The precedent for the use of expert witnesses in English law is *Folkes* v. *Chadd* (1782), where an engineer gave evidence on why a harbour had silted up. This established that expert opinion was admissible, but only within strict, judicially controlled limits. Ever since, courts have sought to constrain experts' influence, through such means as the 'hearsay' rule, which limits witnesses to giving evidence based upon their own direct knowledge and observations; and the 'ultimate issue' rule, which prevents witnesses from giving opinions on the main issue at stake (*R* v. *Wright* [1821]; Jones 1994: 104).[1] Throughout the centuries English judges have repeatedly warned of the apocalyptic consequences if 'trial by jury' were to metamorphose into 'trial by expert', yet as the sciences began accumulating knowledge more systematically, and as mastery of that corpus of knowledge became the criterion of professional status, it became increasingly hard for courts to exclude such knowledge, even though it was technically 'hearsay' (Jones 1994: 106-7).

Adversarial proceedings tend, however, to foster simplistic notions of 'scientific objectivity'. To forestall attacks on the validity of the expert evidence they have obtained, lawyers structure their submissions so as to conceal, as far as possible, the contingent nature of 'their' expert's conclusions and methods (Jones 1994: 14; see Clifford 1988: 321). Such processes may be understood in terms of the general insight that legal cases are 'constructed' through discretionary selection of the evidence to be presented, rather than providing a transparent window through which the facts in dispute are viewed (Jones 1994: 11; McBarnet 1981; Redmayne 2001: 1). Experts are therefore under pressure to profess greater certainty than they really feel. Their discomfort may, however, be partly ameliorated by the knowledge that whereas, for them, 'objective' generally means external to the observer, with all the philosophical complications that such a notion entails, lawyers use it merely to evoke the subjectivity of the 'reasonable man' (Kandel 1992: 3). In other words, an expert is expected to assess matters as any reasonable person sharing their expertise would assess them, rather than to provide accounts which are 'true' in any metaphysical sense.[2] As the US Supreme Court noted in *Daubert*: 'Rules of Evidence [are] designed not for the exhaustive search for cosmic understanding but for the particularized resolution of legal dispute'.

The admissibility of expert evidence is a legal rather than a factual matter, and hence subject to judicial discretion (Edmond 2004*b*: 140). In the United States, admissibility was governed from 1923 onwards by the *Frye* test: only after the scientific community had agreed that a particular technique was valid would evidence produced thereby be admissible in court. In the 1993 case of *Daubert*, however, the Supreme Court ruled that *Frye* had been superseded by the new Federal Rules of Evidence, and needed to be reassessed. The Federal Rules state that ordinary witnesses cannot express 'opinions or inferences' (Rule 701), but that experts may do so providing these are based on facts or data obtained using reliable methods reliably applied (Rule 702), and 'of a type reasonably relied upon by experts' (Rule 703). Experts may even address the ultimate issue (Rule 704), except that they may not testify as to the link between a defendant's 'mental state or condition' and the crime he or she is charged with. This final caveat could of course prevent experts from testifying on cultural matters, if culture were seen as some kind of 'mental state or condition', but I am not aware of this argument ever being used.

In its *Daubert* decision, the Supreme Court set out to delineate a new test based on Popperian notions of falsifiability as well as general acceptance:

1. Ordinarily, a key question to be answered in determining whether a theory or technique is scientific knowledge that will assist the trier of fact will be whether it can be (and has been) tested. [citing Popper 1989: 37]
2. Another pertinent question is whether the theory or technique has been subjected to peer review and publication. Publication ... is not a *sine qua non* of admissibility; it does not necessarily correlate with reliability ... [citing Jasanoff 1990: 61-76]
3. Additionally, in the case of a particular scientific technique, the court ordinarily should consider the known or potential rate of error ...
4. Finally, 'general acceptance' can yet have a bearing on the enquiry.

Although Popper's views were already seen as old-fashioned by specialists, the Court seems to have felt that he provided a rigorous yet simple standard for determining admissibility. The fact that *Daubert* incorporated Jasanoff's constructionist views too, however, illustrates that common law is pragmatic, and not necessarily concerned with philosophical coherence (Edmond & Mercer 2004: 20; Jasanoff 1995: 63).

The change in approach between *Frye* and *Daubert* exemplifies a general shift from a *disciplinary* approach to objectivity, grounded in 'tacit learning, experience, social relations and trust, insight, and the need to link solutions to their specific contexts', to a *mechanical* approach, relying on 'quantification, formal rules and a fixation with methodological review' (Edmond & Mercer 2004: 8, citing Porter 1995), in an attempt to limit the acceptability of individual (read unreliable) opinions. English courts are less precise in specifying reliability criteria for expert evidence, but their behaviour is broadly consistent with US principles (Hodgkinson 1990: 138).

Despite their differences, both the *Frye* and *Daubert* approaches define reliability in terms of technique rather than content (Edmond 2004*a*; 2004*b*). Some argue that such a focus is relatively unproblematic for anthropologists, given their broad acceptance of the basic methods of participant-observation (Donovan & Anderson 2003: 102; Kandel 1992), yet it is equally arguable (Stafford, this volume) that no anthropological techniques meet *Daubert*'s falsifiability criterion, however flexibly applied. Moreover, while it seems reasonable to expect that expert opinions in 'soft' sciences should receive even more judicial scrutiny for reliability than is applied to the 'hard' sciences (Murphy & Cuccias 1997), it is by no means clear that the same reliability tests can be applied in both cases. For example, Jasanoff highlights the particular problems posed by ethnographic 'intersubjectivity', and the uncertain 'cognitive status' of the field notes upon which ethnography is based (1996: 110-11). Crown lawyers in a Canadian First Nation land case even sought to have anthropological evidence excluded as 'unscientific' (Culhane 1998: 132), and although the judge did admit it, he reserved the option to attach little weight to it. MacCrimmon (1998) suggests, however, that social scientists' expertise should not be equated with that of physical scientists, but with 'the specialized knowledge of ... the fire inspector who testifies about the cause of a fire'. It is, in short, best defined in terms of the extent of their experience, rather than the falsifiability of their disciplinary techniques. But while such an approach might meet wide acceptance in the United Kingdom, it is less helpful in the United States, where practical experience does *not* necessarily make one an expert (Jasanoff 1995: 60).

Experts' evidence may be excluded if their testimony goes beyond the bounds of their legitimate expertise, and there is always the risk of the court ruling that it is inadmissible because it falls 'within the common stock of knowledge of a lay jury' (Jones 1994: 109). In *R* v. *Turner*, for example, Lawton LJ stated: 'Jurors do not need psychiatrists to tell them how ordinary folk who are not suffering from any mental illness are likely to react to the stresses and strains of life'. Where decisions are made by judges themselves, however, as in asylum appeals, there is less emphasis on exclusion because they are assumed to be less impressionable than lay juries (Redmayne 2001: 3). One might expect anthropologists to be as vulnerable as psychiatrists to such exclusionary arguments, because their knowledge, too, risks being deemed part of the 'common stock', but no such generalized legal critique has been mounted in the UK (but see *R* v. *Jameel Akhtar*, below).

Legal pluralism

One recurring theme in the anthropology of law has been legal pluralism, the study of the coexistence of diverse legal cultures. This originated among Dutch scholars in Indonesia (von Benda-Beckmann & Strijbosch 1986), and was introduced into anglophone anthropology by M.G. Smith (L. Kuper & Smith 1969; see also Pospisil 1971: 107).

Early pluralist approaches led to a recognition that state law almost always coexisted with forms of 'customary' law, but the very universality of this finding entailed the risk that legal pluralism became a mere 'just so' story, lacking explanatory value in particular cases (Fuller 1994). This danger is largely avoided by the greater ethnographic specificity of what Sally Merry (1988: 872) terms 'new legal pluralism', a series of detailed studies of the American legal system as experienced by ordinary litigants. The work of Moore (1973), Conley and O'Barr (1990), and Merry herself (1990) shows how different understandings of law coexist even within mainstream American society, and draws attention to the importance of studying law not just as a set of processes but as 'a system of thought' (Fuller 1994: 11); in short, to the importance of studying legal discourses (Humphreys 1985).

'New' legal pluralists adopt an interpretative approach which draws upon Geertz's account of law as a cultural phenomenon, a set of 'symbols ... through whose agency [legal] structures are formed [and] communicated' (1983: 182). This helped give rise to the 'rights as culture' approach, discussed below. But while Geertz certainly seems right in arguing that legal reasoning places events into broader contexts, thereby suggesting principled courses of action to be undertaken in response, other aspects of his approach are harder to accept. Far from 'the cultural contextualization of incident' being 'a critical aspect of legal analysis ... as it is of ... sociological analysis' (Geertz 1983: 181), it is arguable that almost the reverse is true: that formal legal proceedings in Western common law downplay specific contexts as much as possible in the interests of attaching events to general principles of law. Similarly, the second part of Geertz's claim, that law 'makes life's nebulous events tangible and restores their detail' (1983: 182), seems utterly mistaken. One core difference between anthropological and legal analyses is that the former treat ambiguity and complexity as immanent aspects of all real-life situations, while the latter seek to prune away 'extraneous' details, so as to identify the abstract, general, *de*-contextualized legal principles assumed to lie within (see Good 2004*b*; Kandel 1992; Rigby & Sevareid 1992).

Problems also arise over the degree to which law constitutes an autonomous domain, rather than being embedded in broader discourses and cultures. Rosen, for instance, contrasts *qadi* courts in Morocco, which appeal to 'concepts that extend across many domains of social life' (1989: 5), with Western common law systems, whose relationship to broader ethical concerns is problematic (1989: 72). Too great a focus upon its embeddedness within the broader culture makes the study of law indistinguishable from anthropology in general, however (Rosen 1989: 5). Malinowski, for example, defined law so broadly – 'the configuration of obligations, which makes it impossible for the native to shirk his responsibility without suffering for it in the future' (1926: 59) – as to make it indistinguishable from all other kinds of normative social relationship. Geertz and Rosen can also be criticized for excessive idealism. While it is sometimes helpful to see law as a set of symbols, it is also 'about repression just as much as imagination' (Fuller 1994: 11). Finally, such approaches risk portraying culture as static rather than processual and contested.

Culture talk and rights talk

Anthropologists differ among themselves, of course, in their understandings of 'culture'. It was Franz Boas who first made 'culture' a central trope of American anthropology, but current American understandings owe more to Talcott Parsons. He made culture 'the central project' in post-war American anthropology (A. Kuper 1999: x), likened by its proponents to the theory of gravity in explanatory importance (Kroeber & Kluckhohn 1952: 3). Culture was a symbolic discourse shared by every member of a community, and while Parsons himself did not believe that culture *determined* people's actions, his successors Sahlins, Geertz, and Schneider stand accused of often writing as though their ethnographic subjects actually inhabit Parsonian symbolic worlds in which they 'live only for ideas' (A. Kuper 1999: 16-17). By contrast, British social anthropologists of that period mostly followed Radcliffe-Brown (1940) in viewing culture as merely a 'vague abstraction', and seeing many American uses of the term as 'hyper-referential' (A. Kuper 1999: ix), a difference which may help explain why the 'cultural defense' debate, below, has far less salience in the UK than across the Atlantic.

Despite such historical disagreements, most contemporary anthropologists would, I imagine, agree with Zygmunt Bauman that culture 'does not *cause* behaviour, but summarizes and abstracts from it, and is thus neither normative nor predictive' (1996: 11). Unfortunately, precisely the opposite is assumed by many legal treatments of 'culture', driven, as common law systems tend to be, by a modernist penchant for pragmatic essentialism.

A very different but equally essentialist teleology permeated the rights-orientated international bodies which proliferated after the Second World War (Dembour 2001; Eriksen 2001). This sudden upsurge of rights-based discourse aroused the suspicion of many anthropologists, who saw its universalistic principles as being in potential or actual conflict with cultural relativism. By the time they began coming to terms with these developments – as in the American Anthropological Association's attempt to reconcile human rights with cultural differences by making the right to be different itself a basic human right (American Anthropological Association 1999; Turner 1997) – the ground was again shifting beneath their feet, as rights discourse came under increasing challenge in the name of new notions of 'culture' having little resonance for anthropologists on either side of the Atlantic.

Cowan, Dembour, and Wilson identify three approaches to this culture/rights impasse. The first, which they label rights *versus* culture, posits an unavoidable opposition between rights-based universalism and cultural relativism, yet, ironically, both sides in this debate – the Germanic Romantic nationalists who see cultural diversity as 'a problem to be solved' (Cowan *et al.* 2001: 3) *and* the 'multiculturalists' who celebrate it – take for granted an essentialist understanding of cultural communities as clearly bounded and internally homogeneous. More fundamentally, the framing of rights and culture as inevitably opposed illustrates a general feature of legal positivism, which starts from the premise that laws are universally applicable, only to find that real-life situations resist any such essentializing of social categories.

In the second approach, exemplified by the American Anthropological Association response, the right *to* culture is itself made one of those universal rights guaranteed by rights discourse. Here too, culture is reified, as 'another "thing" that an ... actor is entitled to "have" and "enjoy" ' (Cowan *et al.* 2001: 8). Paradoxically, yet characteristically, Article 22 of the 1948 Universal Declaration of Human Rights defined this right in individualistic terms, rather than with reference to communities: 'Everyone, as a member of society ... is entitled to realization ... of the economic, social and cultural rights indispensable for his dignity and the free development of his personality'. This approach, too, came under increasing pressure in relation to the recognition of minority rights, cultural diversity, and claims voiced by, or on behalf of, 'indigenous' peoples. Such claims may concern rights to land, political autonomy, or religion, and may be expressed in terms of culture, race, ethnicity, custom, or tribe. They may also, as in the 'cultural defense' discussed below, 'be invoked to argue for exemption from laws binding other citizens ... or for legal interpretations that take into account the claimants' particular cultural identities' (Cowan *et al.* 2001: 9). There is a double essentialization at work here: cultural activists often essentialize the cultures which they claim to represent, sometimes as a conscious strategy, and this tendency is encouraged by the '*essentializing proclivities*' of law itself (Cowan *et al.* 2001: 11, original italics).

The third approach, more the preserve of analysts than practitioners, sees rights discourses and practices themselves as *cultural processes*. This approach resembles, and partly derives from, the 'law as culture' analyses already discussed. Like legal 'facts', the 'facts' adduced by rights discourse are socially constructed, and far from criticizing this approach on the grounds that the cultural processes arising out of rights discourse are less 'organic' and more artificial than those of 'real' cultures, Cowan *et al.* see this as a virtue, a constant reminder that supposedly more 'real' cultures are not 'organic' either (2001: 12-13).

Building upon their assessment of these three approaches, Cowan *et al.* suggest (and exemplify) yet a fourth (meta-)perspective, whereby culture is 'a heuristic analytical abstraction ... a *means* of analysing and better understanding the particular ways that rights processes operate as situated social action' (2001: 4, original emphasis).

And yet, despite their long history of scholarly work on the matter, anthropologists find themselves increasingly bypassed by debates about culture within Western-orientated cultural studies, or between supporters and critics of multiculturalism. The latter presents a particularly 'subversive challenge' to anthropologists because it often marks a resurgence of 'the popular ideas that ... cultural identity must be grounded in a primordial, biological identity' (A. Kuper 1999: 239). The tensions thereby created are reflected in Turner's (1993) attempt to distinguish between *critical multiculturalism* – a counter-hegemonic critique of dominant cultural prejudices – and the supremacist posturing of *difference multiculturalism*.

The loss of anthropological 'market share' (A. Kuper 1999: 228) in recent debates about culture is thus partly explicable in terms of the interactions between rights-based and culture-based approaches to law and morality. Anthropologists are likely to be at odds with other approaches to culture, including legal ones, insofar as these are linked to notions of primordiality. Indeed, it has even been asserted that '[t]he modern concept of culture is not ... a critique of racism, it is a form of racism' (Michaels 1995: 129). Yet if anthropologists respond to the racializing of culture by insisting that cultural identities are themselves socio-cultural constructs, they risk falling back into the alternative reductionist trap of making discourse the explanation for everything (A. Kuper 1999: 242; cf. Hall 1996).

Legal essentialism and the 'cultural defense'

When one searches for recent uses of the word 'culture' by judges and advocates in a legal database such as LexisNexis, one is initially struck by the frequency of its use. Closer inspection reveals, however, that it appears mostly in dead metaphors like 'overtime culture' or 'culture of disbelief', and that on the few occasions when the term itself is problematized, this is generally in the context of the so-called 'cultural defense',[3] a legal strategy based on the premise that a criminal defendant, 'usually a recent immigrant to the United States, acted according to the dictates of his or her "culture," and therefore deserves leniency' (Volpp 1994: 57; see also Maguigan 1995; Coleman 1996). The aim of that strategy is to show that persons sharing the offender's cultural background would approve of, endorse, or at least condone such behaviour in that particular context (Van Broeck 2001: 5). This is not so much *legal* pluralism in either sense discussed above, but a kind of 'cultural pluralism' whereby the same laws arguably impinge differently upon persons of different 'cultural' backgrounds.[4]

Such situations rarely entail a straightforward dichotomy between a monolithic dominant cultural code and an equally monolithic and opposed 'traditional' or 'foreign' code. For example, the behaviour in question may not be viewed as 'morally right' by those from the perpetrator's own cultural milieu, but merely as 'unavoidable'. It may or may not accord with written or customary law in their country of origin, or with standard practice among persons of similar background. The 'general view' among persons from their own cultural milieu is what counts here (Van Broeck 2001: 15), and while it may appear to anthropologists that identifying 'general views' is often impossible or misleading, failure to carry out such an exercise in legal contexts may be detrimental to justice, as the example of female circumcision in France illustrates. Some Senegalese and Malian women remain isolated from French society, unaware of French laws and culture, and totally dependant on others from their own cultural background. Because women actually perform female circumcisions, they are generally the very ones to face the most serious criminal charges where these arise, yet even if they knew that their actions were contrary to French law, any refusal on their part would have jeopardized the entire social network upon which they depend. Consequently, they are 'prosecuted for acts in which they had no free choice, even if they did not agree with them' (Van Broeck 2001: 14).

In mounting a cultural defense, it is not merely a matter of showing behaviour to be *consistent with* cultural norms; the offence must have been directly 'motivated by' the norms which persons of their cultural background apply to the context in question

(Van Broeck 2001: 21). The demarcation of cultural offences therefore depends upon the general theory of criminality held by those performing the assessments: for example, those who see socio-economic deprivation as a causal factor in criminal behaviour may be less willing to consider cultural explanations. Either way, such labelling is often arbitrary, because motives are usually complex and multi-stranded. Furthermore, the possibility of classification as a 'cultural offence' only arises when the act in question conforms to moral norms *different from* those of the dominant legal culture. This may sound obvious, but its implications merit consideration. Lawyers and judges, when making such classifications, are inevitably constituting their own culture in opposition to that of the litigant (Volpp 1994: 81). This othering process is almost bound to lead to reification, especially when the lawyers' own culture remains, unexamined, in the background.

Cultural evidence in court

Van Broeck and Renteln both propose three-stage reasoning processes for lawyers seeking to identify cultural offences, which can be summarized as follows:

1. What are the stated motives of the accused?
2. Do other members of the relevant group agree?
3. Do these motives differ from those of the dominant culture? (Van Broeck 2001: 23-4)

1. Is the litigant a member of the ethnic group in question?
2. Does that group have such a tradition?
3. Was the litigant influenced by the tradition when s/he acted? (Renteln 2004: 207)

While discussing step (2), Van Broeck remarks that '[a]nthropologists can intervene as experts in this stage' (2001: 24). After noting research findings that 'instrumental' offences involving personal gain are far less likely to be seen as culturally motivated than 'expressive' offences, motivated, for example, by notions of 'honour' (Van San 1998), Van Broeck comments again that '[a]nthropologists could play an important role in this by functioning as cultural experts' (2001: 26, citing Winkelman 1996). Renteln, too, envisages a key role for anthropologists in demonstrating the 'authenticity' of cultural beliefs or practices (2004: 207). Surprisingly, however, given the growing literature on the topic, neither author considers the implications for anthropologists of taking on such roles, or the ethical and methodological problems this may cause (Loeb 2005: 301).[5]

Moreover, what exactly is understood by 'culture' in legal contexts? Issues of scope and definition are legally crucial because it must first be shown that behaviour is indeed 'cultural' before any cultural defence can be mounted. It is therefore surprising how much writing on 'cultural defenses' either takes the notion of 'culture' itself more-or-less for granted (Volpp 1994; Renteln 2004) or adopts a reified notion of cultural causality which seems to rule out individual agency (Torry 2000).[6]

Judges and advocates are, of course, unaware of the methodological and moral dilemmas posed for anthropologists from one culture, especially a hegemonic one, when required to represent or speak for people from another. In Australia, where anthropologists have long experience of acting as experts, the pitfalls of so doing became especially apparent during the Hindmarsh Island Bridge controversy. There, the fact that core cultural knowledge was held secretly by particular individuals and groups not only posed difficult ethical issues, but raised basic questions about how anthropologists might set about convincing the courts to view cultural values as dynamic responses to contemporary circumstances, rather than recognizing only those cultural features whose historical continuity could be established (Kirsch 2001; Weiner 1999). This issue of 'cultural continuity' arises in Canadian land claims cases too (Culhane 1998).

The literature on 'anthropological advocacy' deals largely with involvement in legal proceedings over land rights, cultural artefacts, or anatomical specimens (Culhane 1998; Paine 1985; Wade 1995).[7] Almost invariably, it involves anthropologists mediating between 'indigenous' cultures and hegemonic politico-legal systems; a key issue is therefore whether, or to what extent, they are reporting on pristine cultures 'out there', or whether those cultures are actually generated by the interaction between the culture-bearers and the courts – or, for that matter, between their supposed adherents and the anthropologists (Weiner 1999: 202). In asylum claims, anthropologists are often cast as pundits on micro-politics rather than interpreters of cultures. Even when 'culture' becomes relevant, however – as with the stigma of rape, and its social consequences – asylum courts are not concerned to understand these matters in indigenous cultural terms, as land claims hearings in Australia or North America might be. Instead they cut directly to the chase: what are the implications of all this 'culture' for the well-foundedness of the applicant's fear of persecution, and the 'real risk' they might face if returned to their state of origin?

Few British anthropologists have experience of acting as experts across a range of jurisdictions. Roger Ballard, who acts not only in asylum appeals but also in family law and criminal matters affecting British Punjabis, reports (pers. comm.) striking contrasts between different branches of law, which seem (as noted in the earlier discussion on admissibility) closely linked to the presence or absence of a jury. Thus, civil courts are prepared to receive ethnographic evidence about context, whereas criminal courts are far more restrictive.

For example, the evidence in *R* v. *Jameel Akhtar*, a heroin-smuggling case, included a conversation in Urdu, taped by Customs officers. The transcripts naturally omitted the speakers' tones and styles, but from the tapes Ballard concluded that Mark, the Customs informer, was leading the conversation, and that many 'incriminating' statements by the accused were actually polite grunts of agreement such as Punjabis make when harangued by political or economic superiors. The judge ruled, however, that this was not evidence of fact, but a commentary on matters which were the sole responsibility of the jury. This decision was upheld by the Court of Appeal, which noted that

> juries in this country often find themselves trying cases of this sort, and with assistance from the judge ... they are able to do that perfectly fairly. [I]nsofar as Dr Ballard's evidence was going to be relied upon by the defence to seek to elucidate the truth or plausibility of what Mr Akhtar gave as the explanation of his various conversations with Mark [it] was evidence of cultural background which, in our judgement, would not be admissible in any event when the issue in the case was whether when they met on those occasions Mark and Akhtar had been discussing heroin or herbal remedies: a matter in our judgement not illuminated at all by any expert in any discipline whatsoever.

Although the conversation was in a language they did not speak or understand, the Worcestershire jurors were deemed capable of assessing its significance for themselves.

In apparent contrast, the 1951 Refugee Convention requires that whenever asylum claims are evaluated, applicants' stories should be placed within their cultural, socio-economic, and historical contexts (UNHCR 1992: ¶42; cf. Barsky 2000: 58). Even so, culturally grounded misunderstandings are common in asylum hearings (see also Kalin 1986). I have witnessed actual, apparent, or potential misunderstandings over such matters as: inconsistent transliterations of personal names from languages with non-Roman scripts, leading to doubts over whether the appellant was indeed the individual referred to in the documentation; inconsistencies by appellants and other witnesses in dating particular events, resulting from inaccurate mental conversions from non-Gregorian calendars; variations in the structures of kin relationship terminologies; different systems for naming parts of the body; and different classifications of illnesses and diseases.[8]

Such misunderstandings are important if allowed to stand, because the Home Office representatives always seize upon apparent inconsistencies in asylum applicants' accounts, so as to call their credibility into question. None the less, the cited examples all concern fairly straightforward aspects of cultural difference, which could largely be explained away if the court were aware (which it generally is not) that there *was* a confusion, and had access to an explanation of why that confusion arose. Far more complex and hard to resolve are suggestions that certain acts which seem odd to British eyes are explicable in terms of appellants or others following their own 'traditions' or 'cultures'. Consequently, 'country experts' often find themselves being asked to explain, or explain away, culturally specific differences in behaviour.

Legal practitioners routinely seek to conceal the optative and contested nature of cultural practices, which they see as fatally weakening asylum claims dependent upon persecution resulting from such practices (Akram 2000; McKinley 1997). Such legal resorts to cultural essentialism place social science expert witnesses in a quandary, as with the anthropologists pressured to give yes/no answers to the question 'are the Mashpee a tribe?' (Clifford 1988: 318-22). Schwandner-Sievers, who not only acts as an expert in asylum appeals, but is also often approached by police seeking the 'cultural background' to violent crimes involving Albanians, discusses the practical and ethical difficulties associated with 'communicating "culture" (and its social consequences) without reproducing essentialist representations' (2006: 224). In her case, the risk lies in being led to portray exotic cultural features like 'blood-feuds' as 'causes' of delinquent behaviour. Faced with police and courts seeking to explain crimes in terms of 'Albanian traditions of violence', does she grit her teeth and accept the premise that culture itself is the explanation for strange or questionable behaviour, thereby contributing to 'the reification of these contexts by articulating them within the constraints of ... legalism' (Hepner 2003), or try to explain the fluid and processual character of culture, and thereby risk raising doubts as to the validity of the appellant's motives?

* * *

This chapter is concerned above all with notions of 'evidence' in the narrow legal sense. These are matters of some importance, given the momentous decisions which courts are frequently called upon to make, and, as such, they merit rather more intensive study by social scientists than they have generally received in the past. Law is too important to be left solely to lawyers – even academic lawyers.

As we have seen, lawyers view evidence in ways which seem quaintly empiricist and positivistic to social scientists weaned on notions of postmodern reflexivity. Up to a point, however, this legal stance reflects understandable practical imperatives rather than metaphysical naïvety. After all, legal proceedings must produce definite outcomes – verdicts or judgments – within quite short time spans. Judges do not enjoy the same luxury as scholars of being able to refine their views on particular matters throughout lifetimes of research and scholarship, and existential doubt is incompatible with the need to decide there and then.

Law's modernist empiricism may indeed be pragmatically justifiable in, for example, its use of the testimony of eyewitnesses to establish the chains of events leading up to accidents, or during the perpetration of crimes. Yet such an approach seems so fundamentally misguided when dealing with 'cultural' phenomena – which are, as we have seen, generally agreed by social scientists to be matters of contextual and contested interpretation, rather than being sufficient, or even necessary, causes of particular actions – that it is almost bound to produce distorted understandings and, in many cases, miscarriages of justice. It is for this reason that law's reifying approach to 'culture' gives grounds for concern.

NOTES

Field research was supported by ESRC Research Grant no. R000223352.

[1] The ultimate issue rule was formally abolished in civil cases by the *Civil Evidence Act 1968* (Henderson 2003: 218), but continues in practice to affect the acceptability of expert reports in asylum appeals.

[2] In other words, legal devices for 'guaranteeing truthful knowledge' (Bloch, this volume) operate by downgrading the notion of 'truth' from metaphysical to pragmatic status.

[3] I retain this spelling because this notion is largely confined to American legal scholarship (Phillips 2003 is a rare exception for English law). In continental Europe the stress is more upon cultural *offences*, a difference which Van Broeck (2001) explains in terms of contrasts between common law systems and the Code Napoléon.

[4] In such arguments culture is equated with 'strange beliefs' in just the way discussed by Keane (this volume). There are also legal debates over notions of 'acculturation'. How much should be expected, and how soon?

[5] Loeb mentions Deloria (1969), Pocock (2000), Sandoval (2000), and Tuhiwai Smith (1999), to whom may be addded Clifford (1988), Edmond (2004a), Paine (1985), Schwandner-Sievers (2006), and Weiner (1999).

[6] '[Y]outh gangs, new-immigrant traditionalists, religious sects and cults, old working-class communities, and other subcultural enclaves ... *indisputably foster cultural dictation*' (Torry 2000: 68, my italics).

[7] 'Advocacy' is often an inappropriate term, as common law systems specifically prohibit expert witnesses from engaging in advocacy – although in the Hindmarsh Island Bridge litigation, Australian courts alternated in practice between treating anthropologists as advocates and as experts (Edmond 2004a).

[8] There is nothing to suggest that such confusions express cognitive differences of the kind whose existence is debated by Stafford (this volume). They generally result from different interpreters making different decisions over how to translate particular words lacking precise equivalents in English. Problems may be exacerbated by marked differences in class, generation, cultural background, or gender between appellant and interpreter.

REFERENCES

Cases cited

DAUBERT V. MERRELL DOW PHARMACEUTICALS, (92-102), 509 US 579 (1993) [USSC].
FOLKES V. CHADD, (1782) 3 Douglas K.B. 157.
FRYE V. UNITED STATES, 54 App D. C. 46, 293 F. 1013 No. 3968 (1923) [CADC].
R V. JAMEEL AKHTAR, 9701082/Z2, 10 March 1998 [CA].
R V. TURNER, 17 October 1974, [1975] QB 834, [1975] 1 All ER 70, [1975] 2 WLR 56 [CA].
R V. WRIGHT, (1821) Russ. & Ry. 456, 168 ER 895.

Printed sources

AKRAM, S.M. 2000. Orientalism revisited in asylum and refugee claims. *International Journal of Refugee Law* **12**, 7-40.

AMERICAN ANTHROPOLOGICAL ASSOCIATION 1999. Declaration on anthropology and human rights (available on-line: *http://www.aaanet.org/stmts/humanrts.htm*; accessed 1 January 2008).

BARSKY, R.F. 2000. *Arguing and justifying: assessing the Convention refugees' choice of moment, motive and host country*. Aldershot: Ashgate.

BAUMAN, Z. 1996. From pilgrim to tourist – or a short history of identity. In *Questions of cultural identity* (eds) S. Hall & P. du Gay, 19-36. London: Sage.

CLIFFORD, J. 1988. *The predicament of culture*. Cambridge, Mass.: Harvard University Press.

COLEMAN, D.L. 1996. Individualizing justice through multiculturalism: the liberal's dilemma. *Columbia Law Review* **96**, 1093-167.

CONLEY, J.M. & W.M. O'BARR 1990. *Rules versus relationships: the ethnography of legal discourse*. Chicago: University Press.

COWAN, J.K., M.-B. DEMBOUR & R.A. WILSON 2001. Introduction. In *Culture and rights: anthropological perspectives* (eds) J.K. Cowan, M.-B. Dembour & R.A. Wilson, 1-26. Cambridge: University Press.

CULHANE, D. 1998. *The pleasure of the crown: anthropology, law and first nations*. Burnaby, B.C.: Talon Books.

DELORIA, V. 1969. *Custer died for your sins: an Indian manifesto*. New York: Oklahoma University Press.

DEMBOUR, M.-B. 2001. Following the movement of a pendulum: between universalism and relativism. In *Culture and rights: anthropological perspectives* (eds) J.K. Cowan, M.-B. Dembour & R.A. Wilson, 56-79. Cambridge: University Press.

DONOVAN, J.M. & H.E. ANDERSON, III 2003. *Anthropology and law*. New York: Berghahn.

EDMOND, G. 2004a. Thick decisions: expertise, advocacy and reasonableness in the Federal Court of Australia. *Oceania* **74**, 190-230.

——— 2004b. Judging facts: managing expert knowledges in legal decision-making. In *Expertise in regulation and law* (ed.) G. Edmond, 136-65. Aldershot: Ashgate.

——— & D. MERCER 2004. Experts and expertise in legal and regulatory settings. In *Expertise in regulation and law* (ed.) G. Edmond, 1-31. Aldershot: Ashgate.

ERIKSEN, T.H. 2001. Between universalism and relativism: a critique of the UNESCO concept of culture. In *Culture and rights: anthropological perspectives* (eds) J.K. Cowan, M.-B. Dembour & R.A. Wilson, 127-48. Cambridge: University Press.

FULLER, C.J. 1994. Legal anthropology. *Anthropology Today* **10**, 9-12.

GEERTZ, C. 1983. *Local knowledge*. New York: Basic Books.

GOOD, A. 2004a. 'Undoubtedly an expert'? Country experts in the UK asylum courts. *Journal of the Royal Anthropological Institute* (N.S.) **10**, 113-33.

——— 2004b. Expert evidence in asylum and human rights appeals: an expert's view. *International Journal of Refugee Law* **16**, 358-80.

——— 2006. *Anthropology and expertise in the asylum courts*. London: Routledge-Cavendish.

HALL, S. 1996. Who needs identity? In *Questions of cultural identity* (eds) S. Hall & P. du Gay, 1-17. London: Sage.

HENDERSON, M. 2003. *Best practice guide to asylum and human rights appeals*. London: Immigration Law Practitioners Association/Refugee Legal Group.

HEPNER, T.R. 2003. Expert witnessing: anthropology and Eritrean asylum seekers in the United States. Unpublished paper, American Anthropological Association meeting, Chicago, November.

HODGKINSON, T. 1990. *Expert evidence: law and practice*. London: Sweet & Maxwell.

HUMPHREYS, S. 1985. Law as discourse. *History and Anthropology* **1**, 241-64.

JASANOFF, S. 1990. *The fifth branch: science advisors as policymakers*. Cambridge, Mass.: Harvard University Press.

——— 1995. *Science at the bar: law, science and technology in America*. Cambridge, Mass.: Harvard University Press.

——— 1996. Research subpoenas and the sociology of knowledge. *Law and Contemporary Problems* **59**, 95-118.

JONES, C.A.G. 1994. *Expert witnesses: science, medicine and the practice of law*. Oxford: Clarendon Press.

KALIN, W. 1986. Troubled communication: cross-cultural misunderstandings in the asylum hearing. *International Migration Review* **20**, 230-41.

KANDEL, R.F. 1992. How lawyers and anthropologists think differently. In *Double vision: anthropologists at law* (*NAPA Bulletin* **11**) (ed.) R.F. Kandel, 1-4. Washington, D.C.: American Anthropological Association.

KIRSCH, S. 2001. Lost worlds: environmental disaster, 'culture loss', and the law. *Current Anthropology* **42**, 167-98.

KROEBER, A.L. & C. KLUCKHOHN 1952. *Culture: a critical review of concepts and definitions*. Cambridge, Mass.: Papers of the Peabody Museum 47: 1, Harvard University.

KUPER, A. 1999. *Culture: the anthropologists' account*. Cambridge, Mass.: Harvard University Press.

KUPER, L. & M.G. SMITH (eds) 1969. *Pluralism in Africa*. Berkeley: University of California Press.

LOEB, E. 2005. Review of Alice Renteln, *The cultural defense*. *Anthropological Quarterly* **78**, 297-302.

McBARNET, D. 1981. *Conviction: law, the state and the construction of justice*. Oxford: Macmillan.

MacCORMICK, N. 1994. *Legal reasoning and legal theory*. Oxford: University Press.

MacCRIMMON, M.T. 1998. Fact determination: common sense knowledge, judicial notice, and social science evidence. *International Commentary on Evidence* (available online: *http://www.bepress.com/ice/vol1/iss1/art2/*, accessed 1 January 2008).

McKINLEY, M. 1997. Life stories, disclosure and the law. *Political and Legal Anthropology Review* **20**, 70-82.

MAGUIGAN, H. 1995. Cultural evidence and male violence: are feminist and multiculturalist reformers on a collision course in criminal courts? *New York University Law Review* **70**, 36-99.

MALINOWSKI, B. 1926. *Crime and custom in savage society*. New York: Harcourt Brace.

MERRY, S.E. 1988. Legal pluralism. *Law and Society Review* **22**, 869-96.

———— 1990. *Getting justice and getting even: legal consciousness among working-class Americans*. Chicago: University Press.

MICHAELS, W.B. 1995. *Our America: nativism, modernism, and pluralism*. Durham, N.C.: Duke University Press.

MOORE, S.F. 1973. Law and social change: the semi-autonomous social field as an appropriate subject of study. *Law and Society Review*, Summer, 719-46.

MURPHY, K. & M. CUCCIAS 1997. The application of Daubert or Frye analysis to expert testimony in the 'soft sciences'. *Federation of Defense and Corporate Counsel Quarterly* **47**, 331.

PAINE, R. (ed.) 1985. *Advocacy and anthropology: first encounters*. St John's: Memorial University of Newfoundland.

PHILLIPS, A. 2003. When culture means gender: issues of cultural defence in the English courts. *Modern Law Review* **66**, 510-31.

POCOCK, J.G.A. 2000. Waitangi as mystery of state: consequences of the ascription of federative capacity to the Maori. In *Political theory and the rights of indigenous peoples* (eds) D. Ivison, P. Patton, & W. Sanders, 25-35. Cambridge: University Press.

POPPER, K. 1989. *Conjectures and refutations: the growth of scientific knowledge* (4th edn). London: Routledge & Kegan Paul.

PORTER, T. 1995. *Trust in numbers: the pursuit of objectivity in science and public life*. Princeton: University Press.

POSPISIL, L.J. 1971. *The anthropology of law: a comparative theory*. New York: Harper & Row.

RADCLIFFE-BROWN, A.R. 1940. On social structure. *Journal of the Royal Anthropological Institute* **70**, 1-12.

REDMAYNE, M. 2001. *Expert evidence and criminal justice*. Oxford: University Press.

RENTELN, A.D. 2004. *The cultural defense*. New York: Oxford University Press.

RIGBY, P. & P. SEVAREID 1992. Lawyers, anthropologists, and the knowledge of fact. In *Double vision: anthropologists at law* (NAPA Bulletin **11**) (ed.) R.F. Kandel, 5-21. Washington, D.C.: American Anthropological Association.

ROSEN, L. 1989. *The anthropology of justice: law as culture in Islamic society*. Cambridge: University Press.

SANDOVAL, C. 2000. *Methodology of the oppressed*. Minneapolis: Minnesota University Press.

SCHWANDNER-SIEVERS, S. 2006. 'Culture' in court: Albanian migrants and the anthropologist as expert witness. In *Applications of anthropology: professional anthropology in the twenty-first century* (ed.) S. Pink, 209-28. Oxford: Berghahn.

TORRY, W.I. 2000. Culture and individual responsibility: touchstones of the culture defense. *Human Organization* **59**, 58-71.

TUHIWAI SMITH, L. 1999. *Decolonizing methodologies: research and indigenous peoples*. New York: Zed Books.

TURNER, T. 1993. Anthropology and multiculturalism: what is anthropology that multiculturalists should be mindful of it? *Cultural Anthropology* **8**, 411-29.

———— 1997. Human rights, human difference: anthropology's contribution to an emancipatory cultural politics. *Journal of Anthropological Research* **53**, 273-91.

UNHCR 1992. *Handbook on procedures and criteria for determining refugee status under the 1951 Convention*. Geneva: UNHCR.

VAN BROECK, J. 2001. Cultural defence and culturally motivated crimes (cultural offences). *European Journal of Crime, Criminal Law and Criminal Justice* **9**, 1-32.

VAN SAN, M. 1998. *Stelen en stelen: delinquent gedrag van Curaçaose jongeren in Nederland*. Amsterdam: Spinhuis.

VOLPP, L. 1994. (Mis)identifying culture: Asian women and the 'cultural defense'. *Harvard Women's Law Journal* **17**, 57-101.

VON BENDA-BECKMANN, K. & F. STRIJBOSCH (eds) 1986. *Anthropology of law in the Netherlands: essays on legal pluralism*. Dordrecht: Foris.

WADE, P. (ed.) 1995. *Advocacy in anthropology*. Manchester: Group for Debates in Anthropological Theory.

WEINER, J.F. 1999. Culture in a sealed envelope: the concealment of Australian Aboriginal heritage and tradition in the Hindmarsh Island Bridge affair. *Journal of the Royal Anthropological Institute* (N.S.) **5**, 193-210.

WINKELMAN, M. 1996. Cultural factors in criminal defense proceedings. *Human Organization* **55**, 157-8.

5

The antinomies of political evidence in post-Apartheid Durban, South Africa

SHARAD CHARI *London School of Economics and Political Science/University of KwaZulu-Natal*

Post-Apartheid South Africa has witnessed an outpouring of various forms of evidence documenting past and present inequities. Whether using the tools of the novel, memoir, poetry, polemics, political economy, social surveys, biophysical science, or photography, testimonies to post-Apartheid inequality have had a mixed success in calling into question remnants of the Apartheid and anti-Apartheid past. In certain respects, this is not surprising. A long history of segregated 'cultures', and associated spaces and practices, continues to have a powerful afterlife during South Africa's transition to democracy. Despite some spatial and class mobility, particularly among the de-racializing elite, the employed middle classes, and those among the poor who can access social services, most livelihoods and forms of politics continue to be structured through the remains of racially segregated 'Indian', 'Coloured', 'African', and white areas and populations. To say this is not to assert the claim that all things South African must necessarily concern 'race', as, for instance, all things Indian must be about 'caste'. Rather, it is to insist that we interrogate mutations in state-sanctioned racism and ethno-racial discourse as they structure work, housing, crime, environment, public health, or almost any aspect of South African society.

This chapter focuses on the processes through which residents of a Coloured township adjacent to an oil refinery on the racial borderlands of the post-Apartheid city of Durban devise and deploy evidence of subjection to racism in the hope of a post-racial future. I attend to a range of evidence devised and used by Wentworth's residents, from ethnographic and historical contextualization to scientific data. At first glance, the forms of evidence are not that specific, nor are they grounded in a conception of evidence that is peculiar to a Coloured population quarantined by Apartheid next to polluting industry. However, the means by which political evidence is deployed takes specific form in relation to the industrial Goliaths, and in relation to official and corporate dissimulation. The specificity of local attempts at devising political evidence only becomes clear in relation to a broader political economy of dissimulation through which certain racialized populations remain subject to toxic exposure, despite their best efforts at documenting the facts of pollution. For Wentworth's residents, 'speaking truth to power' remains a fraught affair.

This chapter gives pause to consider the antinomies of witnessing and documenting evidence of state-sanctioned racism in a post-Apartheid township subject to toxic exposure. I use Albert Memmi's (2000) general theory of racism as a practical logic through which certain differences are isolated, valued hierarchically, and the consequent hierarchy of values is used to legitimate projects of group-targeted exploitation or harm. Memmi insists that racism is not the only way to approach difference. Anti-racism can be considered in these terms as a practical logic which values differences in order to mitigate harm and promote solidarities. In practice, both racism and anti-racism require valuation and knowledge production. In other words, questions of ethnography and evidence are important not just to anthropologists but also to broader publics engaged in anti-racial practice or other forms of social activism. In this volume, Webb Keane reminds anthropologists that ethnographic knowledge has to treat categories as contextualized in wider semiotic constellations. Outside academic work, knowledge about cultural difference and social context is usually less rigorous in addressing Keane's requirement. Various publics contextualize categories in broader semiotic constellations to counter persisting ethno-racial or gender inequalities, to varied effect. As Good (this volume) shows with respect to 'cultural evidence' in courts of law, for instance, the anthropologist's conception of culture can be in tension with the rather more blunt essentialisms employed in legal systems. Value clashes between varied academic and folk conceptions of ethnography in the public realm remain under-researched.

What I suggest is that if ethnography today strives for empathetic, yet critical, solidarity with the other, as Daniel Miller (2005) argues, there is an affinity between anti-racist practice and contemporary critical ethnography. While anthropology has been obsessed with the auto-critique of its colonial and Eurocentric baggage over the past three decades, the question of critical ethnography as a precondition for a politics of solidarity is rather less researched, with a few notable exceptions (e.g. Graeber 2002; 2004). This chapter concerns challenges faced by people involved in social justice work that they variously call 'activism', 'community work', or 'political work'. I ask how various residents in Wentworth formulate evidence for social transformation, in confronting what they perceive to be mutations in state-sanctioned racism after Apartheid.

Participants mobilize evidence for political work through specific tools and authorizing discourses, marking certain kinds of evidence as political evidence orientated to the transformation of persisting inequalities. The compensatory dispute is the dominant form of political evidence constructed in Wentworth. I question the efficacy of this form of political evidence in relation to the broader social relations that afford racism its power. People engaged in political work periodically confront the ways in which racism utilizes contextual as well as decontextualized evidence about formerly racially designated population groups and spaces. In certain instances, Wentworth's residents have found ways to call such connections into question. At other moments, residents amass evidence while waiting for opportune moments to act in a climate of uncertainty. When faced with official dissimulation and wilful silencing from corporate and state power, collecting political evidence may simply be a means to demonstrate patience and resolve against the inefficacy of compensatory politics.

The city of Durban has become something of a laboratory for post-Apartheid struggles for de-racialization and social justice. This chapter is part of a broader research project on former racial Group Areas of Indian Merebank and Coloured Wentworth, within the patchwork residential-industrial geography of Durban. Of similar sizes and populations, Wentworth and Merebank have the distinction of being surrounded by the polluting industry of the South Durban Industrial Basin.[1] While apparently similar, however, these townships have been built through divergent histories of dispossession, work, welfare, belonging, and activism. Merebank was an old village of ex-indentured Indian peasant-workers on the urban fringe, and despite a rich and multi-layered history of anti-Apartheid activism, it has demobilized after Apartheid. On the other side of Duranta Road, Wentworth was created as a Coloured township to house a large number of mixed-race tenants thrown out of informal backyard tenancies along the advance of Apartheid's forced removals in Durban. Over time Wentworth has become more trapped and parochial, despite the wide trajectories taken by its industrial migrants. Wentworth's men have been South Africa's pre-eminent industrial artisans, and Apartheid's racial labour markets made occupations like pipe-fitting and boiler-making the prized jobs for Coloured men. After Apartheid, Wentworth has become a hotbed of environmental justice and labour activism, among other forms of unpaid political work. Over the past five years, I have been engaged in documenting the past and present transformations of these very different Apartheid townships. My research traces the contemporary effects of divergent histories of race, space, and activism in past and present South Durban.[2]

People engaged in political work in Wentworth make complicated decisions about types and tactics of evidence, with implications for possibilities of both mutuality and harm. I will argue that while attempting to fight collectively around certain issues, Wentworth's residents also create new forms of differentiation within the neighbourhood. I focus on institutionalized forms of political mobilization in environmental justice organization but also on the sporadic and ongoing political work orientated to transforming social conditions.

I will begin with a brief discussion of some of the lessons of environmental activism, the most important arena of political work to emerge from Wentworth. In the wake of official dissimulation, some of Wentworth's residents have come to professionalize themselves, presenting evidence of their resolve to engage the structures of the state. In the second section, I draw lessons from moral debates precipitated by the arrival of a city government official to the neighbourhood. I note the uses of evidence in these debates, and also the ways in which political evidence is used to differentiate Wentworth internally. I then turn to some of the ways in which people maintain archives in order to claim land and a rightful place in history. These situations demonstrate both the limits of legalism and the focus on compensation, as well as the openness of the ethnographic impulse to contextualize evidence in wider histories and imaginations. To conclude, I offer general observations about the ways in which struggles over political evidence in places like Wentworth make space for critique of knowledge production in the wake of a racially fragmented archive, and of emergent forms of state racism.

Environmental evidence and official dissimulation

The fight for clean air is the most important form of post-Apartheid political activism in Wentworth.[3] The industrial giants that surround the neighbourhood of Wentworth provide little consistent employment to local labour. However, the refineries have steadily contributed to long-term ill-health in this 'fenceline community'. The refinery has for the most part disavowed that it is self-evidently a producer of pollution. In response, activists have tried to demonstrate how persisting ties between corporate power and city government, bequeathed from the Apartheid era, continue to structure the corporation's power to pollute in the democratic era.

Historical research on pollution politics shows how older environmental activism from the white population on the nearby Bluff had the pernicious effect of pushing the brunt of industrial pollution onto the segregated black communities of South Durban (Sparks 2004; 2005). Post-Apartheid environmental activism in the South Durban basin began in 1995, when the iconic leader of the new nation, Nelson Mandela, stopped *en route* to the Engen refinery to speak to protesters outside. The South Durban Community Environmental Alliance (SDCEA) was formed in 1997 to link environmental groups across the racial divides, to fight a demon that knows no colour: air pollution. With its strongest base in Wentworth, through the Wentworth Development Forum (WDF), SDCEA has tried to represent all communities of the South Durban Industrial Basin. Bobby Peek of SDCEA has since helped found South Africa's main environmental justice organization, groundWork, in 1999, with its key concerns in oil and air pollution from chemical industries, health care waste and incineration, and hazardous waste.[4] GroundWork has since become a branch of the global network called Friends of the Earth. A persisting strength of the SDCEA/WDF/groundWork alliance is that it can link scales and forms of activism, from militant protest to legal struggle to transnational advocacy, and in relation to all levels of government.

Environmental activists in South Durban have long stumbled over problems of evidence, and corporate and governmental obstinacy in attributing responsibility for ill-health to polluters. An important set of newspaper articles by Tony Carnie reported that the rate of leukaemia for children under the age of 10 in neighbouring Merebank was twenty-four times the national average. Carnie knocked on doors collecting information for his articles, and called South Durban a 'cancer alley'. Both the city and industry dismissed this and subsequent survey research as unscientific and anecdotal. Since then, scholars from the University of KwaZulu-Natal Medical School and the University of Michigan School of Public Health have conducted a rigorous study of air pollution flows at a primary school in the middle of the industrial basin, showing that 53.3 per cent of students suffered from respiratory ailments. This has not met with response either from government or from the corporations. The corporations' position has been that statistical probabilities show imperfect causality between pollution and ill-health. GroundWork's response is that 'the struggle is really against official silence and the willful ignorance that serves to frustrate ... demands that industry must clean up and compensate those it has harmed' (Hallowes & Munnik 2006: 149).

The trio of WDF, SDCEA, and groundWork have stood firm as critics of corporate dissimulation, refusing to accept 'corporate social responsibility' programmes from the refineries as consolation. They continue to collect evidence, through community monitoring via low-tech 'bucket brigade' sampling of pollutants, and through documentary evidence of pollution-related ill-health. One response of the refineries has been to question whether these organizations can rightfully stand in as representatives of 'community', even if this is necessary for collecting evidence of ill-health next to an oil refinery.

The mixed tactical approach of these organizations has meant that evidence that organizations actually represent 'community' is important. SDCEA-WDF show evidence of popular support through numbers at demonstrations and meetings. However, given that SDCEA is meant to be an organization fighting across racial lines in what ought to be a truly post-Apartheid struggle against an enemy that knows no colour, SDCEA/groundWork attend to sceptics with some caution. Interracial activism always challenges the boundaries of formerly racialized 'communities'.

While there have been some victories, most notably a new Air Pollution Act, environmental justice activists like Bobby Peek are painfully aware that environmental gains are geographical, and that a victory in one place might take its toll by shifting burdens elsewhere. The activists have therefore held to legal guarantees, such as the constitutional guarantee for a clean environment for all (Constitution of South Africa 1996). As Bobby Peek sees it, the challenge for South Durban is to link environmental and labour activism, to bring together problems of pollution and jobless growth in the toxic sink that is the South Durban Industrial Basin. Such a moment of confluence did appear briefly, in militant community labour action in 2003. As Peek warns, 'The environmental movement is just beginning to challenge the economic system'.[5]

A large section of Wentworth is not mobilized by this environmental activism. Neither does it collect evidence of air pollution through the informal 'bucket brigade' system. The silence of the state and corporations has meant that many people see environmentalism as an alien language that is not bound to lift Wentworth's residents out of their current condition. Bobby Peek sees this as a problem of mass organization and education to fight the dominant dynamics of dissimulation about pollution and ill-health. What is also at work is distrust of juridical mechanisms alone to resolve persisting racial inequalities so deeply etched into the landscape. While many of Wentworth's residents are distrustful of governmental and legal instruments, however, some of them have also become savvy in their engagements with the state. The moral debates that have emerged from tense interactions with the state reveal ways in which people engaged in political work demonstrate their professionalism as agents of 'development' as well as their difference from those in need of betterment.

Moral debates and the productivity of professionalism

Xolani Zondi[6] was perplexed. He had come as a representative of the municipality's Poverty Alleviation Programme to talk to residents in Wentworth about his mandate. He was welcomed and made to sit in the courtyard of Diane Brown's home. The fifteen other people introduced themselves as labour organizers, community workers, and two social workers from the Department of Mental Health and the Department of Social Services. They spoke in turn about the many problems of the community. The social workers spoke of 'uncontrollable children', glue sniffing, HIV/AIDS, domestic violence, and depression brought on by chronic unemployment. Diane Brown spoke about her organization's financial need to fund its gardening project, as a way of dealing with depression and the problems of juvenile delinquency identified by the social worker. Lenny Stevens, a labour organizer for limited-duration contract workers employed periodically by the refineries for repairs and retrofits, spoke for a while, situating the problems of the community in a specific account of the effects of a dominant labour regime. He spoke of 'growing out of gangsterism to sustaining families', and he insisted that for a family, living on less than R1,500 per month (about £100) is poverty, 'whether you want to admit it or not'. Stevens elaborated on the union's attempts at starting co-operatives 'to meet basic needs – the rent, the lights, the school fees'. After he and others spoke, everyone turned expectantly to Mr Zondi from Poverty Alleviation.

A bit taken aback by his outspoken interlocutors, the soft-spoken Mr Zondi praised Wentworth for being a counter-example to the 'level of demobilization in civil society'. He explained the city's approach to Poverty Alleviation and its programmes for the poor, and he informed the residents that the city was developing indigent registers, based on assessments by social workers, to identify households living under the poverty line to qualify for special programmes. He drew a pyramid with small entrepreneurs in the middle, to be targeted by the city's Economic Development department, and with the poor at the bottom, to be targeted by Poverty Alleviation. Lenny responded in his slow and booming voice, 'We have come up with these ideas ourselves. We've done research and we have workshopped most of these ideas and we have done a pyramid like yours and found we're on the bottom'. Another member of the meeting said, 'People are already starving here, and there are competent bodies, like Women of Wentworth, so how can the city help?' 'What is the new dispensation doing for level 1 of your pyramid?' asked another. Mr Zondi made a few brief remarks about targeting 'breadwinners' and measuring the level of indigency, before beating a hasty retreat. Diane Brown assured him, and the members of the community whom she had called to the meeting, that she would 'liaise telephonically'.[7]

Several dilemmas about political evidence are apparent in this vignette. First, what is striking is the way in which Lenny Stevens, Diane Brown, and others laid claim to the same bureaucratic language of the representative of the state, who, incidentally, was a former 'struggle comrade' of Diane's brother. Stevens and Brown spoke of 'workshop-ping' and 'liaising', and indeed they have taken me to several workshops and meetings during my research trips over the past five years. This is precisely not what James Ferguson (1990) calls an 'antipolitics machine' that uses bureaucracy as a means for de-politicizing questions of poverty and inequality. Practices of professionalism and bureaucratization sustain the ongoing mobilizations in Wentworth around a variety of social, political, and environmental issues. Something else is at work in these gestures: evidence of professionalism that clearly marks certain people in Wentworth as morally charged agents of 'development' or betterment.

Second, one of the undercurrents in the meeting was that several members felt that they had been left out of the city's development priorities as a constituency, as 'Wentworth Coloureds' who are insignificant to the ruling political party alliance as well as to the city's coffers. Several people made asides to this effect before and after the meeting, and indeed Mr Zondi made indirect reference to the perceived marginality of Wentworth, with unrecognized levels of poverty *here*, in a forgotten Coloured neigh-bourhood. The afterlife of Apartheid's racially 'separate development' is a rhetorical balancing act as people point to persisting inequalities, unsure of how to reference them in non-racial terms. In asides, people in Wentworth often say things like 'we were too black in the past, not black enough in the present', but these individuals become much more careful in interracial exchanges, such as in the meeting with Mr Zondi. In other words, racial references are often only part of quite volatile value struggles.

Third, a recurring concern among Wentworth's activists is that they not reproduce various kinds of stereotypes about this place as inevitably ridden by gangs, drugs, and illicit sex, and yet these sentiments continue to recur in local moral debates. Hence, Lenny Stevens, Diane Brown, and others at the meeting seemed to confirm elements of the stereotype – with respect to juvenile delinquency, alcohol abuse, or domestic violence – as if the evidence was unnecessary or simple common sense. Working-class Coloureds are assumed to have a propensity for certain things that do not require evidence. At closer glance, participants diverged not so much in the content but in their rationale for deploying evidence of poverty and marginality in Wentworth. The social workers tended to reproduce shocking stories that circulate about Wentworth both in the neighbourhood and in the media, of child abuse, drug use, and sexual violence. In the first instance, these are stereotypes posited on Wentworth, which add to its stigma and confinement (Wacquant 2004). However, as in Diane Brown's turn to the same values, these are productive discourses that circulate within the division of labour in political work. Both Diane Brown and Lenny Stevens make reference to stereotypes about Wentworth, but they also use them to make a more specific case for *family* breakdown. As Diane said to me of her own community work, her organization centres on 'family preservation'.[8] What, precisely, are these debates over the morality of family values about? In what follows, I turn to a series of events and processes that link the stakes in local debates about bureaucratization, stigma, and family values to practices of political work in Wentworth.

Just before the meeting with the Poverty Alleviation representative, Lenny spoke to me at length about how his life was shaped by the dominant regime of industrial migrant labour, which had placed intense stress on his family life. Several of the biographies of Wentworth's migrant industrial artisans that I have collected since 2002 centre on familial anxieties. As Hylton White (2001: 468) suggests, based on fieldwork north of Durban, there are many variants across South Africa of the figure of the migrant absconder referred to by isiXhosa speakers as the *Itshipa* or cheap, who neglects emotional and financial responsibilities to the household. Fear and loathing of the absconder recurs in Wentworth narratives when people speak of industrial artisans on long-distance contracts at refineries across South Africa, or in engineering projects across the continent. Various former migrants and their kin have spoken to me about how these long-distance projects brought bursts of income to migrant men, who then squandered the money on new cars, clothes, guns, and new drugs such as Mandrax. According to these narratives, the local street-gang culture shifted with the entry of guns and Mandrax, and gangsterism became something else by the 1990s: less youth culture than organized drug trade controlled by powerful drug lords.

Elements of this narrative are shared with other South African migrants, but there are important differences. African migrant histories are linked to quite different social dynamics of kinship, generation, marriage, and bridewealth. There is a strong historical and ethnographic tradition recording these complex dynamics between migration and family dynamics with respect to black African but not Coloured populations, to the extent that these histories are separable. While African migrant histories can draw from this ethnographic knowledge to assert claims about threats to 'Zulu' or 'Pondo' 'culture' in relation to migrant labour, there are no analogous narratives of South African Coloureds to draw from. The result is an ethnographic blindspot that adds to the notion that Coloureds, as Grant Farred puts it, 'have no a priori or pre-lapsarian moment; [nor can they] retreat into a mythic precolonial "innocence". Coloured difference is ... insufficiently different for them to conceive of themselves as anything but South African' (2001: 186).

While drawing from contextual knowledge – their own experientially based observations about migrant labour and its effects on family and household – Wentworth's residents deploy this knowledge in general terms of family breakdown. The reason for not seeing themselves as similar to other black migrants is a segregated historical consciousness produced by a long history of racially segregated living, education, work, politics, leisure, and intellectual production. Hence, what ought to be presented as historical ethnographic evidence is deployed instead as generic analysis. This 'general knowledge' risks reproducing the stigma posited on Wentworth Coloureds as a whole. As a strategy of risk aversion, political workers often uncritically reproduce internal distinctions within Wentworth in which the stigma lies within a certain fraction of the population. Evidence of social distinctions among a population similar in class terms becomes central to this task.

Hence, when President Thabo Mbeki visited Wentworth on a pre-election trip with various communities in Durban in 2004, a group of residents who met him poured forth narratives about the 'degeneration of the family' and of the rising exchange of sex for survival, themes that have been written about in other poor neighbourhoods in the province (Hunter 2002). Members of the Wentworth Development Forum (WDF), the most vocal civic organization, were livid. WDF saw this characterization as an affront to a community that has been stigmatized enough, and it started a 'family preservation unit' as a response. Once more, what remains uncommented upon is the reason 'family crisis' becomes the centre of attention in moral debate, let alone its historical basis in the dominant migrant labour regime. Moral debates about family values are not recognized by Wentworth's residents as evidence of shared ground with other South Africans whose lives have been fundamentally altered by twentieth-century migrant labour regimes. However, both moral debates about family and gestures to profession-alism work to foment internal divisions within Wentworth. These family values and gestures to bureaucratization converge in practices of political work.

I drove around with the late Skido Joseph as he put together his portfolio as a 'development consultant', to transform his situation as an unemployed person who seemed genuinely interested in helping the lot of his neighbourhood. He printed his portfolio in one community organization, used the phone to make an appointment in another, and had a friend in a third organization look over the format of his profile.[9] Skido had a chequered past as a labour organizer and community activist, though the precise details are difficult to verify. What was clear, as he drove around Wentworth in his old car blaring anti-Apartheid 'struggle music', was that he was bitter about not being able to use his struggle credentials to access jobs in the post-Apartheid state, as many of his former comrades had. Skido's asides to me were contradictory – sometimes racialized, and at other times cosmopolitan; sometimes extremely conservative on gender and sexuality, yet often encouraging of women's activism. Skido was a charmer and one got the sense that he could work the system, at least enough to get through his everyday movements. Most of his labours were unpaid, and we often met while stealing a cup of tea from a kind host in Wentworth.

What is important is that Skido went out of his way to display evidence of his professionalism as a way of distinguishing himself from those in need, many of whom were not materially that different from himself. This evidence was always both docu-mentary and performative. Skido's documentary evidence, in the form of a visiting card, a CV, or a business plan, demonstrated his commitment to the new rules of professional conduct with power. However, his body language, his narrative or musical asides, and the packed gun that he often revealed stuck in his jeans under his T-shirt reminded people that he was once a militant. The juxtaposition of documentary and embodied evidence is multi-registered. Anyone could read the documents to know of

Skido's qualifications or of his various plans. Wentworth's residents were meant to see the combination of evidence as confirming that he was a forgotten struggle hero who was learning the rules of post-Apartheid politics. Like many others, Skido was invested in a process of internal differentiation of Wentworth's residents, separating community workers and activists, on the one side, from 'the poor', on the other. The boundary line is tenuous. I have encountered many people who, like Skido, employ a moral discourse of professionalism to mark distinctions while carefully negotiating their own conduct with respect to these markers. Several people I have interviewed turn to similar documentary evidence of their professionalism, particularly by bringing out 'business plans' that outline various ventures for which they might seek funding from businesses, international labour unions, state institutions, or non-governmental bodies.

Lenny Joseph and others ran a metal workers co-operative for a while and they wrote proposals that described this enterprise as a development organization. The proposals themselves are evidence of professionalism, as Lenny and his colleagues sought to appeal to progressive funding sources as socially conscious innovators. Diane Brown has written multiple proposals through a computer donated to her by an international visitor. She maintains connections, and sends documentary evidence of her ongoing involvement as a community worker engaged in social transformation.

Others, like Frank Henry, a community HIV/AIDS caregiver, give their time to community work without payment, and with little recognition. Frank has moved through various community organizations in Wentworth, fighting the fierce Christian currents that promote abstinence as the primary means for tackling the pandemic. Along with some other stalwart community AIDS workers, Frank has maintained a presence in part by building evidence of his professionalization as what he now calls a 'family health counsellor'. Frank's professionalism comes from participation in a variety of free workshops held by the city and by non-governmental organizations, through which he has a good general understanding of various issues with respect to HIV/AIDS. When he took me to visit some of the poorest residents of Wentworth in a homeless shelter called The Arc, he expressed some reserve on whether these people could be reintegrated into society. Frank straddles the boundary between dispensers and receivers of community work, and our visit to The Arc was a rare instance in which he could take a clear stance on one side.

As I have suggested, several people in Wentworth – unemployed, underemployed, or with steady incomes – put some of their labour into various kinds of community or political work. This is usually unpaid work in the service of regenerating the lives of various less fortunate residents. Sometimes, it affords access to sources of funding from the city or from private donors, most impressively the 'social responsibility programmes' from the oil refineries and the pulp and paper mill that surround Wentworth.

Diane Brown is an expert at writing up proposals, at holding meetings, and at 'liaising telephonically' with various city officials like Xolani Zondi, and she has managed to turn a small organization into a centre for women and children, an after-school programme, a dance school funded by a successful Coloured pop-star, and now a family resource centre. Diane speaks emotionally about the plight of the poor, and I have gone with her to visit poor families in the flats on Hime Street and Alabama Road. She has told me horror stories about men selling their wives and daughters as prostitutes, about drug abuse, and about children suffering innumerable forms of violence. What I am suggesting is that her practice of demonstrating this evidence is primarily meant to be evidence of her own respectability as a social worker, tirelessly working for the uplift of the poor around her.

Only one leader of a community organization has said to me quite frankly that in his estimation a large share of Wentworth's population ought to be written off because they are irredeemable, and efforts ought to be concentrated on the few who can be redeemed. Most people involved in community or activist organizations hedge their bets by walking the thin line between those who dispense betterment and those in need of it.

What is striking in all these cases is the way in which people portray themselves as working, when in fact they are not employed in waged labour. Engagement in community organizations does not enable these people to earn a wage for their necessities. These ongoing, repetitive labours for the means to rejuvenate life are socially necessary. While Wentworth's unemployed residents may not find waged work, they cannot help but labour to find the means for their physical and emotional survival. Material remuneration for this labour works in a highly mediated way, through grants, donations, cups of tea, and a little bit of food distributed through organizational networks. People are forced to play their expertise to 'earn' the right to this remuneration. Professionalism is a kind of cultural capital that provides evidence of commitment to political work, for as long as the individual can stay on the right side of the divide between dispensers and receivers. These concerns exemplify an involution of politics in the wake of official silencing of evidence of toxic suffering in a neighbourhood surrounding an oil refinery. This is one kind of response to the limits of juridical means for ending environmental injustice. In the following section, I turn to a few instances in which people maintain historical evidence in personal archives as political evidence of a different sort. While apparently centred on compensation for the loss of land, these personal archives open much larger questions of access to knowledge and power in a fractured society with a segregated historical consciousness.

Historical evidence and archival challenges

I have suggested that a segregated historical consciousness is one of the central artefacts of a long history of state-sanctioned racism in South Africa. There have been some attempts to situate the plight of Wentworth's residents in a historical context, but with specific challenges. The notion of history as a commons is alive and well in contemporary South Africa, particularly after the Truth and Reconciliation Commission and the flood of memoir-writing in the past decade.[10] The critical archivist Verne Harris (2002) notes perceptively that the dominant understanding is that inherited from nineteenth-century archival science, which continues to treat archives, archivists, and records as things rather than as creative, productive, and open processes. Harris has stood for open access to the records of the Truth and Reconciliation Commission, as with other records to aid in struggles for redistribution and redress, and he sees the importance of maintaining historical records as a contested commons. The notion of reclaiming the commons is most sharply posed in narratives about land and territory, particularly in accounts of forced dispossession and imagined restitution.[11] Some residents in Wentworth have engaged in testimonials of the remains of histories of dispossession and segregation, sometimes through the aid of various objects, and through the careful maintenance of personal archives.

While narrating his long and complex story of transition from the countryside to the city, of the loss of his family land, and of his frustrated attempts to work within Apartheid political structures, Jan Fynn makes sure to stress his deep roots in what he considers his ancestral property. Fynn narrates his life as powerfully hinged by his ancestry, as the descendant of Henry Francis Fynn, an Englishman who negotiated with multiple sovereignties so as to receive both a grant of land from the British Crown and a chieftaincy and a royal wife from the Zulu King Shaka. Jan Fynn considers himself the main heir to these legacies, connecting his own trajectory of dispossession to a collective responsibility as the key patrilineal descendent of Henry Francis Fynn's 'Coloured' family. When I met him, Jan Fynn was a retired politician, managing a school in the peri-urban south of Durban. As we spoke, he opened a small briefcase and displayed his personal archive across his bed, next to a sleeping cat. Among the objects in his collection were photocopies from various books, material on the Fynn clan, and maps and documents attesting to his right to land and chieftaincy. Fynn showed me a newspaper clipping in which he dons Zulu garb to protest ethnic exclusion of non-Zulus from holding chieftanships. He confronted the Zulu chief in the area near Umbumbulu, which he claims is his ancestral right. He told me how he demanded to see this competitor's historical evidence to weigh it against his own records that the chieftaincy ought rightly to be his. Fynn claimed even to have phoned up doyen of Zulu history, Professor Jeff Guy of the University of KwaZulu-Natal, to ask him to support the authenticity of his claim, to which he reports that Guy apologized that this is a matter not of history but of politics.

Clearly, this separation of history and politics is a rhetorical rather than analytical point, although Fynn presents it without irony, as a lack of support from a noted historian. Significantly, Fynn continues his painstaking work in assembling archival evidence even when his attempts have been frustrated by a broader political economy of Zulu chieftaincy that is unlikely to take on his counter-claim.[12] Among Fynn's records are documents about his ancestral land titles as well as secondary material photocopied from books and dissertations that he thinks support his case. Fynn insists that his historical evidence ought to be authoritative, because these are documents that bear witness to the truth through the careful conventions of historical research. Fynn is not alone in assuming the power of documentary evidence. He demonstrates a faith in archival technologies to vindicate the truth, if not now, then at some point in the future. Of importance is the philosophy of history that bolsters this certitude about archival maintenance, but also the dogged realism through which he sees documentary evidence. Despite a deeply segregated official archive and popular historical consciousness, Fynn persists in maintaining documentary evidence ostensibly to reveal the cosmopolitan possibility for a Coloured claimant to chieftaincy, presumed to be a Zulu privilege. An ideology of Coloured indigenism undergirds this authoritative discourse, as it seeks to combat resurgent Zulu ethnic nationalism by claiming deeper historical roots in the territory south of Durban.

A more modest effort more narrowly concerned with land has been undertaken by a lady whom I call Louise Landers, who also supplemented her life history to me by drawing out her personal archive of documents. Landers had also made an unsuccessful claim on her ancestral property as a descendant of Adam Kok, founder of the city of Kokstad. Like many Griqua, Landers places her life in a communal narrative of dispossession by the Orange Free State in the 1850s, followed by a great trek across the Drakensberg, and reconstitution of the short-lived polity of East Griqualand (Beinart 1986). Griqua alienation of land followed the period after Adam Kok's death in 1875, and the failed rebellions in the last decades of the nineteenth century. Significantly, the Landers's family was dispossessed before the 1913 Land Act, the cut-off date for restitution through the Land Claims Court. She showed me various bits of documentary evidence not unlike Jan Fynn's, including her own land title documents as well as background chapters photocopied from books on the Griqua. Landers is less interested than Fynn in demonstrating her status as an indigene, despite her evident pride and interest in her Griqua background. She is more concerned to show how colonial-era dispossession remains outside the 1913 cut-off date for land claims. Included in her personal archive was also the polite official letter from the Land Claims Court that affirmed her history but refused her inheritance, purely on the basis of the 1913 cut-off. To add insult to injury, she also showed me an advertisement for a farm called Die Kroon that invites tourists to experience a real Afrikaans outdoor experience on what she considers her ancestral property.[13]

Most Coloured residents in Wentworth do not have recourse to such direct claims to land as do Jan Fynn and Louise Landers, and certainly not to chieftaincy. As atypical as these cases are, it is important to note that the evidence of dispossession and segregation is relegated to a colonial past. As White (2001) argues, it is important to note which pasts are remembered and forgotten in the present. In Fynn's case, a colonial past is used to critique Zulu claims to property, and to deflect from his involvement in the Coloured political parties that participated in Apartheid government. Most of Wentworth's residents had been tenants prior to coming to the Coloured township in the 1960s, and most had been dispossessed far before. Louise Landers is therefore a rare individual with a documented property claim, and she maintains her records in the hope of revision of the 1913 cut-off date.

What is important is that these and a few other individuals in Wentworth continue to collect historical evidence not just for compensation of loss of land and title, but also to demonstrate the wrongfulness with which these arguments have been dismissed. In this respect, these appeals to historical evidence share common cause with others who maintain documentary evidence of participation in Apartheid and anti-Apartheid politics, in varied ways of claiming the right to political participation.

Derrick McBride, a former anti-Apartheid militant who was incarcerated on Robben Island, maintains files on various topics, including papers on his activist son's time on Death Row for his sabotage activities as a member of Umkhonto we Sizwe (MK), the armed wing of the African National Congress (ANC). I have collected McBride's life history over several interviews, and at various points he referred to newspaper clippings, background material for his memoir in process, and documents that comprise various campaigns that he is involved in as an active community organizer in Wentworth. Most recently, McBride has been collecting newspaper clippings on police corruption in Wentworth. From the polar opposite side of the political spectrum but just a few minutes away in Wentworth, a man I call Gerard Jones, who also served on Apartheid government bodies and fought to bring the white supremacist National Party *into* Wentworth in the first democratic elections, has a dramatic collection of papers and clippings in the corner of his living room.[14] Both McBride and Jones maintain documentary archives of their political involvements to demonstrate their standing as authorities on politics, both in the past and in the present.

When I interviewed McBride, what was striking was that he began with a lengthy imaginative journey to an *ur*-past, before the category 'Coloured' could have been meaningful, to an interracial Indian Ocean proletariat in the region that would become the Cape Colony (Chari 2006b). He apologized for his lack of archival evidence as a poor person who had been trapped in a ghetto, then incarcerated on Robben Island, and he presented a profoundly cosmopolitan narrative that blended South Africa's long history of racialized dispossession with the events of his specific life. Despite retaining a wide-angle view of the totality of the social formation, McBride also interjects this narrative with asides that speak to the specific injuries he faced growing up as a dark-complexioned boy in a Coloured family. These 'intimate injuries' are important as devices that display the gendered underside of racial hegemony (Stoler 2002: 40). This emotional evidence is as important as the documents McBride can point to, and it adds a specific pathos to his narrative, drawing his audience to either identify or reject his appeal to common cause.

These limited archiving experiments in Wentworth show how some people try to support their political claims – whether individual or communal – by supplementing notions of agency with the careful maintenance of documents. While Louise Landers maintains evidence of her land claim, she also sees it as part of a broader project of Coloured land restitution, and she clips newspaper articles on similar restitution and recognition efforts elsewhere in South Africa. Jan Fynn, Derrick McBride, and Gerard Jones have all participated in public politics in one way or another – two as agents of Apartheid government and one as an anti-Apartheid saboteur. What is interesting is that the former anti-Apartheid activist most viscerally attends to the dilemmas of persisting ethno-racial markers, while engaging in new arenas of political activism, such as his current preoccupation of police corruption. Appeals to historical documentary evidence reveal important things when the evidence fails to deliver. On the one hand, Fynn and Landers show us how a faith in history inspires the maintenance of evidence precisely to mark ongoing state injustice. There is a utopianism in Fynn's claim against Zulu nationalism, and for a possible future as cosmopolitan as a past in which his English ancestor could have been offered a chieftaincy by King Shaka. On the other hand, McBride demonstrates not simply the maintenance of historical records but the importance of the performative and emotional evidence that cannot be documented. McBride embodies evidence of ongoing racial injury as another resident waiting in a state of uncertainty in the shadows of corporate and governmental dissimulation. For someone who spent time on Robben Island to be 'freed' into a society that he cannot recognize, 'post-Apartheid' appears littered with obstacles to justice. McBride's documentary and extra-documentary witnessing is retrospective without being nostalgic, and it is always critical of the injustices of the present.

Conclusion: antinomies of political evidence

Reflecting on the effects of South Africa's Truth and Reconciliation Commission (TRC), the writer and public intellectual Njabulo Ndebele (1998) argues that the TRC has brought into public debate a set of dilemmas concerning memory, responsibility, and realism. In contrast to literary-theoretic treatments of TRC *stories*, Ndebele thinks back to the importance of realism in Apartheid-era writing on the daily indignities of life, especially when these indignities verged on the utterly bizarre or the unimaginable. On stage, the playwright Athol Fugard captured the tension between realism and unimaginable horror through the conventions of Brechtian *Verfremdungseffekt*, the alienation effect through which the performer forces realization of the illogic of empathetic identification with the other, and the necessity of critique. After the allure of the TRC's Christian narrative of redemption has properly receded, Ndebele's argument is that its more important effect may be an incitement to many forms of realist, personal narrative.

Ndebele is cautious about the political content of the incitement to realist narrative. What remains central are the ways in which knowledge of the other either produces solidarity or harm. The evidence deployed in Wentworth's crucible of political work is mixed, but what Wentworth demonstrates is the incredible productivity of ordinary men and women in producing a diversity of forms of political evidence orientated towards a possible anti-racial future, in Memmi's terms.

I have considered three domains of political work in which markers of racism persist in pernicious ways: in the fight for a clean environment in a 'fenceline community' next to an oil refinery, in the moral politics of dispensing betterment in community organizations, and in attempts to archive and wield historical material politically. In the case of environmental activism, racism is confronted as a social and spatial process of differentiation. Here, political evidence confronts most clearly the domain of the powerful alliance of petrochemical refineries and post-Apartheid government. Environmental justice struggles clarify the barriers of official dissimulation in curtailing the efficacy of political evidence as it is brought to bear on state-sanctioned racism in the present.

Responses to official dissimulation about social and spatial injustice in Wentworth are varied. On the one hand, stigma posited on Wentworth is understood through contextual means, but reframed in a generic defence of family values, prompting further differentiation of the local population as dispensers and receivers of political work. On the other hand, attempts at maintaining archival evidence point to the limits of claims-making, but also the limited efficacy of this evidence in demonstrating official intransigence and the layers of stigma and marginality. The antinomies of political work demonstrate the mutability of racism, as ethno-racial and gender difference rears its head to divide attempts at transforming social inequalities.

For many of Wentworth's residents, life in the shadow of dissimulation requires patient endeavour, often against the odds. Several people walk a fine line through the moral politics of dispensing and receiving community or political work, demonstrating evidence as political workers when the need arises. I have sought to show ethnographically how political evidence takes specific form in the creative attempts, despite various obstacles, of stigmatized Coloured neighbours of polluting industry to battle wider forces that seek to keep them on the margins of the post-Apartheid city.

NOTES

This research is part of a broader project, for which I am grateful for research funding from the University of Michigan, the Geography Department at the LSE, and the School of Development Studies at UKZN, South Africa. Thanks to Matthew Engelke for the invitation to participate in the conference from which this chapter originates, and for his useful comments on earlier drafts.

[1] In 2001, both Wentworth and Merebank had roughly similar populations of 27,000 for Wentworth and 21,000 for Merebank.

[2] I have conducted fieldwork in these areas periodically between 2002 and 2007, and have an ongoing relationship with individuals and organizations. I have been collecting oral histories, less structured interviews, and have been observing various contexts in daily life.

[3] This section draws from Chari (2006a).

[4] Bobby Peek, pers. comm., 31 October 2004.

[5] Bobby Peek, pers. comm., 22 April 2004.

[6] All names have been converted into pseudonyms unless I have been advised otherwise by my interview subject.

[7] Poverty Alleviation Meeting, Wentworth, 18 November 2002.

[8] Diane Brown, Wentworth, 13 November 2002.

[9] Skido Joseph, Wentworth, 14-15 November 2002.

[10] For instance, the essays in Nutall & Coetzee (1998), Hamilton & Harris (2002), and, from Wentworth's growing tradition of memoir-writing, Lottering (2002).

[11] There is a vast canon on forced removals, and a more recent set of works that utilize oral histories and personal narratives to reconstruct these processes. The work around the District Six Museum in Cape Town (*http://www.districtsix.co.za/*) and the Centre for Popular Memory at the University of Cape Town is particularly important in this respect (e.g. Field 2001), as is the work in the rebuilding of Constitution Hill in Johannesburg, particularly in the former women's prison (*http://www.constitutionhill.org.za/*).

[12] Interview with Jan Fynn, 29 November 2004.

[13] Interview with Louise Landers, 19 December 2002.

[14] Gerard Jones, Wentworth, 6 September 2004.

REFERENCES

BEINART, W. 1986. Settler accumulation in East Griqualand from the demise of the Griqua to the Natives Land Act. In *Putting a plough to the ground: accumulation and dispossession in rural South Africa 1850-1930* (eds) W. Beinart, P. Delius & S. Trapido, 259-310. Johannesburg: Ravan Press.

CHARI, S. 2006a. Post-Apartheid livelihood struggles in Wentworth, South Durban. In *The development decade? Economic and social change in South Africa, 1994-2004* (ed.) V. Padayachee, 427-43. Cape Town: HSRC Press.

——— 2006b. Life histories of race and space in the making of Wentworth and Merebank, South Durban. *African Studies* **65**, 105-29.

CONSTITUTION of SOUTH AFRICA 1996. Chapter 2 – Bill of Rights, Section 24 – Environment (available on-line: *http://www.info.gov.za/documents/constitution/1996/96cons2.htm#24*, accessed 2 January 2008).

FARRED, G. 2001. Where does the rainbow nation end? Colouredness and citizenship in post-Apartheid South Africa. *New Centennial Review* **1**, 175-99.

FERGUSON, J. 1990. *The anti-politics machine: 'development,' depoliticization, and bureaucratic power in Lesotho.* Cambridge: University Press.

FIELD, S. (ed.) 2001. *Lost communities, living memories: remembering forced removals in Cape Town.* Cape Town: David Philip.

GRAEBER, D. 2002. *Toward an anthropological theory of value: the false coin of our own dreams.* New York: Palgrave.

——— 2004. *Fragments of an anarchist anthropology.* (Prickly Paradigm **14**). Chicago: Prickly Paradigm Press (available on-line: *http://www.prickly-paradigm.com/paradigm14.pdf*, accessed 2 January 2008).

HALLOWES, D. & V. MUNNIK 2006. The groundWork Report 2006. Poisoned spaces: manufacturing wealth, producing poverty. Pietermaritzburg: groundWork (available on-line: *http://www.groundwork.org.za/Publications/Reports.asp#groundworkreport*, accessed 2 January 2008).

HAMILTON, C. & V. HARRIS (eds) 2002. *Refiguring the archive.* Cape Town: David Philip.

HARRIS, V. 2002. The archival sliver: a perspective on the construction of social memory in archives and the transition from Apartheid to democracy. In *Refiguring the archive* (eds) C. Hamilton & V. Harris, 135-60. Cape Town: David Philip.

HUNTER, M. 2002. The materiality of everyday sex: thinking beyond prostitution. *African Studies* **61**, 99-120.

LOTTERING, A. 2002. *Winnifred and Agnes: the true story of two women.* Cape Town: Kwela Books.

MEMMI, A. 2000. *Racism* (trans. S. Martinot). Minneapolis: University of Minnesota Press.

MILLER, D. 2005. Materiality: an introduction. In *Materiality* (ed.) D. Miller, 1-50. Durham, N.C.: Duke University Press.

NDEBELE, N. 1998. Memory, metaphor, and the triumph of narrative. In *Negotiating the past: the making of memory in South Africa* (eds) S. Nutall & C. Coetzee, 19-28. Cape Town: Oxford University Press.

NUTALL, S. & C. COETZEE (eds) 1998. *Negotiating the past: the making of memory in South Africa.* Cape Town: Oxford University Press.

SPARKS, S. 2004. '*Stink, maar uit die verkeerde rigting*': pollution, politics and petroleum refining in South Africa, 1948-1960. History and African Studies Seminar, Department of Historical Studies, University of Kwa-Zulu Natal, Durban, South Africa, 27 April (available on-line: *http://www.history.ukzn.ac.za/?q=node/587*, accessed 2 January 2008).

——— 2005. Civic culture, 'environmentalism' and pollution in South Durban: the case of the Wentworth Refinery. History and African Studies Seminar, Department of Historical Studies, University of Kwa-Zulu Natal, Durban, South Africa, 19 April (available on-line: *http://www.history.ukzn.ac.za/?q=node/611*, accessed 2 January 2008).

STOLER, A.L. 2002. *Carnal knowledge and imperial power: race and the intimate in colonial rule.* Berkeley: University of California Press.

WACQUANT, L. 2004. Ghetto. In *International encyclopedia of the social and behavioral sciences* (eds) N. Smelsner & P. Baltes, 1-10. London: Pergamon Press.

WHITE, H. 2001. *Tempora et mores*: family values and the possessions of a post-Apartheid countryside. *Journal of Religion in Africa* **31**, 457-79.

6

Three propositions for an evidence-based medical anthropology

STEFAN ECKS *University of Edinburgh*

Is depression rising?

This chapter tries to disentangle some problems of 'evidence' that I encountered during research on medical responses to mental illness in Kolkata (Calcutta, India). What is the relation between anthropological and medical ways of gathering evidence? Are they nicely separated, or are they mingled in complicated ways? To answer these questions, let me start with a classic anthropological way of presenting evidence, a short 'I was there' story (see Engelke, this volume). Between June and August 2005, I interviewed two types of doctors, fifteen psychiatrists and fifteen general physicians, about how they diagnose and treat depression. In previous research, I had focused on popular perceptions of low moods and on the marketing of antidepressants in India (Ecks 2005). In this phase of research, I wanted to find out how these two groups of doctors might have similar, or opposing, views. Psychiatrists were an obvious choice for doctors treating depression. GPs might appear as a less obvious group of prescribers, but UK-based studies show that depression is predominantly diagnosed and treated by general practitioners, not by psychiatrists (Henry 1993).

The current perception among experts of global mental health is that there is a large 'treatment gap' between developed and less developed countries (World Mental Health Survey Consortium 2004). It is believed that in countries like India, the number of mental health specialists is small, and that local GPs are not integrated into global treatment strategies. Hence I expected that Kolkatan GPs would be relatively uninterested in mental health problems. In turn, I expected to find that psychiatrists, although small in number and not easily accessible to poorer people, were getting more clients than previously. I thought that psychiatrists were the chief prescribers of antidepressants, while GPs would tend to treat only physical symptoms.

All the interviews were done one-to-one and in medical chambers. All the doctors were Bengalis, all were trained at least partly in Kolkata, and almost all of them had received their first medical degree, the MBBS (*Medicinae Baccalaureus et Baccalaureus Chirurgiae*), from Calcutta Medical College. All of them had at least five years of professional practice. Work experience abroad, mainly in the UK, was common among the younger psychiatrists, but not among the GPs and older psychiatrists. These thirty doctors disagreed on many points, but there were also several questions where the answers turned out to be highly similar.

One of the questions that triggered similar responses in each group was: 'Is the number of people suffering from depression rising?' Medical claims that depression is 'rising' is a cornerstone of current policies for global mental health. This rise refers either to an *absolute* rise in the number of people suffering from depression or to a *relative* rise because of a decrease in other diseases. For example, the World Health Organization (WHO) reckons that depression will become the world's second most prevalent health problem in the year 2020 (cardiovascular diseases are expected to be the number one problem), *relative* to other diseases. But there is also an argument for an *absolute* rise: for example, in 2003, the US President's Council on Bioethics published a report which holds that up to 20 per cent of all Americans were suffering from 'some form of depression' (President's Council on Bioethics 2003: 240). The report diagnoses a constant rise in the *absolute* number of depressed patients and argues that this rise is neither an artefact of new diagnostic criteria nor an artefact of new survey methods.

I asked for the doctors' opinions about this alleged 'rise' of depression to contextualize their statements on how they prescribe (or do not prescribe) antidepressants. I also wanted to find out how they relate their own daily practices to statistical evidence. Before starting the interviews, I expected that the psychiatrists would have read a few of the statistics published by the WHO and quote them as evidence. In turn, I presumed that the GPs would emphasize primary health problems instead of depression, not least because so much has been written on 'somatization' and the tendency of patients in non-Western countries to present psychiatric problems as physical problems (e.g. Kleinman & Kleinman 1985; Patel 2001; see Kohrt *et al.* 2005). My expectation was that the GPs would worry little about mental health and would tend to emphasize that there is no evidence of more depression. All these expectations were contradicted by the empirical evidence.

The psychiatrists said that there was no reliable evidence available to prove or disprove the hypothesis of rising depression: 'we do not have proper statistics in this country' was a common reply. By contrast, nearly all the GPs said that depression was rising rapidly, especially over the past ten years. They saw a clear causal link between depression and India's socio-economic transformation. The GPs described how people feel financially more insecure than ever before, how competition for education and jobs has increased tremendously, and how the joint family system – the bedrock of traditional life – is crumbling.

The GPs often switched back and forth between talking about *actual* socio-economic changes and changes in people's *perceptions* of them. For example, they might first argue that life is hard and, therefore, full of reasons to feel depressed. Then they might say that life has always been hard, but that *sensibilities* have changed: Bollywood movies and TV programmes showing affluent lifestyles created great expectations that could only be disappointed by harsh realities. Let me quote one of the GPs, Dr Mukherjee (a pseudonym), whose chamber was located right next to a *bustee* (slum):

Their [patients'] attitude has increased. Their aspirations are higher. Earlier people would say 'OK, I am in the slum, I remain in the slum, my aspirations are not high'. But nowadays, with all these electronic media, the coverage and all that, the younger generation has a higher aspiration. If someone was a rickshaw puller, his son wouldn't mind being a rickshaw puller, but now the son doesn't want to become a rickshaw puller. He wants a motorcycle. That is the basic problem. They are more prone to depression.

Dr Mukherjee expressed a view of depression as a multi-dimensional problem that could not be reduced to genetics or neurotransmitters. In the short statement quoted above, no less than four factors that cause depression are mentioned: (1) social inequality (the slum and beyond); (2) intergenerational change (grandfather, father, and son); (3) consumer desires (the motorcycle); and (4) the noxious influence of the mass media. For this GP, to suffer from depression is not reducible to physical pathology, but is a form of *social* suffering. Implied in this is also a notion of social marginality as *relative* to changing levels of wealth. Take, for example, the desire for a motorcycle: in terms of access to commodities, poor people might be better off in *absolute* terms than previous generations, but they feel increasing deprivation *relative* to other people's lifestyles (see Ecks & Sax 2005).

Importantly, neither the GPs nor the psychiatrists quoted any *medical* evidence for a rise of depression. Instead, GPs like Dr Mukherjee cited as evidence their own quasi-sociological observations of interactions with patients and of living in urban India today. By contrast, the psychiatrists stressed the *lack* of any reliable data. They also frequently mentioned social problems of all sorts, but if pressed on the issue, they did not admit these as *medical* evidence. This reveals a different stance towards the evidential status of social processes: should 'social change' be allowed to count as part of the medical evidence? For the GPs, the notion of 'social transformation' was clearly permitted as evidence for a rise of depression, while the psychiatrists hesitated. It is not the case that the GPs saw links between social suffering and depression that the psychiatrists did not see. The difference is that GPs *admitted* social factors to count as evidence, whereas the psychiatrists did not.

Who makes a more convincing argument about depression, the GPs or the psychiatrists? Anthropologists would rarely ask such a question about medical evidence directly; causal links between physical and social ills seems to lie outside our disciplinary boundaries. But in fact, anthropologists make such claims all the time. If I sided with the GPs and accepted the evidence of 'social change' as evidence for a rise in mental distress, most anthropologists would agree without blinking an eye. Yet the invocation of 'society' by medical doctors should surely make us *more* cautious about 'evidence', not less.

In the following, I want to rethink the evidence for or against the rise of depression in urban India. To do this fruitfully, I need to ask a series of questions about both anthropology and medicine. First, what are the current standards of gathering medical evidence? This will lead, first, into a discussion of evidence-based medicine (EBM), probably the most powerful movement in biomedicine since the 1990s. My examples will be mostly drawn from psychiatry. The second question to be asked is: do evidentiary standards in medicine have an impact on those in medical anthropology? My answer to this question has three parts, each of which becomes a proposition for an 'evidence-based medical anthropology'. This chapter, then, does not draw a line between how the people we study use evidence, as against how anthropologists use evidence (Engelke, this volume). Rather, it asks how medicine *changes* how anthropology looks at evidence – before asking how anthropology might change medicinal evidence in turn.

Evidence-based medicine

Establishing itself as one of the natural sciences in the nineteenth century, biomedicine has long given highest authority to the best available 'evidence', in various definitions. Since the mid-twentieth century, definitions of best evidence became increasingly linked to randomized controlled trials (RCTs) (Williams & Garner 2002). For example, a large study on the treatment of depression conducted in the early 1960s by the US Medical Research Council compared the benefits of electroconvulsive therapy, imipramine, phenelzine, and placebo. The study showed that the tricyclic antidepressant imipramine was the most effective treatment, and subsequently imipramine became the 'gold standard' for antidepressant trials for decades afterwards. That the efficacy of new drugs had to be shown statistically (based on large samples) and in comparison to placebo control groups became the hallmark of best evidence (Timmermans & Berg 2003). Other forms of evidence, such as clinical case studies, have been delegated to a lower level of significance (Sinclair 2004: 187). The rise of EBM can be interpreted as one more phase in a systematic devaluation of immediate visibility as a reliable source of scientific evidence (Pape 2002; see Bloch, Pinney, both in this volume). Doctors are trained to believe more in statistical evidence than in what they observe in clinical practice.

Doctors have been expected to keep up with the latest research findings ever since the laboratory revolution of the nineteenth century (Cunningham & Williams 1992). But the situation that doctors find themselves in today is not a scarcity of evidence, but an excess of it. By some estimates, more than 5,000 medical research papers are published *each and every day*. No doctor could possibly read even a fraction of them. Moreover, as several authors have argued, no active physician can afford more than thirty minutes *per week* for reading articles or textbooks. Plainly speaking, the truth *might* be out there, but if no one has the time to read about it, it is useless. EBM is an attempt to make available condensed research findings for busy clinicians. It focuses not just on the procedures of creating good evidence, but also on efficient data management and swift retrieval.

One of the most popular on-line sites of EBM, the Cochrane Library,[1] is a database of meta-analyses of existing publications (Lambert 2006a: 2613). These short texts try to give quick answers to quick clinical questions. For example, 'Are antidepressants effective in the treatment of bulimia nervosa?' can be put to the database, and be answered instantly (the answer is 'yes'). To bring this kind of information into everyday practice, EBM supporters lobby for the use of computers that can be taken along on ward rounds.

Questions put to the database need to be succinct and treatment-orientated: for example, does drug *X* work for symptom *Y*? The skills of asking such questions are now a compulsory part of medical training in many countries, including the UK (Lambert 2006b: 2638-9; Sinclair 2004). For example, the Royal College of Psychiatrists (UK) incorporated a 'Critical Appraisal' paper in its curriculum for the Membership Examination (MRCPsych Exam) in 1999.[2] To be skilled in EBM also means to be skilled in the critical analysis of statistical data. Are there flaws in the sampling? What does '50% remission rate' mean? Is there sufficient evidence to show that a drug is more effective than a placebo? The reflexive appraisal of statistics gives rise to what is perhaps EBM's most characteristic statement, namely 'there is *not enough* evidence' to recommend a particular treatment. (As shown earlier, the rhetoric of 'not enough' evidence is also used by Kolkata psychiatrists.)

Given this drive to standardize all phases in the production, distribution, and consumption of evidence, critics point out that EBM tends to be conservative about what should count as good evidence and what should not. EBM has an in-built tendency to favour established treatments over new ones, because fewer RCT data are available for whatever is new. To counter this critique, EBM publications now include disclaimers such as 'absence of empirical evidence for the effectiveness of a particular intervention is not the same as evidence for ineffectiveness' (National Institute for Clinical Excellence 2004: 8). But on balance, extensive quantitative evidence is always preferred.

EBM databases also tend to re-inscribe existing diagnostics, because the data from various studies can be compared only if disease entities and trial procedures are taken as stable. The validity of a diagnostic label such as 'depressive disorder' cannot be questioned by EBM procedures. Even if it is acknowledged that terminologies and diagnostic criteria are changing, and that 'depression' covers a heterogeneous group of disorders, EBM must rely on clearly defined categories (cf. National Institute for Clinical Excellence 2004: 13). Key questions of transcultural psychiatry, such as if 'depression' can be diagnosed in India in the same way as in Europe, cannot be asked within the confines of EBM.

The evaluation of treatment options uses particular types of statistical evidence: for example, the 'number needed to treat' (NNT). This is a measure of medical efficacy that expresses how many patients need to be given a medication before one of them has a positive result. Questions about the prevalence of particular diseases (e.g. 'is depression rising?') are a part of this approach, because to know about disease prevalence helps doctors to make more accurate diagnoses. A dedicated field of 'evidence-based public health' that looks at these questions in more detail is currently emerging.

The quick adoption of EBM in biomedicine has taken many by surprise. EBM mission statements are often couched in an anti-authoritarian, grass-roots manner. Evidence-based medicine is said to be a great improvement over the 'ego-based' medicine of individual clinicians. It aims to dislodge the 'eminence-based' medicine that puts the subjective opinions of hierarchically superior doctors over independent evidence. EBM is also said to break the stranglehold of pharmaceutical marketing on medical practice, because product-specific bias is neutralized by comparing all available evidence (see de Vries & Lemmers 2006).

There are several examples of how the introduction of EBM is shifting relations of power between clinicians, pharmaceutical companies, regulating governments, public health authorities, and patients. For example, there has been 'anecdotal' evidence since the early 1990s that giving SSRIs (selective serotonin reuptake inhibitors) to children and adolescents increases their risk of suicide. In 2003, the UK Committee on the Safety of Medicines initiated an EBM-style review of available studies and concluded that the 'balance of risks and benefits' of treating depression with SSRIs in under-18-year-olds is 'unfavourable' for all SSRIs, except Prozac (fluoxetine) (Medicines and Healthcare Products Regulatory Agency 2004: 6). Doctors were advised to be more careful about giving antidepressants to young patients than previously. The report is seen as a good example of how EBM helps to standardize best practice in psychiatry, against individual doctors' prescription patterns, and against the vested interests of pharmaceutical companies, which have long denied these risks. (Conclusions from this report were also discussed at the Annual Conference of Psychiatrists of West Bengal in 2005, confirming that EBM is a global project.) There are also, of course, good reasons to argue that gains in transparency are bought at the high price of marginalizing any type of treatment not sponsored by pharmaceutical corporations.

Despite its quick adoption, doctors continue to debate the strengths and weaknesses of EBM with great fervour. Many of EBM's advantages are seen as its greatest drawbacks. One commonly mentioned problem is that EBM constricts autonomous decision-making by the experienced clinician. Critics of EBM, such as a spoof group named Clinicians for the Restoration of Autonomous Practice (2002), abbreviated CRAP, argue that clinical practice which is sensitive to the individual patient and local circumstances is irreducible to the evidence from RCTs. They also point out that EBM gives too much power to health bureaucrats, hospital administrators, and insurance analysts.

But it has also been argued that the revolutionary powers of EBM are overstated. Now that the dust is settling, EBM might look more like medical business as usual. In his ethnography of psychiatric training in the UK, Simon Sinclair concludes that much of EBM's critical potential had already been 'absorbed and accommodated within ordinary professional life' (2004: 179).

'Evidence' in medicine and medical anthropology

The medical literature on EBM has grown to enormous proportions over the past years, and it would take several EBM-style meta-analyses to digest all the arguments presented. Instead of discussing further what EBM is, I now want to shift the question towards its implications for *anthropological* approaches to medicine, especially towards engagements with 'evidence'. Helen Lambert notes that 'notions of evidence remain implicit and unexamined in disciplines such as anthropology' (2006b: 2641), and that this resistance even to address evidence is a hindrance in talking to scientists, for whom such truth claims are essential. What I will argue in the following is that a profound change in how medicine assesses evidence also means that anthropology has to reconsider its own ideas.

The relation between medical anthropology and biomedicine is usually seen as one of asymmetrical power (see Good, in this volume, on the asymmetries between anthropology and law). Anthropological observers usually think of themselves as far less powerful than the medical practitioners they are observing, and every anthropologist will have experienced moments when medics shrug off anthropological findings as 'mere anecdotes' that cannot be 'generalized' – especially when medics are criticized.

When anthropologists reflect on the impact of this power asymmetry for their own practice, they usually respond in one of two ways. They either think that biomedicine is fundamentally different from anthropology and, therefore, that medics have no right to tell them about what is good or bad evidence. Or they think that anthropology has inched so close to medicine that its integrity as an autonomous discipline is threatened. For example, C.H. Browner (1999) warned against the 'medicalization of medical anthropology', that is, the growing tendency of anthropologists to let biomedicine determine their research agenda. The emergence of anthropological studies of, say, reproductive technologies is a working example of this. In turn, it would be hard to find a medical doctor warning against the 'anthropologization' of medicine. The term 'medicalization' is used frequently and almost self-evidently by anthropologists. We have all read (or have even written ourselves) studies on the medicalization of mental health, the medicalization of ageing, the medicalization of menopause, and so on.[3] But an 'anthropologization' of medicine is practically unheard of, although this notion was used by no one less than Michel Foucault (1970: 348; Gane 2002). The power difference between the two fields is impossible to deny. So if I speak of links between medicine and medical anthropology, I am not suggesting that there is a level playing field. This means that changes in biomedicine are likely to be recorded in anthropology, but *not* vice versa.

Common to both these positions is the notion that findings from medical anthropology have little or no impact on the field they are describing. The 'hardness' of biomedicine looks so overwhelming that 'soft' field notes seem not to make any difference. The supposition of asymmetrical power strengthens the false perception of biomedicine as a kind of passive object. The comfortable feeling that anthropologists can describe, analyse, and 'deconstruct' biomedicine in any way they like provides them with a deceptive sense of evidentiary autonomy. If the relation between observer and observed is constituted as asymmetrical, it strengthens the assumption that medical procedures of gathering evidence are entirely different from anthropological ones. Indeed, this idea has been entrenched since the late 1970s, when medical anthropologists insisted on recovering subjective 'illness' experiences from below medicine's overpowering definitions of objective 'disease' (Eisenberg 1977; Kleinman 1980). The problem with this division of labour is that medical anthropologists who want to speak of 'evidence' face a clear choice: either they subscribe to biomedical notions of good evidence; or they are forced to insist that 'qualitative' evidence is just as robust as that gathered in the medical sciences through quantitative methods.

Byron Good once said that 'medical anthropology is one of the primary sites within anthropology where alternative responses to the confrontation between historicism and the natural sciences are being worked out' (1994: 24). What I want to do in the following is try to go beyond both historicism and the natural sciences and think through the possibility of an 'evidence-based medical anthropology'. Is it possible for anthropologists to speak of 'evidence' without accepting only medical standards as 'gold' standards? I suggest that it is necessary to re-assemble what should count as 'evidence'.

It might sound absurd to speak of an evidence-based medical anthropology. To begin with, the *scaling* of evidence in the two disciplines seems incompatible (Engelke, this volume). EBM is based on randomized controlled trials, and on the conviction that good trials are conducted with large samples. Medical anthropology does not conduct trials, and usually insists on the soundness of small samples, which can sometimes consist of just one patient or healer. If I do not advocate large samples, statistical methods, databases, and meta-analyses, what is 'evidence-based medical anthropology' (EBMA) supposed to be?

First proposition: EBMA is an anthropology *of* EBM

The first proposition is rather straightforward: EBMA is the anthropological study of how evidence is used by medical practitioners. Defined in this way, EBMA is first of all a kind of anthropology *of* EBM. This leaves the usual split between the observer and the observed intact, at least at first.

Whenever medicine introduces new practices, new fields of inquiry open up for medical anthropology. The anthropologies *of* genetics or *of* reproductive technologies are current examples of this. Given that EBM is heralded as a profound transformation of medicine, it is only a matter of time before medical anthropologists will look at it in greater detail (Lambert 2006a). Ethnographic studies on how the training of doctors is changing through EBM (e.g. Sinclair 2004), how 'evidence' from RCTs can be manipulated (Lakoff 2007), how the demand for RCT data is increasingly off-shored to developing countries (Petryna 2007), or how patients' perceptions are transformed by being exposed to EBM-type reasoning are just beginning. I expect that the most fruitful studies on EBM will be those located at the intersections between EBM, clinical practice, and patients' participation. It will be useful to broaden the discussion from narrowly defined clinical settings to broader social questions. To look at EBM in relation to emerging notions of citizenship (Jasanoff 2004; Rose & Novas 2004), such as 'biological citizenship' (Petryna 2002; Rose 2006), 'therapeutic citizenship' (Nguyen 2004), or 'genetic citizenship' (Petersen & Bunton 2002), will be especially productive. I want briefly to introduce one more project of this kind, which I call 'pharmaceutical citizenship' (Ecks 2005).

Pharmaceutical citizenship revolves around two questions: how do different notions of citizenship determine the *rights* to receive pharmaceuticals and the *duties* of using them? In turn, how does the taking of pharmaceuticals have an impact on a person's status as a citizen? The spread of EBM leads to specific co-constitutions of pharmaceuticals and citizenship, making them far more visible than previously. Public discussions on the 'evidence' behind medical claims are critical events in the constitution of pharmaceutical citizenship (see Hayden 2007). What is happening through the growing importance of EBM is that the sources of evidence, and the procedures of making evidence, are becoming more transparent than before. The current legal struggle around the anti-cancer drug Herceptin is a good example of this. Until recently, representatives of the National Health Service (NHS) were denying this expensive drug to patients in the early stages of breast cancer because there was 'not enough evidence' to prove its effectiveness. Trying to overturn the decision by the NHS, Elisabeth Cook, a 59-year-old patient, took her plea to receive the drug to the High Court. In early April 2006, this court ruled that the NHS should provide the drug after all. A few weeks later, the European Medicines Agency adopted 'positive opinions' about extending the use of Herceptin to the early stages of breast cancer.[4] In June 2006, the National Institute for Health and Clinical Excellence (NICE), the new NHS evidence-based medicine body, approved Herceptin for women with early-stage breast cancer. These decisions did not directly force NHS trusts to pay automatically for the drug, and legal disputes continue.[5] However, the pressure on NHS trusts across the UK to pay for Herceptin in the early stages of breast cancer has greatly increased because of the lobbying by patient activists (some of them in tandem with Roche, the producer of Herceptin – citizens and corporations are more often aligned than it might seem).

It is not new to see the formation of lobby groups around diseases. What is new is that a specific drug is at the centre of attention. If certain drugs had been singled out before, this usually happened in only two situations: either there was strong evidence that a drug was doing *damage* and should be stopped (e.g. Grünenthal's Thalidomide or Merck's Vioxx); or there was good evidence that a drug was effective, but poorer people could not afford it (e.g. antiretroviral drugs). Yet in the Herceptin case, a particular drug is invested with the highest *hopes* by patients who are otherwise medically fully treated. What is also new is that one can see televised debates in which an array of experts take part, all of them presenting 'best evidence' for or against making the drug available. Until the Herceptin case, few people would have heard of the existence of NICE. Now the Institute, and its procedures of making evidence, is front-page news. EBM might not be a household name yet, but public engagement is growing. Elisabeth Cook's claim was that she has got better *evidence* than the NHS, evidence that shows how Herceptin will be an effective anti-cancer drug in her stage of the disease. The basis of her claim was *not* her bodily suffering as such, but conflicting sources of evidence for drug efficacy.

It might be argued that questions of evidence have long been discussed by medical anthropologists in terms of how different types of actors explain what they are doing and what kinds of evidence they allow to speak (e.g. Lévi-Strauss 1963: 175-81). But it seems clear that the spread of EBM draws far more attention to how different actors, both medical and non-medical, use various sources of evidence, and to what kinds of evidence are *allowed* and what kinds of evidence are not.[6] This also includes the question of how some actors use evidence *vis-à-vis* other actors. A doctor might quote certain types of evidence in face-to-face interactions with colleagues, others in scientific papers, yet others when talking to patients. Evidence is not only selective; it is also strategic, and always used in relation to a particular audience. These performative aspects of evidence cannot be predicted by EBM itself, and can be studied ethnographically only by an evidence-based medical anthropology.

Second proposition: EBMA is an anthropology *with* EBM

Doing an anthropology *of* EBM is one area of an evidence-based medical anthropology, but it should not stop there. Hence my second proposition is that we should try to do medical anthropology *with* EBM. This means to allow EBM to look *back* at medical anthropology and let it reflect on our own concepts. I argue that the introduction of EBM is bound to change how medical anthropologists provide evidence for their own assertions.

Even more than before, we need to ask how medical anthropology is *related* to biomedical practices. I would argue that the two fields are not as far apart in how they gather evidence as is usually thought. Biomedicine is not a passive object of the anthropological gaze. Instead, biomedicine defines most of the parameters within which we are working. Biomedicine informs anthropology on all levels of inquiry, from the definition of what we aim to study, to the way we write field notes, and to the way we stake our claims in arguments with medicine. On each level, questions of 'evidence' are crucial.

(1) *Objects of study*: Biomedicine defines most objects of study for anthropologists, especially in the form of disease entities. Even if medical anthropologists try to show the historical and cultural contexts of medical classifications, they still have to work within medical parameters. An anthropological study of 'depression' that does not engage with psychiatric definitions is bound to produce the 'wrong' kind of evidence. Even if an anthropologist conducts a purely ethnomedical study of a culture-specific illness concept that seems to have no biomedical equivalent (e.g. *susto*, a kind of low mood caused by 'soul loss' in Latin America), the domain of what is 'purely ethnomedical' is still defined by biomedicine; what cannot be translated into medical categories appears as 'culture-bound' by default.

(2) *Relevance*: Anthropologists use medical evidence to show that they produce *relevant* knowledge. Many anthropological funding proposals start with epidemiological

statistics to show that the problem they are going to study is widespread and pressing. You have already heard me present evidence like this a moment ago when I referred to WHO statistics about the rise of depression as a public health problem. Indeed, the choice of research topics in medical anthropology is often guided by statistics like this.

(3) *Sample*: Medicine defines the samples to be studied. For example, when I started studying popular notions of 'depression' in Kolkata, one of the usual comments from doctors was that I had to work with them to know who was depressed and who was not.

(4) *Setting*: Medicine defines the settings in which we gather evidence. Medical anthropologists usually divide settings into 'clinical' and 'community' settings. The possibility of making this distinction hinges on the presence of biomedicine's clinical settings; community settings are much harder to delineate and are often just any place outside the clinic.

(5) *Research ethics*: More and more, medicine is setting the standards for what is good or bad ethical practice in anthropology. Getting research subjects to sign 'informed consent' declarations is starting to become common in our discipline as well, and there are many examples of how ethics developed for clinical research are transforming the ethics of ethnographic research. Anthropological evidence cannot be published in medical journals if one cannot show proof of good research ethics.

These five points may suffice to show that changes in biomedicine also change medical anthropology. There is bad news and good news in this. The bad news is that medical anthropology is inextricably tied to biomedical practices, for better or worse. To deny this influence would only mean to strengthen it.

But there is a lot of good news, too. Probably the best is that anthropologists can draw on the *same* sources of evidence as medicine. A legacy of the approach founded by Bronislaw Malinowski is the fixed idea that every bit of evidence that an anthropologist presents has to come from her own presence in the field. Findings from different ethnographies are said to 'resonate' with one's own, but are not expected to build a shared evidence base. This is also why the genre of the 'meta-analysis' is practically non-existent in anthropology.[7] Although an emphasis on the 'local' is at the heart of the fieldwork approach, the taken-for-granted view that it provides *all* the relevant evidence is ludicrous. In practice, anthropologists quote other studies as evidence all the time, although they were *not* 'there' themselves. Anthropologists can put fieldwork findings highest in their hierarchy of evidence without excluding all other sources of evidence. So why not also draw on 'medical' evidence for one's own claims? There is no fundamental difference between the sources of anthropological and medical evidence. There are only different ways of assembling the evidence and presenting an argument.

All of the above examples seem to address methodological questions, perhaps creating the false perception that our theoretical foundations remain untouched. However, medical hegemony can also be detected in many of our core concepts. What is fascinating about the emergence of EBM is how some of medical anthropology's foundational ideas appear in a new light, showing marks of the historical contexts in which they arose.

Take, again, the distinction between 'disease' and 'illness': this division clearly bears the mark of 'eminence-based' medicine. The encounter between the doctor and the patient in a clinical setting was seen as the dramatic moment when two sets of knowledge confronted each other. This notion might have been plausible at a time when the practising doctor seemed to be the highest authority to decide on the available evidence. Yet in times of EBM, it is impossible to uphold this. Even when the disease/illness division was first formulated in the late 1970s, it was already a fiction that doctors knew all the evidence. Since EBM created, or at least deepened, the rift between practitioners' knowledge and available published knowledge, the disease/illness distinction looks even more implausible. The debate about EBM is one more example of the fact that health is a field of *multiple* truth claims, instead of a simple opposition between doctors' knowledge (in the singular) and patients' beliefs (in the plural).

The disease/illness opposition does not just entail a questionable division between the bearers of knowledge, the doctors, and the bearers of beliefs, the patients. It also entails an implausible partition between 'disease' as something to be *explained* by the natural sciences and 'illness' as something to be *understood* by a hermeneutic approach. Illness seems to gather the meaning of suffering, whereas disease appears as its hard, objective, biomedical reality. One of the analytic consequences of privileging 'meaning' (or 'social construction' or whatever else it might be called) is that it seriously limits the scope of evidence that can be drawn on. If we speak about meaning, all we can use is evidence from meaningful humans, while *things* drop out of the picture. But it is *things* that give stability to human-human interactions.

Bruno Latour (2005) argues agency should not be seen as limited to meaningful, intentional humans. Instead of asking only about meaningful action, Latour suggests that we should also ask: does the presence of this agent – either human or non-human – *make a difference* to the course of another agent's action or not?

If we use this insight for EBMA, we should not limit our sources of evidence to meaningful illness concepts of humans. Instead, we should always look specifically for artefacts and other non-humans as sources of evidence (see Bloch, Pinney, Chari, Keane, this volume). EBMA should not carry on using the same sources of subject-centred evidence as previously, but should re-assemble what it counts as evidence (see below).

Third proposition: EBMA changes EBM epistemologies

My first proposition is that EBMA should study evidence-making practices in medicine. The second proposition turns the tables and suggests that anthropologists should take the emergence of EBM to reflect more carefully on how they themselves are making evidence. The third proposition turns the perspective around again and suggests that an evidence-based medical anthropology would be in an excellent position to question EBM epistemology. This last project is only possible if we first have ethnographic accounts of what EBM does (the first proposition) and have done some substantial rethinking of our own concepts (the second proposition). The third proposition is the most difficult and most uncharted part of EBMA.

Perhaps the most commonly raised argument by anthropologists in regard to EBM is that it excludes, or at least marginalizes, social dimensions of disease and illness. Summarizing social scientific engagements, Helen Lambert underlines that EBM lacks 'a place for – or even acknowledgement of – social structural influences and social, cultural, political and economic dimensions, despite their critically important role in determining health status and outcomes' (2006b: 2642). What many authors point out is that social factors should be incorporated into medical evidence-making procedures. Anthropologists can only do so if they do not simply reject EBM. For example, there could be better ethnographic evidence that socio-economic factors, such as unemployment or violence, increase the risk of depression. But I think that an evidence-based medical anthropology should also try to go beyond this, not to weaken 'social' perspectives within EBM, but to strengthen them.

When we speak of 'social factors' contributing to a rise of depression, we seem to be talking about disease causation: for example, 'unemployment causes depression'. Yet this has already gone one step too far. What is at stake is causality more generally defined. In relation to depression, this means that we should not just ask *why* depression is rising, but for what reasons some *doctors* believe that it is rising, and what evidence is available for that claim.

As we have seen before, one weakness of EBM is that it does not allow questioning diagnostic criteria and disease entities. It can only produce reviews and meta-analyses if all the studies incorporated are assumed to speak to the same problem. This further entrenches one of biomedicine's greatest blindspots, namely that diseases are believed to exist independently of medical interventions. But it has been shown convincingly that, for example, millions of patients were only diagnosed as 'depressed' *after* antidepressants were available (e.g. Healy 2004).

The common-sense model of disease causation and treatment runs as follows: diseases are caused by various objectively existing forces, such as bacteria or viruses. This leads to a particular experience of not feeling well in patients. In order to get better, they seek the advice of a doctor. Relying on scientific training and clinical experience, a doctor diagnoses the disease and prescribes an appropriate remedy. This remedy, usually a pharmaceutical substance, contains active ingredients that change the patient's physiology in a way that makes him feel better.

This model emerged from traditional 'eminence-based' practice, but EBM fully subscribes to it as well. All that EBM does differently is to chart a new path for the doctor to find an appropriate remedy. Instead of her own clinical experience, she is advised to trust in meta-analyses. If some EBM discussions address how to include 'patients' preferences' on a par with research evidence and clinical experience (e.g. Haynes, Devereaux & Guyatt 2002), it can only do so if these are taken as stable and indifferent by medical practice.

The same common-sense model also informs research in medical anthropology. Its classic formulation is the 'explanatory model' (Helman 2000; Kleinman 1980: 104-18). Even if fewer people nowadays use the term itself, it is still commonsensical to ask, first, how sickness symptoms are perceived, then to ask what causes the symptoms, and then to ask what kind of treatment would be best to cure sickness. But just like the disease/ illness division, the explanatory model is an epistemic side-effect of eminence-based medicine. The model presupposes that sickness episodes truly *start* with a patient's perception of symptoms, which are then given diagnostic meaning by a doctor, and which are then treated with the best available medicines.

If the explanatory model is derived from an idealized biomedical decision-making process, it comes as no surprise that the GPs in Kolkata also start with symptoms, *then* explain causes, and *then* move on to appropriate treatments. The way they describe rising rates of depression is as follows: first, they diagnosed more patients with depression than previously. Then they wondered why that is the case, and interpreted the occurrence of these symptoms in relation to socio-economic factors. Finally, they prescribed the best available treatment. But what *is* this treatment?

When I first juxtaposed the GPs' warm-hearted concerns about India's socio-economic upheaval to the psychiatrists' cold-hearted concerns about the lack of proper statistics, most anthropologists' gut feeling would have been to take sides with the GPs, who appear to have an intense awareness of social factors. For them, depression is a form of social suffering, not an abstract statistic. This explanation of depression might be greeted with universal acclaim by medical anthropologists, who have long argued that sickness must be seen in its cultural contexts, and that the unequal distribution of capital is a root cause of suffering. In short, the GPs seem to be on the leading edge of social-sensitive reformulations of EBM.

What might change this evaluation is another piece of evidence: the treatment of depression actually used. While the GPs lamented socio-economic circumstances, they also said that the use of antidepressants was by far the best response. They told me that they were prescribing these drugs much more often than in previous years. The introduction of SSRIs had, in their opinion, made it possible to take the treatment of depression out of the domain of specialized psychiatry and into general practice. While they found previous types of antidepressants too hard to handle, SSRIs were 'easy' to prescribe and 'safe' to use. When I asked how many of their patients were given antidepressants, many of them said 'up to 20 per cent', and that they 'routinely' prescribed antidepressants to elderly patients and those suffering from chronic diseases. The GPs also said that they tended *not* to tell their patients about either the diagnosis or about the medicines, in order to avoid hostile reactions. To be honest with patients resulted, in their experience, in denial and refusal ('Depression? I am not mad!').

But if we start with the evidence from artefacts – here, from pharmaceuticals – another story about the alleged rise of depression becomes more plausible.[8] Depression seems to have been of marginal importance to Indian GPs before the late 1980s. Psychiatrists had treated symptoms of depression before, mostly with tricyclics, while GPs would at most use basic tranquillizers, such as amitriptyline. Then, during the 1990s, the arrival of 'safe and easy' SSRIs greatly expanded the reach of antidepressants to non-specialized doctors. Pharmaceutical companies' marketing efforts were playing a central role in this. With these pills at hand, the GPs started to diagnose more and more patients with 'depression', all made possible by the presence of drugs. The next phase, namely the dissemination of a biomedical view of depressive symptoms among patients, is now underway. It is becoming common that people in Kolkata diagnose themselves as 'depressed' and go to a doctor. This is *only* possible because they are promised that the doctors can give them a pill. The way I reconstruct this process (first the pill, then the symptom) presents the exact reversal of how both EBM and orthodox medical anthropologists would usually describe the therapeutic process. With the standard model (first the symptom, then the pill), one would never be able to see this.

If we start reconstructing the evidence from the actual drugs prescribed, instead of starting from symptoms and their 'meanings', the GPs' concern about social change suddenly appear like an elegant justification for their increasing use of pills. There is not even the need to say that they are 'concealing' their true opinions. What I find most striking about the GPs is their honest conviction that depression *is* rising, and that depression *is* caused by social pressures. But the 'evidence' that the GPs are drawing on is primarily an artefact of their own prescription habits. They are literally *making evidence* by how they are prescribing drugs.

That is why this chapter can end where Nancy Scheper-Hughes's 'three propositions for a critically applied medical anthropology' also ended: 'Praxis must not be left in the hands of those who would only represent the best interests of biomedical hegemony' (1990: 197). Anthropology can only achieve this if it rethinks its idea of evidence.

NOTES

[1] *http://www.cochrane.org/reviews/clibintro.htm* (accessed 5 January 2008).

[2] *http://www.mrcpsych.com/critical.htm* (accessed 6 January 2008).

[3] To use Google as an *ad hoc* evidence database: on 31 July 2007, there were nearly one million hits for 'medicalization'/'medicalisation'. Anthropologization'/'anthropologisation' attracted fewer than 600 hits.

[4] *http://www.medicalnewstoday.com/articles/42542.php* (accessed 21 February 2008).

[5] 'Concerns over cancer drug cost', BBC, 24 November 2006, *http://search.bbc.co.uk/cgi-bin/search/results.pl?scope=all&edition=d&q=herceptin&go=Search* (accessed 5 January 2008).

[6] In the language of Actor-Network-Theory (ANT), these twin opportunities have been discussed either as 'extending' networks or as 'cutting' them (Latour 2005; Strathern 1996).

[7] With their emphasis on cross-cultural comparison and 'quick access' to gathered evidence, Human Relations Area Files, Inc. (HRAF) and allied projects are an exception to this. Yet even HRAF-style meta-analyses never reach the level of statistical sophistication that EBM developed.

[8] To make this claim fully, I would of course need to present far more evidence than in this chapter.

REFERENCES

BROWNER, C.H. 1999. On the medicalization of medical anthropology. *Medical Anthropology Quarterly* 13, 135-40.

CLINICIANS FOR THE RESTORATION OF AUTONOMOUS PRACTICE WRITING GROUP 2002. EBM: unmasking the ugly truth. *British Medical Journal* 325, 1496-8.

CUNNINGHAM, A. & P. WILLIAMS (eds) 1992. *The laboratory revolution in medicine.* Cambridge: University Press.

DE VRIES, R. & T. LEMMERS 2006. The social and cultural shaping of medical evidence: case studies from pharmaceutical research and obstetric science. *Social Science & Medicine* 62, 2694-706.

ECKS, S. 2005. Pharmaceutical citizenship: antidepressant marketing and the promise of demarginalization in India. *Anthropology & Medicine* 12, 239-54.

——— & W.S. SAX 2005. The ills of marginality: new perspectives on health in South Asia. *Anthropology & Medicine* 12, 199-210.

EISENBERG, L. 1977. Disease and illness: distinctions between professional and popular ideas of sickness. *Culture, Medicine & Psychiatry* 1, 9-23.

FOUCAULT, M. 1970. *The order of things: an archaeology of the human sciences* (trans. anonymous). London: Tavistock.

GANE, M. 2002. Normativity and pathology. *Philosophy, Psychiatry, & Psychology* 9, 313-16.

GOOD, B. 1994. *Medicine, rationality, and experience: an anthropological perspective.* Cambridge: University Press.

HAYDEN, C. 2007. A generic solution? Pharmaceuticals and the politics of the similar in Mexico. *Current Anthropology* 48, 475-95.

HAYNES, R.B., P.J. DEVEREAUX & G.H. GUYATT 2002. Clinical expertise in the era of evidence-based medicine and patient choice. *Evidence-Based Medicine* 7, 36-8.

HEALY, D. 2004. *Let them eat Prozac: the unhealthy relationship between the pharmaceutical industry and depression.* New York: University Press.

HELMAN, C.G. 2000. *Culture, health and illness: an introduction for health professionals.* (Fourth edition). Oxford: Hodder Arnold.

HENRY, J.A. 1993. Debits and credits in the management of depression. *British Journal of Psychiatry* 163, S20, 33-9.

JASANOFF, S. 2004. Science and citizenship: a new synergy. *Science and Public Policy* 31: 2, 90-4.

KLEINMAN, A. 1980. *Patients and healers in the context of culture: an exploration of the borderland between anthropology, medicine, and psychiatry.* Berkeley: University of California Press.

——— & J. KLEINMAN 1985. Somatization: the interconnections in Chinese society among culture, depressive experiences and meaning of pain. In *Culture and depression: studies in the anthropology of cross-culture psychiatry of affect and disorder* (eds) A. Kleinman & B. Good, 419-90. Berkeley: University of California Press.

KOHRT, B.A., R.D. KUNZ, J.L. BALDWIN, N.R. KOIRALA, V.D. SHARMA & M.K. NEPAL 2005. 'Somatization and 'comorbidity': a study of *jhum-jhum* and depression in Nepal. *Ethos* **33**, 125-47.

LAKOFF, A. 2007. The right patients for the drug: managing the placebo effect in antidepressant trials. *BioSocieties* **2**, 57-71.

LAMBERT, H. 2006a. Introduction: gift horse or Trojan horse? Social perspectives on evidence-based health care. *Social Science & Medicine* **62**, 2613-20.

——— 2006b. Accounting for EBM: notions of evidence in medicine. *Social Science & Medicine* **62**, 2633-45.

LATOUR, B. 2005. *Reassembling the social: an introduction to Actor-Network-Theory.* Oxford: University Press.

LÉVI-STRAUSS, C. 1963. *Structural anthropology* (trans. C. Jacobson & B.G. Schoepf). Harmondsworth: Penguin.

MEDICINES AND HEALTHCARE PRODUCTS REGULATORY AGENCY 2004. Report of the CSM Expert Working Group on the safety of selective serotonin reuptake inhibitor antidepressants (available on-line: *http://www.mhra.gov.uk/home/groups/pl-p/documents/drugsafetymessage/con019472.pdf*, accessed 5 January 2008).

NATIONAL INSTITUTE FOR CLINICAL EXCELLENCE 2004. Depression: management of depression in primary and secondary care (National Clinical Practice Guideline **23**) (available on-line: *http://www.nice.org.uk/CG023*, accessed 5 January 2008).

NGUYEN, V. 2004. Antiretroviral globalism, biopolitics, and therapeutic citizenship. In *Global assemblages: technology, politics, and ethics as anthropological problem* (eds) A. Ong & S. Collier, 124-44. Oxford: Blackwell.

PAPE, H. 2002. *Die Unsichtbarkeit der Welt: eine visuelle Kritik neuzeitlicher Ontologie.* Frankfurt am Main: Suhrkamp.

PATEL, V. 2001. Cultural factors and international epidemiology. *British Medical Bulletin* **57**, 33-45.

PETERSEN, A. & R. BUNTON 2002. *The new genetics and the public's health.* London: Routledge.

PETRYNA, A. 2002. *Life exposed: biological citizenship after Chernobyl.* Princeton: University Press.

——— 2007. Clinical trials offshored: on private sector science and public health. *BioSocieties* **2**, 21-40.

PRESIDENT'S COUNCIL ON BIOETHICS 2003. Beyond therapy: biotechnology and the pursuit of happiness. Washington, D.C. (available on-line: *http://www.bioethics.gov/reports/beyondtherapy/beyond_therapy_final_webcorrected.pdf*, accessed 5 January 2008).

ROSE, N. 2006. *The politics of life itself: biomedicine, power, and subjectivity in the twenty-first century.* Princeton: University Press.

——— & C. NOVAS 2004. Biological citizenship. In *Global assemblages: technology, politics, and ethics as anthropological problem* (eds) A. Ong & S. Collier, 439-63. Oxford: Blackwell.

SCHEPER-HUGHES, N. 1990. Three propositions for a critically applied medical anthropology. *Social Science & Medicine* **30**, 189-97.

SINCLAIR, S. 2004. Evidence-based medicine: a new ritual in medical teaching. *British Medical Bulletin* **69**, 179-96.

STRATHERN, M. 1996. Cutting the network. *Journal of the Royal Anthropological Institute* (N.S.) **2**, 517-35.

TIMMERMANS, S. & M. BERG 2003. *The gold standard: the challenge of evidence-based medicine and standardization in health care.* Philadelphia: Temple University Press.

WILLIAMS, D.D.R. & J. GARNER 2002. The case against the 'evidence'. *British Journal of Psychiatry* **180**, 8-12.

WORLD MENTAL HEALTH SURVEY CONSORTIUM 2004. Prevalence, severity, and unmet need for treatment of mental disorders in the World Health Organization World Mental Health Surveys. *Journal of the American Medical Association* **291**, 2581-90.

7

Definitive evidence, from Cuban gods

MARTIN HOLBRAAD *University College London*

Ethnographic evidence

In Cuba people seem concerned with the evidence gods give. Much ethnographic evidence could be adduced to show this, though, with that intention, I take a detailed vignette (see also the Introduction to this volume). This is Jorge, a well-established actor and tango singer in his 50s, speaking to me in his flat in the Old City of Havana in 2005 about Afro-Cuban religion, and particularly about what he calls *pruebas*, or, in rough English, 'proofs':

> I love this religion and I love all the deities (*santos*), because they've given me a lot of *pruebas*. Shall I tell you the story? I'd been wanting to move here to the centre for many years – too many buses to work – but it wasn't easy [referring to the legal ban on house purchases in Cuba, which prevents people from moving home unless they can persuade someone to swap their own with them]. So four years ago, when I was on tour in Santiago with the troupe, I went to see the Virgen de la Caridad del Cobre [the patron saint of Cuba whose sanctuary outside Santiago de Cuba is the focus of pilgrims' devotion, and who is often identified with Ochún, the Afro-Cuban deity of sexual love and rivers]. We were standing there with two pals of mine – I wasn't really into it at that time. One of them goes to me, 'ask her for what you want, ask her', and I thought all I want is to move house, so I did ask her, and I said that if she helped me I would come back and bring her her flowers [the Caridad del Cobre particularly likes offerings of sunflowers]. When I get back home to Havana my neighbour tells me that a man had been by my home and had made enquiries about a house-swap (*permuta*). And really, I'm not joking, ten days later here I was in my new apartment and, well, here we all are and here is Ochún with her flowers.

Jorge was pointing at the ceremonial pot inside of which Ochún is placed, in the form of a beautiful river stone, as part of consecration ceremonies in Santería – the most widespread Afro-Cuban religious tradition in Havana, on which this chapter focuses. Jorge's Ochún – the decorous pot with its consecrated contents – was on display alongside a number of other *santos* (Changó, Yemayá, Oyá, Obatalá, etc.), each with his or her ritual insignia and paraphernalia, to form what is called a 'throne' (*trono*), a ceremonial display that Santería initiates (*santeros*) mount for special occasions (Brown 2003). The occasion in this case was Jorge's third anniversary of initiation – his third 'birthday', as *santeros* put it, to emphasize that Santería initiation is about 'giving birth' to the neophyte and to the deities he or she 'receives' as part of the ceremony: the ones Jorge is now displaying in his *trono*. In fact, the occasion of his third birthday and the story of Ochún's *prueba* are not unrelated. Jorge continued:

> I've had so many *pruebas* it's hardly worth counting. A few months after moving into this house I started getting headaches all the time, the light would bother me ... a lot of pain. I told a friend of mine who is a spiritist and she said that I should check to see if there's a dead spirit (*muerto*) bothering me in the house ... So I went to see a woman who had attended me before in these matters, a *santera*, and she came here and cleaned me up and the house too [namely a ritual cleansing referred to as *limpieza*] and everything was fine after that ... It was these things that brought me closer to the whole story of Santería and the spirits, so I decided that it would be good for me to do it [to 'make himself *santo*', namely to get initiated into Santería].

Jorge's story is one of persuasion – conversion even. Four years ago, on tour with his troupe, he was 'not really into' Santería. Then, with the *pruebas* mounting, three years ago he decided to be initiated himself. And now, surrounded by his gods on his birthday, he tells me of their *pruebas*.

Arguing with evidence

To introduce the argument of this chapter, we may begin by noting that recounting Jorge's story at the outset is supposed to do two things at once, both of which are characteristic of anthropological ways of arguing. First, suitably contextualized, Jorge's story is supposed to provide 'ethnographic evidence', in this case of religious practice in contemporary Cuba, and particularly of the role of *pruebas* in the practice of Santería. To the reader unversed in Afro-Cuban religion, Jorge's story is meant to serve as a descriptive entry into a set of ideas and practices that are to a degree unfamiliar, and to provide some of the data that the reader will have to bear in mind in order to understand the argument that is 'built upon the data', as we might say, and to judge its merits.

Secondly, as well as providing ethnographic evidence, Jorge's story serves to set up an 'ethnographic problem'. For while the degree to which what Jorge had to say may appear unfamiliar to the reader would depend on what the reader happens to know about *pruebas*, Santería, or similar phenomena in other parts of the world,[1] Jorge's story, presented as an ethnographic vignette, is also meant to be unfamiliar in a more deliberate or principled sense. Much like the classical 'problems' of cross-cousin marriage, magic, or gift exchange, Jorge's account of *pruebas* is anthropologically interesting at least partly because it conflicts with assumptions the anthropologist may fairly deem, for the sake of argument, to share with his readers (e.g. that promises to a saint are not an efficient way of securing a flat, that headaches are not due to spirits and cannot be cured by ritual cleansings, and that none of this is evidence of the *santos'* powers). Here unfamiliarity is not a matter of a reader's psychological state or cultural background but rather an analytical condition that resides in the difference between a set of assumptions, on the one hand, and, on the other, ethnographic data that appear to contradict them. For all I care (anthropologically), you, or I, may actually think spirits give headaches and so on – indeed, you may happen to be Jorge. The point is that such notions are anthropologically interesting – they constitute a 'problem' – insofar as they are entertained 'critically', which is to say in relation to their alternatives. By way of convention, we may call the constitutive unfamiliarity of ethnographic data 'alterity'.

It is my contention in this chapter that the idea that ethnography can both constitute 'evidence' and be an index of 'alterity' is in a crucial sense incoherent, and that much anthropological argument is hostage to this muddle. Since I take it that a concern with alterity as outlined above lies at the heart of anthropological thinking (although my argument does not depend on the stronger claim that alterity must be the only concern of anthropology), it would follow that the notion of ethnographic evidence requires revision. In the main body of the chapter this is done with reference to *pruebas* and what Jorge had to say about them. As will be explained, notions of *pruebas* are both close enough to anthropological ideas about evidence to warrant comparison, and different enough from them to occasion a revision. Before getting to this, however, it is necessary to make clear why anthropologists' joint concern with evidence and alterity is incoherent.

The issue, I argue, turns on how one interprets the notion of alterity. As we saw, alterity can be articulated in formal terms (rather than cultural or psychological ones) as an apparent divergence between ethnographic data and the assumptions that are taken as initial for purposes of analysis. For example, Jorge's story is 'alter' since, as we shall see in more detail, it appears to negate a number of common assumptions about the nature of evidence, much like, say, for Mauss the ethnography of Maori exchange seemed to negate common assumptions about the market, or for Evans-Pritchard Zande witchcraft seemed to negate common assumptions about causation.[2] But what do these apparent negations amount to? Logically speaking, there are two possibilities. One is that the apparent negations are indeed genuine. For example, the reason for which Jorge's story appears to contradict, say, the assumption that head-aches are not caused by spirits may be that Jorge is in fact asserting that headaches are caused by spirits. There is, however, an alternative possibility. The appearance of contradiction between Jorge's comments and our initial assumptions may just as well be due to misunderstanding. Jorge may appear to be asserting that headaches are caused by spirits but may in fact be saying something quite different – something we fail to grasp, not because it contradicts our assumptions, but rather because it goes beyond them. Like hammers to which everything looks like nails, we may be thinking that Jorge is talking about what we understand as 'headaches', 'causation', 'spirits', and so on, while he may in fact be attaching quite a different meaning to such notions – a meaning that is unavailable to us from within the framework of our own assumptions. Jorge may, in other words, be talking not against us but rather past us.

In view of the distinction between the alterity of genuine negation and that of misunderstanding, it is plain to see that the notion of ethnographic 'evidence' is compatible only with the former. Ill-understood data can hardly serve as evidence that may 'inform' (let alone 'support') an argument. It follows that if ethnography is to serve as evidence, as anthropologists habitually assume, then its alterity must take the form of a genuine (and therefore straightforward) negation of the analytical assumptions anthropologists take for granted for the purposes of their arguments.

While such a formal definition of alterity may seem somewhat technical, the strategy it describes is arguably a very familiar one in anthropology. For example, if I were to say that in this chapter my objective is to understand why Jorge might think spirits cause headaches, I doubt many anthropologists would bat an eyelid. Universalists among them would perhaps expect me to go on to identify the processes (existential, psychological, evolutionary, or what have you) that explain how Jorge may have come to hold such a view. Relativists, on the other hand, would tend to expect an answer with reference to other local ideas and practices with which Jorge's views may be shown to cohere. In either case it is assumed that Jorge's views are understood as such, so that the anthropological problem they pose is why he might hold them.

I suggest that this assumption is both unwarranted and pernicious. It is unwarranted because, as we have seen, there is an alternative to assuming that the content of ethnography is understood, namely that it is not. In fact, the idea that the alterity of ethnography must lie in its negation of our own assumptions smacks of a crime most anthropologists – universalists and relativists alike – proclaim as capital, namely ethnocentrism. If the fallacy of ethnocentrism turns on reading onto another 'ethnos' (or 'culture') assumptions drawn from one's own, at issue here is a similar projection. The ethnographic dog, imagined as the locus of alterity, is in fact wagged by the tail of the analyst's own assumptions, albeit by negation. Moreover, what makes this fallacy of 'negative projection' particularly pernicious is that what it projects onto ethnography – i.e. onto people like Jorge – is essentially falsehood. On this view, after all, ethnography poses analytical problems just because it negates what we, for whatever analytical reason, take to be true (e.g. why might Jorge think that headaches are caused by spirits, given that, as we assume, they do not?). Smarter-than-thou chauvinism, fairly taken as the brunt of ethnocentric sin, here emerges as a constitutive principle of anthropological reasoning.[3]

So, provided one wishes to avoid the unwarranted assumption that what makes the people we study interesting is that they get things wrong, we are left with the idea that, far from constituting evidence, ethnographic data consist in misunderstandings. The job of anthropological analysis, then, is not to account for why ethnographic data are as they are, but rather to understand *what* they are – instead of explanation or interpretation, what is called for is conceptualization. And note that such a task effectively inverts the very project of anthropological analysis. Rather than using our own analytical concepts to make sense of a given ethnography (explanation, interpretation), we use the ethnography to rethink our analytical concepts (see also Corsín Jiménez & Willerslev 2007; Henare, Holbraad & Wastell 2007; Viveiros de Castro 2003). This follows directly from the formal definition of the problem of alterity. If our misunderstandings of ethnography stem from the fact that it is incongruous with the assumptions we take as initial, then it must be those assumptions that require analytical attention.

Furthermore, the fact that these initial assumptions lead us to misrepresent ethnographic data as a series of falsehoods (i.e. negations of assumptions we take to be true) suggests an appropriate method for the work of conceptualization, namely that of altering those assumptions in such a way as to arrive at the position of being able to represent the ethnographic data as truths. If, for example, the assumption that spirits do not cause headaches leads me to misrepresent Jorge as claiming the opposite, then the onus is on me to rethink my assumptions about spirits, causation, headaches (and their relevant corollaries) in a way that would allow me to formulate Jorge's views as statements of truth. So the question would be: what must we take 'spirits', 'causation', and 'headaches' to be in order to be able to assert truly that spirits cause headaches? Elsewhere I have called this approach 'ontographic' (Holbraad 2003), to indicate that, by contrast to some habitual anthropological strategies, it addresses alterity in ontological terms (e.g. what is a spirit?) rather than epistemic ones (e.g. what do Cubans – or whoever – think about spirits?).

The rest of this chapter illustrates and further explores such an approach with reference to the ethnography of *pruebas*. Its argument serves as an example inasmuch as *pruebas* present the problem of alterity in the terms already outlined. As we shall see, while the best translation of *pruebas* is 'evidence', Jorge's comments on *pruebas* (and other relevant ethnography) conflict with our common understanding of the notion of evidence to such an extent that they appear absurd. Illustrating the approach I have outlined, the latter half of the chapter seeks to reconceptualize the idea of evidence in such a way as to remove this apparent absurdity.

It will be noted, however, that by addressing an ethnography of evidence, the chapter adopts a strategy that could be described as 'recursive' (see also Henare *et al.* 2007: 15). Unlike other concepts one might seek to conceptualize anthropologically ('spirit', 'person', 'gift', or what have you), the concept of evidence pertains to the very process of anthropological analysis, as already shown. For, as will be detailed, the assumptions with which the ethnography of *pruebas* conflicts (and which render the idea of *pruebas* absurd) are integral to habitual ways of thinking about the role of evidence in anthropology. It follows that if the present analysis uses the ethnography of *pruebas* to rethink the concept of evidence, it also uses it, effectively, to rethink *itself* – or at least its own evidential procedures.

Indefinite evidence

My dictionary translates the Castellan *prueba* as 'proof', and that is how people in Cuba often use it. But Jorge, speaking of his *pruebas*, seems to be describing evidence – the evidence gods gave him. If, as we ordinarily understand it, proof is meant to be an incontrovertible demonstration of a hypothesis, then Jorge's plural usage of *pruebas* (proofs) as a succession of events ('hardly worth counting') that cumulatively 'brought him closer' to Santería and the spirits seems redundant. In his reckoning, gods are not proven once and for all – like a theorem might be in mathematics, or like God might have been for some scholastic theologians – but rather slowly, as if by a process of induction, or perhaps, to switch from logical analogies to legal ones, by deposition (see Good, this volume). In either case (induction or deposition), what is at issue is not proof but evidence, understood as facts that lend a hypothesis support (see, e.g., Howson 2000). Jorge, one might surmise, is speaking loosely, much like I do when I say that my kettle 'proves' that water boils at 100°, or that our inability to find weapons of mass destruction in Iraq 'proved' that Saddam did not have them and therefore – more loosely – that the war in Iraq was illegal.

The impulse that makes us think of Jorge's mind as a kind of lab or courtroom allows us to assume the same of anthropology. Indeed, the scientific analogy is particularly intuitive to anthropologists, as the instituted aggrandisement of the discipline as a 'social science' indicates – hackneyed objections notwithstanding (e.g. Geertz 2000; Sperber 1985, for critical comment see Strathern 2005: 33-49). Our notion of evidence is integral to the intuition. Anthropology is scientific mainly inasmuch as it admits ethnographic evidence that may offer support for theoretical hypotheses. When Ernest Gellner wrote, from the borders of anthropology and philosophy, of the 'legitimation of belief', he also had in mind the merits of *ethnographic* legitimation for theoretical belief (Gellner 1974: 149-67). In doing so, he was fortifying a connection (self-evident to him) between anthropologists' interest in ethnographic particulars and philosophers' concern with the rigours of evidence in science – concerns with verification, falsification, prediction, and so forth.[4] So, on this premise, if Jorge's *pruebas* can be translated as 'evidence' by analogy to kettles and boiling-points, it can do so by analogy to anthropology too.

It would seem, then, that Jorge's interest in the evidence the gods give him is basically similar to the evidence he and other 'informants' may give to us about, say (and this is where my argument turns recursive), the concept of evidence itself. We hypothesize that Jorge's notion of *pruebas* concerns the relationship between a hypothesis and its evidence. Our hypothesis to this effect is supposed to be supported by my ethnographic vignettes about Jorge on *pruebas*. For is he not doing the same thing? In his case the hypothesis in question regards the efficacy of the gods at the first instance and maybe, by implication, their existence. The evidence, cumulative in character, is the *pruebas*: Ochún's help with the house swap, the headaches caused by spirits and the *santera*'s cure, and all the help the *santos* have given Jorge since his initiation. If, as Imre Lakatos put it, 'the hallmark of scientific behaviour is a certain scepticism even towards one's most cherished theories' (1978: 1), then Jorge's approach to his gods has something of science about it.

For Lakatos, however, such a comparison, though apposite, does not serve to elevate Jorge's concerns with *pruebas* as scientific, but only to denigrate scientists' concerns with evidence as superstitious. In the famous lecture from which the quotation is taken, titled 'Science and pseudoscience', Lakatos makes a point of refuting the idea that willingness to provide evidence for hypotheses may in itself qualify as the kind of 'scepticism' he considers the hallmark of science. Pertinently, the discussion is set up with witchcraft in mind: 'If we look at the vast seventeenth-century literature on witchcraft, it is full of reports of careful observations and sworn evidence – even of experiments. Glanvill, the house philosopher of the Royal Society, regarded witchcraft as the paradigm of experimental reasoning' (Lakatos 1978: 2). Bastard sisters spring to mind: as for Frazer, Lakatos's assumption is that Glanvill's concern with evidence could only ever be *pseudo*scientific (cf. Frazer 1911). But while for Frazer what made the comparison between science and witchcraft viable was partly their common appeal to evidence, for Lakatos appeals to evidence were exactly what made witchcraft suspicious from what he would want to deem a properly scientific point of view. Indeed, what is so interesting about Lakatos's argument is the way it attributes the concern with evidence not to a hard-nosed scientific outlook, but rather to an essentially theological mindset – science as bastard sister of magic, so to speak. I quote him at length:

> One can today easily demonstrate that there can be no valid derivation of a law of nature from any finite number of facts; but we still keep reading about scientific theories being proved from facts. Why this stubborn resistance to elementary logic? There is a very plausible explanation. Scientists want to make their theories respectable, deserving of the title 'science', that is, genuine knowledge. Now the most relevant knowledge in the seventeenth century, when science was born, concerned God, the Devil, Heaven and Hell. If one got one's conjectures about matters of divinity wrong, the consequence of one's mistake was no less than eternal damnation. Theological knowledge cannot be fallible: it must be beyond doubt. Now the Enlightenment thought that we were fallible and ignorant about matters theological. There is no scientific theology and, therefore, no theological knowledge. Knowledge can only be about Nature, but this new type of knowledge had to be judged by the standards they took over straight from theology: it had to be proven beyond doubt. Science had to achieve the very certainty which had escaped theology. A scientist, worthy of the name, was not allowed to guess: he had to prove each sentence he uttered from facts. (Lakatos 1978: 2)

There are two strands of argument here, both of which are relevant to Jorge's *pruebas*, though for present purposes one is more interesting than the other. The less interesting point regards the socio-historical psychology of persuasion, as it were: caught up in the transition to Enlightenment, seventeenth-century scientists' naturalism could be made respectable by drawing on already established *theological* concerns with proof. A converse argument could be made about Cubans like Jorge. Insofar as the idiom of evidence is peculiarly salient in the case of Afro-Cuban religion (and this is an open ethnographic question), one may wish to argue that in a Marxist context – incidentally, Lakatos's contemporary bugbear of 'pseudoscience' (1978: 3) – where religions like Santería have been repressed until recently, *santeros*' religiosity may be able to curry more favour by drawing on dominant *scientistic* concerns with evidence (cf. Palmié 2002). For example, the popularity among *santeros* during my fieldwork of a book written before official openings towards Santería in Cuba, titled *Materialism explains spiritism and Santería*, by an author sometimes assumed to have been a *santero* himself (Gaston Aguero 1961), may lend credence to such a hypothesis. And certainly there is no denying the enthusiasm with which my informants recounted their *pruebas* to me in particular, taking me not only as a lucrative potential neophyte (cf. Holbraad 2004), but also for a 'scientist'.

However, in line with Lakatos, this is not the kind of evidence in which we can afford to be interested here, for Lakatos's point about the theological roots of proof from evidence arguably has more implications than he had foreseen, pointing towards a *different concept of evidence*, and thus leaving the door open for an alternative concep-tualization, as outlined above. In particular, we may take up his suggestion that scien-tists' concern with evidential proof is motivated by divine standards of indubitability. For Lakatos, the apparent paradox of this position is a matter of historical contingency. Scientists are caught between two worlds, using the template of a theological past to articulate the aspirations of a scientific future, 'stubbornly resisting elementary logic'. But leaving the historical argument to one side, Lakatos's logical point relies on a clear-cut normative distinction between proof as a theological concern and evidence as scientific one. However, while it may be fair to charge scientists with straddling that divide oxymoronically, it certainly is not fair to Jorge (and presuming the same token, nor is it to Glanvill and the alchemists). His interest in evidence is unapologetically theological. Far from seeking to prove that unprovable, to Lakatos's lights Jorge's concern would emerge as that of providing evidence for the indubitable. But then Jorge's thinking looks not merely fallacious but altogether absurd. One can see why one might aspire to derive a proof from evidence – Lakatos himself gives a plausible account. But as to why one might conspire to provide evidence for a hypothesis that is already defined as being beyond doubt, we are in the dark. If theological knowledge is indubitable, then why bother to provide it with evidence? There are two ways out of this *reductio*. Either theological knowledge is not indubitable or evidence is not what is at issue. Or, limiting the argument to the case in hand, either in Santería the influence of the *santos* is not beyond doubt, or 'evidence' is in some crucial respect a misleading translation of *pruebas*. I shall argue for the latter option.

Infinitive evidence

That the question of indubitability is at the heart of Santería becomes clear when one considers the abiding role of divination in the life of the cult. Practically all aspects of worship, from incidental appeals to the *santos* to help solve everyday problems (like Jorge's headaches) to soliciting divine sanction for the performance of important ceremonies (such as the consecration of neophytes, as in Jorge's 'birth' as a *santero*) require the disclosure of the *santos*' will through divination (Holbraad 2005; in press). Indeed, worshippers' ascent through a series of initiatory steps is largely measured against a scale of divinatory expertise, starting with knowledge of the rudimentary coconut-shell oracle (*los cocos*) that all worshippers are free to use for their own benefit, through the cowry oracle (*los caracoles, diluggún*) that only fully initiated *santeros* are taught to use for themselves or for clients, and up to the most prestigious oracle, that of Ifá, which requires a special initiation reserved for heterosexual men who are chosen as 'fathers of secrets' (*babalawos*) by Orula, the patron deity of divination, through the oracle of Ifá itself.

That divination should be so important in the life of worshippers indicates the essentially 'pragmatic' character of Santería. As is often remarked in the literature, Santería has almost no eschatology, its imperatives are decidedly practical rather than categorical, and even its remarkably rich mythology is interesting to worshippers mainly as a guide for the performance of what they call 'works' (*trabajos*) – often glossed as witchcraft (*brujería*) (see, e.g., Lachatañere 1961 contra Ortíz 1906, cf. Goldman 2005). Divination is integral to this here-and-now orientation, since it provides the principal means by which worshippers can gauge the will of the *santos* regarding their particular concerns, from house moves and headaches to initiations and funerary rites. In fact, it is precisely the pertinence of the *santos'* divinatory pronouncements that worshippers most typically have in mind when, like Jorge, they speak so enthusiastically about the *pruebas* they have had. Inasmuch as it is through divination that the gods typically speak, it follows that evidence that what they say comes to pass is evidence for the efficacy of the oracles. Divination posits hypotheses, it would seem, and *pruebas* confirm them.

Notice, however, how peculiar these 'hypotheses' are. As diviners themselves emphasize, oracles are required to arbitrate on so many aspects of worshippers' lives precisely because their pronouncements are *beyond doubt*. In divination, they often say, the *santos* 'never lie' and they 'never make mistakes'. Diviners themselves may certainly do so – since they are 'imperfect humans', as one practitioner put it – but not the *santos* who speak through them. But if in Santería false divinations are logical oxymorons, it follows that divination here is defined as indubitable. To doubt the truth of a divination is to doubt whether it is really a proper divination, since proper divinations *cannot but be true* (see also Holbraad 2003).

So we are left with the question: why the *santeros'* apparently redundant interest in *pruebas*? Given that, as we saw, providing evidence for the indubitable is absurd, a possible suggestion would be that *pruebas* are relevant to the one question that does admit of doubt in these matters, namely whether any particular divination is a genuine one. On such a view, the more truth one finds – accumulating *pruebas* like Jorge, who has 'had so many' – the more grounds one has for believing that its origin is divine, the trademark of divinity being, precisely, truth. That such a solution to the conundrum commits worshippers like Jorge to the inductive fallacy (*à la* Lakatos, piling up the evidence as if it proved something) is perhaps excusable. The real problem is that the claim is ethnographically untenable. As Jorge indicates at the very outset of his story, his *pruebas* fuel his love of the *santos*, not of the *santeros*! Indeed in his first story, about the house move, doubtful human mediation does not feature at all; it is Ochún's divine power that the *pruebas* are meant to demonstrate.

We are left with the absurdity of evidence. In line with the introductory comments to this chapter, the onus is upon us to reconsider the premises of such a notion, changing our conceptualization of evidence in light of the ethnography of *pruebas*. The key for doing so, I argue, lies in the relationship between *pruebas* and divination, since it is in this connection that the absurdity of providing evidence for indubitable truth emerges. Indeed, the need to reconceptualize evidence in this context is owed to the fact that the concept of truth itself in Santería divination departs radically from common-sense assumptions about truth.

As I have argued in more detail elsewhere, divinatory truths present a problem (that of alterity) because, although practitioners define them as indubitable, they seem to take the form of ordinary statements of fact – i.e. statements that can be *doubted* with reference to facts (Holbraad 2003). For example, the truth of the *santera*'s pronouncement that Jorge's home was occupied by spirits appears to depend on whether Jorge's flat was in fact occupied by spirits – a doubtful matter, to say the least.[5] However, this apparent contradiction depends on our assumption that the *santera* is making what philo-sophers call a 'predicative' statement, that is, that what she is doing is 'ascribing a property' to his house (the property of being occupied by spirits), in the sense Knight and Astuti discuss in their contribution to this volume. Under such an interpretation, the idea that divinatory pronouncements are indubitable appears dogmatic – as if, by cultural fiat, what makes such pronouncements indubitable is the fact that they are pronounced by a diviner.[6] But what kind of truth is this that can be brought about by a mere speech-act?

To avoid the imputation of native dogmatism, I have argued, we need to move away from the assumption that the truth of divinatory statements is meant to be predicative, for an alternative would be to treat them not as statements of fact but rather as *definitions*. On such a view, the truths of divination are to be understood not in epistemic terms, as 'representations' that make claims 'about' the world, but rather as ontological operations. So, for example, when the *santera* says that Jorge's flat is occu-pied by spirits, she is not making a claim about an already existing state of affairs. She is bringing such a state of affairs about, pronouncing a change in 'the world's furniture', to use the ontologists' expression: Jorge's home is *redefined* as one occupied by malevo-lent spirits, his headaches are *redefined* as caused by the spirits, the spirits themselves are *redefined* as vulnerable to the *santera*'s expert cleansing, and so on. Divinatory power, then, resides in the possibility of inventing entities through acts of definition. Following a suggestion by Eduardo Viveiros de Castro (pers. comm.), I propose to call these acts of inventive definition 'infinitions'. Shorthand for 'inventive definition' (cf. Holbraad in press), the term would also indicate that such acts presuppose that entities are infinite in their potential for transformation through redefinition[7] – their only constancy is that they are under permanent ontological reconstruction.

Positing divinatory pronouncements as infinitions gets us out of imputing dogma-tism to the *santeros*. Infinitions are indubitable because they are true by definition, rather like the statements philosophers call 'analytic' (e.g. 'bachelors are unmarried men'). Nevertheless, the idea that infinitions (mere speech-acts like 'your home has spirits in it') can have properly ontological effects may sound mystical or, worse, 'constructivist'. Is it really credible to say that Jorge's home can be brought forth as a new entity (one that is occupied by spirits) just on a *santera*'s say-so? Is this not merely to elevate the very absurdity of divination as an analytical principle? By way of defence, I propose to demonstrate that the idea of 'infinition' is not as logically abhorrent as it perhaps sounds. As we shall see, delving into the logic of infinition also brings us closer to conceptualizing *pruebas*.

Consider what I am doing right now. Stringing meanings together ('definition', 'ontology', 'effect', etc.), I am proposing that you take on board a new concept, appro-priately christened with a new name – 'infinition'. Even if you see no sense in this new concept, surely you can accept that it is at least conceivable that it *may* make sense as such (unless you are a Platonist, in which case you see any sense the concept makes as proof of its prior existence as an immutable Form). In (non-Platonic) principle, then, you accept the possibility of conceptual novelty. You may even agree that the history of ideas is *made* of such instances of conceptual invention – e.g. who had thought of a Form before Plato? Indeed, those philosophers who have followed Nietzsche in think-ing of philosophy as an 'untimely' enterprise have sought to theorize this possibility of conceptual invention (e.g. Deleuze 1994; Heidegger 1968; cf. Nietzsche 1997). And so have anthropologists who see the creation of new meanings not just as a philosophical prerogative, but as an irreducible aspect of social living (e.g. Ardener 1989; Latour 1999; Strathern 1999; Viveiros de Castro 2002; Wagner 1981).

Now, why claim that infinitions must *ipso facto* have ontological effects, bringing forth the objects they define as existing entities?[8] Well, consider the alternatives. One would be to claim that when I, say, define infinitions as inventions of new concepts, I am merely giving a name to a phenomenon that already exists – indeed, how else could I appeal to Plato and his Forms as a convincing precedent of what I have in mind? But this is contradictory. If infinitions already exist, then they do not exist as *new* concepts, which is what they are defined as. Infinitions may be logically quirky, but not as quirky as having the capacity to pre-exist themselves.

The other alternative would be to claim that the concepts that infinitions inaugurate may well be just that, *mere* concepts. On this view, infinitions are treated on a par with 'unicorn', 'the golden mountain' , or 'the current King of France', as at most senses with no reference, in philosophical parlance (e.g. Frege 1980), and hence their purported ontological effects are, quite literally, fanciful. But appealing as it may be to a common-sense viewpoint that would deem diviners' infinitions as unicorn-like psychedelia, such a move is a throwback to the epistemic frame, which insists on treating concepts as 'representations' (here read 'sense') to be contrasted to 'the world' (here read 'refer-ence'). Apart from the question-begging, the problem here is that treating infinitions as representations implicitly pastes over their putative novelty. If one assumes that the ontological effects of infinitions must be measured against the world of 'evidence' that gives them their epistemic purchase, then one precludes novelty on two counts. For one thing, the world to which infinitions might refer is presumed to be already given (as an evidential benchmark, so to speak), so any question of their ontological effects *upon* such a 'world' is already foreclosed. But more to the point, such epistemic litmus tests ('does the new concept refer to an existing entity or not?') also implicitly deny the novelty *of the concepts* they purport to measure against the world. The suggestion that an infinition might not, as it turns out, have a referent gives logical priority to the putatively new concept (read 'representation') over the world to which it may or may not refer *a posteriori*. Thus for the question of an infinition's reference even to be raised, the supposed novel concept must be taken as already given, that is, its novelty, *qua* infinition, must be effaced.

Provided this *reductio* of the alternatives is fair and the alternatives are exhaustive, it follows that by accepting the notion of a new concept we willy-nilly accept that such new concepts must have ontological effects – they must bring forth, into existence, the entities they infine. Now I want to argue that such a move allows us to make sense not only of the *santeros'* claim that what their gods say is indubitable, as we have seen, but also of their apparently paradoxical insistence that these indubitable truths nevertheless admit of a kind of confirmation – I will not say evidence! – by *pruebas*.

A chief reason, perhaps, for which one is tempted to find the idea of infinition psychedelic is what one might call its hyper-nominalism.[9] If nominalism, loosely, is the thesis that every thing is itself and nothing other than itself, then infinitions are hyper-nominalist inasmuch as they are themselves and nothing other *qua new concepts*, and novelty, as we have seen, wears off quickly. No sooner has Jorge's flat been infined as occupied by spirits than the infinition becomes unavailable for *a posteriori* testing, so to speak, lest its novelty disappear. Infinitions pertain to the moment of what Roy Wagner has called 'invention' (1981). Indeed they *are* such moments. This temporal hyper-nominalism, I would suggest, has direct implications for the question of what may count as a 'confirmation' of an infinition, that is, for the question of *pruebas*.

If what *a posteriori* evidence tests is the epistemic purchase of a representation upon the world, then at issue for infinitions must be something like an 'ontological purchase'. Return to the example. As an infinition, the *santera*'s divination brought Jorge's spirit-infested home forth as a new entity. It follows that its confirmation is the existence of Jorge's home *as such an entity*, for example as one that can be cleansed ritually so as to cure Jorge's headaches. However, Jorge's cured headaches cannot be construed as 'evidence' for the existence of his newly defined house-of-spirits, since, as we saw, infinitions do not admit of evidence, at pain of evaporating into thin (epistemic) air. Indeed, since an infinition does not outlast its own novelty (namely it does not outlast *itself*), it would follow that the only way to confirm its ontological purchase is to *re-enact it*: an infinition's 'test' can only be a *further* infinition. In a logical universe where entities are under permanent ontological construction, as we have said, their existence *qua* constructions only has purchase inasmuch as they become implicated in further acts of construction. And such acts of further construction – infinitions in their own right – 'confirm' the existence of the infinitions they transform by showing that they can indeed be engaged *as transformations* – taking them, as it were, for an onto-logical spin. Put in twentieth-century pop science terms: with infinitions, to know something *really is* to change it.

That, then, is how *pruebas* work. The cure of Jorge's headaches confirmed the *santera*'s divination about the spirits not because it provided evidence that it was 'correct', but because it took the entity infined by the divination – Jorge's house-of-spirits – as the baseline for an act of further infinition, namely that of the cure itself. For, just like the divination transformed a seemingly 'ordinary' house into one occupied by spirits, so its *prueba* transformed the alleviation of Jorge's pain into an event of spiritual significance: not simply a disappearance of headaches but a 'cure-of-spiritual-influence'. The ontological purchase of the latter infinition (the existence of Jorge's cure of spiritual influence) confirms that of the former, since it is by appealing to the *santera*'s infinition of his home that Jorge is able to infine his alleviation as a cure of spiritual proportions. But note that this confirmation is not a matter of 'coherence', as it might be articulated were one to think of the infinitions epistemically as represen-tations or, as it is said, 'beliefs' (e.g. Evans-Pritchard 1976; see also Keane, this volume). Jorge's cure confirms the pernicious spirits in his house not by merely presupposing their previous existence, but by actively transforming it – in this case by removing the spirits from the house through the cleansing ritual. His *prueba* takes the form of an infinition that is not just precipitated by the infinitions of the divination, but also (and by that virtue) acts to transform them.

In this sense the relationship between divination and *pruebas*, which so looked like that between 'hypotheses' and 'evidence', elevates the aforementioned 'pragmatism' of Santería to the level of logic. The logic of Santería practice, if you like, is that logic is practical, or even 'pragmatical' – to follow the Greek association of actions (*praxes*) with things (*pragmata*), as infinitions do. The fact that Santería is so orientated to the here and now, rendering doctrinal or cosmologically speculative concerns subservient to 'work' ('witchcraft'), is not a matter of arbitrary local convention. Such an orientation is a function of its 'infinitive' logic. In place of induction (read evidence), deduction (read proof), abduction (read hypothesis), or what have you, the logic of Santería posits *production*, understood as the activity of ontological transformation that infinition involves. Indeed, it is for this reason that practitioners' interest in *pruebas* is far from absurd, as it would have to be if it were glossed as a matter of providing 'evidence' for the gods' indubitable truths. The problem there, as we saw, was that evidence is logically redundant in the face of indubitability. Contrastingly, if *pruebas* are recognized as infinitions, far from redundant, they emerge as an indispensable constituent of the logic of worship, for, as we have seen, *pruebas* are effectively a concomitant of the temporal hyper-nominalism of infinition. Even if providing evidence for divinations were not absurd, it would certainly be optional – representations do not as such *depend* on the provision of evidence for their existence. Infinitions, on the other hand, exist by virtue of being implicated in further acts of transformation, and that is what makes *pruebas* not only logically sensible but also pragmatically necessary.

The infinitive logic of Santería has far-reaching implications, and charting these in diverse areas of worshippers' lives is my ongoing project. That such a project should *remain* ongoing follows from its own infinitive character – a meta-anthropological point raised in the conclusion of this chapter. Before doing so, however, we may note some of the dividends of such an analysis, first for Jorge's story, and then a bit beyond.

Jorge's account, we noted, can be read as one of personal conversion. From a position of relative indifference four years ago at the sanctuary of the El Cobre in Santiago, his *pruebas* helped him get to where he is today, a proud initiate celebrating his 'birthday'. Now, anthropological accounts often present conversion as a matter of 'persuasion' or at least as some kind of change in people's 'beliefs' – an approach that takes off from the kinds of 'epistemic' assumptions we have sought to discard here, and which were no doubt central to Protestant missionaries' thinking on the matter (cf. Whitehouse 2000). However, the emphasis Jorge places on the role of *pruebas* in precipitating his initiation would suggest otherwise. For if initiation itself can fairly be thought of as the apogee of ontological transformation – and what better metaphor for bringing forth new entities than 'birth', which is how *santeros* conceptualize neophytes' initiation (see above and Holbraad in press) – then Jorge's notion that his *pruebas*, in his words, 'brought [him] closer to Santería and the spirits' makes perfect infinitive sense. As infinitions in their own right, *pruebas* brought Jorge closer to initiation not by 'convincing' him that it may be a good idea, but by implicating him into the world of the *santos* through successive acts of ontological reconstruction. Initiation, then, comes as a consummation of a longer trajectory of transformation with which it is logically continuous. Indeed, in this context, the ostentation of the initiate's celebratory *trono* display, which allowed Jorge in the interview literally to point to his *santos* as indicators both of his *pruebas* and of his conversion, illustrates (no, *constitutes*) the ontological productivity of this trajectory in appropriately 'pragmatical' terms – pots, stones, and other beautiful regalia being the *pragmata* of the *santos* (see also Holbraad 2007).

Of course, Jorge's story happens to be a happy one. In fact, much like Evans-Pritchard showed for the Azande (1976: 154-63), in Santería dissatisfaction with divinations is far from uncommon. Horror stories abound in Santería probably as much as those of *pruebas*, with people frequently lamenting how far divinations they were given diverged from how things turned out to be. Considering that oracles in Santería are infallible, it may not be surprising that such divergences provoke reactions ranging from confusion to indignation, and can sometimes cause considerable distress. For example, this is what a young woman told me after a long and particularly important divinatory séance (*itá*), conducted for her as part of an initiatory ceremony:

> It was terrible. [The diviners] said many things that have nothing to do with me ... That I will never prosper until I kneel at my mother's feet and ask for her forgiveness. What is that? I've spent the past hour talking and crying with my mum, trying to work out what I've done to her. I asked her for her forgiveness but she didn't give it because I haven't done anything! We've always been so close, and none of this is going to change that.

Traditionally, anthropologists keen to make sense of native 'belief systems', so called, have felt that such stories pose a problem. Indeed, if one assumes that the diviners' statement is best construed as a representation of the woman's relationship to her mother, then her vehement denials are certainly problematic: the woman appears not to believe in the divination, so, inasmuch as divination is construed as part of the local system of belief, such a case requires explanation. Ingenious analytical footwork such as Evans-Pritchard's 'secondary elaborations of belief' is then produced (1976: 155).[10]

However, an analysis based on 'infinitive' logic dissolves the problem. This is a point in its favour, I take it, since the whole point is that for the natives such cases, distressing as they may be, pose no 'problem' – or not, at least, the kind of 'crisis of representation' that lurks underneath anthropologists' worry that divination might be shown up as a sham to the natives themselves. On an infinitive account, the woman's divinatory fiasco is articulated not as a matter of the world giving the lie to the divination, but rather as a refusal on the woman's part to accept the oracle's reinvention of her. The notion of 'acceptance' is of course used advisedly here. At issue is not some kind of disagreement between neophyte and priest ('you may say I owe my mother an apology, but I don't accept that'), but rather a more literal – or at least 'pragmatical' – sense of 'acceptance'. The woman does not 'take' the diviner's infinition of her inasmuch as she refuses to use it as the basis for further acts of infinition. Nothing is going to change her closeness with her mother, she says. Such stances pose no analytical problem since they are already implicit in a hyper-nominalist characterization of divinations, which premises their purchase not upon accurate depiction, but upon ongoing acts of transformation. In divinatory fiascos the oracle's infinitions are simply *allowed* to dissipate out of existence. So in response to the classical worry about how people can continue to practise divination in the face of its many failures, we may just note that there is no absurdity in allowing some infinitions to drop out of the world, while building whole lives on others. Infinitions make no 'claim' on the world, for they partake of it.

Anthropological evidence

Anthropology, too, partakes of the world. Or so the present mode of analysis would seek to demonstrate. At the outset of this chapter we raised the possibility that the ethnography of *pruebas* could serve as a lever for transforming anthropological assumptions about the nature of ethnographic evidence. The homology between anthropologists' concept of evidence and *santeros*' concept of *pruebas* suggested this possibility, while their difference made it worth pursuing. Given its subject matter, it was proposed, such an approach would in this case have to be 'recursive'. Since anthropologists would assume that the relationship between ethnographic material (such as Cuban notions of *pruebas*) and anthropological analysis (such as the notion of 'evidence') is itself evidential, the merits of transforming the latter in light of the former would have to be borne out in the act. An evidential account of how the notion of anthropological evidence could be cashed in could hardly recommend itself.

So the strategy of this chapter instantiates its argument. We began by testing evidentially the hypothesis that the notion of 'evidence' captures Jorge's concern with *pruebas*. This, we found, would render Jorge's concern absurd, since the indubitable truths of the gods do not, logically, admit of evidence as this is ordinarily conceived. Given that evidence is what *pruebas* nevertheless look like (certainly that is what such concerns have always looked like to classical anthropology), an 'extraordinary' analysis of *pruebas* would be required, which would transform the notion of 'evidence' in a way that could render *pruebas* intelligible. To this end, we found we had to discard the epistemic assumptions upon which ordinary concepts of evidence are founded, in favour of the analytics of 'infinition'. The absurdity of providing evidence for indubitable divinations was thus removed, since the role of infinitions is not to make claims about the world that could be doubted, but rather to populate the world with entities through acts of conceptual transformation. *Pruebas* do not 'test' these acts, but rather consummate them *qua* transformations by prolonging them as such, that is, by transforming them further.

But this is also what *we* have been doing. The conceptual transformation required to arrive at 'infinition' is, of course, itself an infinition. Indeed, the analytical strategy that I have just summarized could be told in the language of Santería. Our 'headache' has been the relationship between ethnography and analysis. Out of an impulse that would appear no less exotic than Jorge's love of the *santos* (it certainly does to non-anthropologists!), we took our ailment to Cuba. Could an ethnography of Santería cure it? Not unless that act was itself understood as part of the cure, was the ethnographic oracle's pronouncement – that is, not unless we accepted that what we were doing was what we were finding: *pruebas*. We could, of course, do like the young woman and simply drop the ethnographic pronouncement, sticking to our initial assumption that ethnography's role is to provide evidence. But that would not remove the headache. So we *took* the ethnographic pronouncement, confirming its ontological purchase by transforming it into the analytics of infinition. Reconceptualizing anthropological analysis as reconceptualization, we transformed ethnographic *pruebas* into anthropological ones. The upshot of the exercise is not only a new anthropological concept (infinition), but also a new concept of anthropology (again, infinition).

To close, we may merely note that the idea of anthropology as infinition effectively draws a line under anthropologists' long-standing insecurities about their relationship to science (see above). On the assumption that the project of science is characterized partly by its investment in the notion of evidence (a contentious assumption perhaps – cf. Latour 1999), our eschewal of this idea here would render the attempt to measure anthropology up to science a straight category mistake. But this is not to throw anthropology into the soft arms of 'interpretation' or 'the arts', as it is often assumed. Rather, the idea of infinition arguably places anthropology much closer to philosophy, inasmuch as philosophy can be seen as a project of conceptual production (see above) by means of what Anglo-Saxon philosophers sometimes call 'conceptual analysis'. But this *is* contentious – though, again, recursively so, since defining philosophy is itself a philosophical problem.

NOTES

Fieldwork in 2005 was funded by the British Academy. I thank Allen Abramson, Viorel Anastasoaie, Patrick Curry, Diana Espirito-Santo, Carrie Jenkins, James Laidlaw, Morten Pedersen, David-Hillel Ruben, Marilyn Strathern, and Eduardo Viveiros de Castro for commenting on drafts of this chapter, and participants in the London School of Economics workshop on evidence, especially Matthew Engelke, Eleonora Montuschi, and Webb Keane, for their many suggestions. I am most grateful to Jorge Luis de Cabo for allowing me to relay his stories.

[1] In fact, nothing is *that* unfamiliar after a century of professional anthropology and other forms of self-conscious travel.

[2] While such 'common-sense' assumptions are often most relevant for gauging the alterity of ethnography, there is no principled reason for assuming they are the only ones. As the anthropological tradition of inter-regional comparison demonstrates, one may set the ethnography of any locality against assumptions prevalent in any other – for an example see Holbraad & Willerslev (2007). (I thank Chloe Nahum-Claudel for thoughts on this matter.) Moreover, since the relation of alterity is to be understood at a logical rather than a cultural level, there is no principled reason even to 'territorialize' geo-culturally either ethnography or the assumptions from which it may diverge (cf. Holbraad 2004).

[3] With respect to the indelicacies of this chauvinism, universalists and relativists part company. While the former tend to bite the bullet, taking it as their task to explain the conditions for the occurrence of native falsehoods, the latter merely refuse to pass judgement, claiming – by liberal dogma – that native views must hold their own 'local' truth. But relativist magnanimity – what Vassos Argyrou calls the stance of 'redemption' (2002: 28-59) – is just an absurd fudge: by law of excluded middle, if the natives contradict our assumptions, only one of us can *actually* be right.

[4] It may not be accidental that the present volume should be associated with the London School of Economics and Political Science, where Gellner's concerns with scientific rigour were formed in (disciplinarily liminal) dialogue with such figures as Popper, Lakatos, Watkins, and Feyerabend.

[5] In his story Jorge did not mention the divinatory origin of the *santera*'s conclusion. But this is only because he assumed that I would know that *santeros* use their cowry oracles to determine (and then to resolve) such problems – divination is the premise of *santeros*' expertise.

[6] For a fully worked-out theorization of this possibility, see Boyer (1990).

[7] An added connotation of the term relates to the philosophical distinction between 'intensional' and 'extensional' theories of meaning. Extensional theories define the meaning of a given expression in terms of its purchase on a world of referents (i.e. in 'epistemic' terms). Intensional theories define meaning with reference to the conditions that would determine such a reference (see, e.g., Chalmers 2002). So in defining x, the extensionist proceeds by asking 'what things are x?', while the intensionist asks 'what counts for a thing to be x?' Infinitions transform intensions (a matter of conceptual definition) rather than merely changing extensions (an empirical concern with the 'application' of a predetermined concept).

[8] It will be clear that this argument is closely related to 'ontological arguments' in theology. As such it deserves a more extended exposition, since such arguments are notoriously difficult to pin down. As Bertrand Russell put it, 'it is easier to feel convinced that [ontological arguments] must be fallacious than it is to find out precisely where the fallacy lies' (1946: 609, cf. Millican 2004). Mindful of the pitfalls, I put this argument up for consideration tentatively, in the hope that criticism might allow me to sharpen it in the future.

[9] I thank Professor David Kirsh for suggesting this.

[10] Compelling as it may have been mid-twentieth century as – effectively – a precursor of Popperian philosophy of science (e.g. Popper 1959; cf. Horton 1967), the analytical armoury of 'secondary elaboration' is just that: a secondary elaboration of Evans-Pritchard's own, which serves to preserve his guiding assumption that oracles make representational truth-claims that could be verified or falsified by evidence. The cost of such a move is charged on the natives. The possibility of falsification, live on Evans-Pritchard's evidential account, is barred only by imputing dogmatism *tout court*: for every oracular 'error' another 'mystical belief' must be added to the natives' tab, its absurd integrity guarded cyclically by its coherence with others.

REFERENCES

ARDENER, E. 1989. *The voice of prophecy and other essays* (ed. M. Chapman). Oxford: Basil Blackwell.
ARGYROU, V. 2002. *Anthropology and the will to meaning: a postcolonial critique.* London: Pluto Press.
BOYER, P. 1990. *Tradition as truth and communication.* Cambridge: University Press.
BROWN, D. 2003. *Santería enthroned: art, ritual, and innovation in an Afro-Cuban religion.* Chicago: University Press.

CHALMERS, D. 2002. On sense and intension. In *Philosophical Perspectives 16: Language and mind* (ed.) J. Tomberlin, 135-82. Oxford: Blackwell.

CORSÍN JIMÉNEZ, A. & R. WILLERSLEV 2007. 'An anthropological concept of the concept': reversibility among the Siberian Yukhagirs. *Journal of the Royal Anthropological Institute* (N.S.) **13**, 527-44.

DELEUZE, G. 1994. *Difference and repetition* (trans. P. Patton). London: Athlone Press.

EVANS-PRITCHARD, E.E. 1976. *Witchcraft, oracles, and magic among the Azande* (abridged by E. Gillies). Oxford: Clarendon Paperbacks.

FRAZER, J. 1911. *The Golden Bough: a study in magic and religion*, part I, vol. I: *The magic art and the evolution of kings*. London: Macmillan.

FREGE, G. 1980. On sense and meaning. In *Translations from the philosophical writings of Gottlob Frege* (eds) P.T. Geach & M. Black, 56-78. Oxford: Basil Blackwell.

GASTON AGUERO, S. 1961. *El materialismo explica el espiritismo y la Santería*. Havana: Orbe.

GEERTZ, C. 2000. *Available light: anthropological reflections on philosophical topics*. Princeton: University Press.

GELLNER, E. 1974. *Legitimation of belief*. Cambridge: University Press.

GOLDMAN, M. 2005. Formas do saber e modos do ser: observações sobre multiplicidade e ontologia no candomblé. *Religião & Sociedade* **25**, 102-20.

HEIDEGGER, M. 1968. *What is called thinking?* (trans. G. Gray). New York: Harper & Row.

HENARE, A., M. HOLBRAAD & S. WASTELL 2007. Introduction. In *Thinking through things: theorising artefacts ethnographically* (eds) A. Henare, M. Holbraad & S. Wastell, 1-31. London: Routledge.

HOLBRAAD, M. 2003. Estimando a necessidade: os oráculos de ifá e a verdade em Havana. *Mana* **9**: **2**, 39-77

――― 2004. Response to Bruno Latour's 'Thou shall not freeze-frame' (available on-line: *http://www. abaete.wikia.com/wiki/Response_to_Bruno_Latour's_%22Thou_shall_not_freeze-frame%22_(Martin_ Holbraad)*, accessed 3 January 2008).

――― 2005. Expending multiplicity: money in Cuban Ifá cults. *Journal of the Royal Anthropological Institute* (N.S.) **11**, 231-54.

――― 2007. The power of powder: multiplicity and motion in the divinatory cosmology of Cuban Ifá (or *mana*, again). In *Thinking through things: theorising artefacts ethnographically* (eds) A. Henare, M. Holbraad & S. Wastell, 189-225. London: Routledge.

――― in press. Relationships in motion: oracular recruitment in Cuban Ifá cults. *Systèmes de Pensée en Afrique Noire*.

――― & R. WILLERSLEV 2007. Transcendental perspectivism: anonymous viewpoints from Inner Asia. *Inner Asia* **9**, 191-207.

HORTON, R. 1967. African traditional thought and Western science. *Africa* **37**, 50-71 and 155-87.

HOWSON, C. 2000. Evidence and confirmation. In *A companion to the philosophy of science* (ed.) W.H. Newton-Smith, 108-16. Oxford: Blackwell Publishers.

LACHATAÑERE, R. 1961. Las creencias religiosas de los afrocubanos y la falsa aplicación del término brujería. *Actas del Folklore* **1**: **5**, 11-15.

LAKATOS, I. 1978. *The methodology of scientific research programmes: philosophical papers volume 1* (eds J. Worrall & G. Currie). Cambridge: University Press.

LATOUR, B. 1999. *Pandora's hope: essays on the reality of science studies*. Cambridge, Mass.: Harvard University Press.

MILLICAN, P. 2004. The one fatal flaw in Anselm's argument. *Mind* **113**, 437-76.

NIETZSCHE, F. 1997. *Untimely meditations* (eds. D. Breazeale; trans. R.J. Hollingdale). Cambridge: University Press.

ORTÍZ, F. 1906. *Los negros brujos*. Madrid: Editorial América.

PALMIÉ, S. 2002. *Wizards and scientists: explorations in Afro-Cuban modernity and tradition*. Durham, N.C.: Duke University Press.

POPPER, K. 1959. *The logic of scientific discovery*. New York: Harper Torchbooks.

RUSSELL, B. 1946. *History of Western philosophy*. London: Allen & Unwin.

SPERBER, D. 1985. *On anthropological knowledge*. Cambridge: University Press.

STRATHERN, M. 1999. *Property, substance and effect*, London: Athlone Press.

――― 2005. *Kinship, law and the unexpected: relatives are always a surprise*. Cambridge: University Press.

VIVEIROS DE CASTRO, E. 2002. O nativo relativo. *Mana* **8**: **1**, 113-48.

――― 2003. *And*. Manchester: Manchester Papers in Social Anthropology.

WAGNER, R. 1981. *The invention of culture*. (Revised and expanded edition). Chicago: University Press.

WHITEHOUSE, H. 2000. *Arguments and icons: divergent modes of religiosity*. Oxford: University Press.

8

The evidence of the senses and the materiality of religion

WEBB KEANE *University of Michigan*

When does evidence seem necessary? Certainly not in every instance. But questions of evidence haunt both anthropology and religions. At least this is so to the extent that they place something imperceptible at the heart of their work. The spirit that possesses a medium, that element of the sacrifice which is received by the god, or the faith that speaks through prayer share this with social order, cultural logic, or hegemonic power: they cannot be directly perceived. One need not insist on any particular ontological dichotomy between matter and spirit, or indeed any universal definition of religion, to recognize the ubiquity of the question posed by the words of Berawan prayer: 'Where are you spirits?' (Metcalf 1989). To find this a question in need of an answer is to seek evidence in experience for something that, on the face of it, is not to be found there but somewhere else.

Yet placing the imperceptible at the heart of religion may obscure certain dimensions of that which we want to understand. To begin, instead, with the materiality of the phenomena in question may set the very demand for evidence on a different footing. This chapter will suggest how an anthropology of 'religion' might benefit from an approach to materiality that does not always expect it to provide evidence of something hidden, such as belief.

In the history of social and cultural anthropology, the category of 'religion' has long stood for the general problem of apparently strange beliefs. Since the beginnings of European expansion, the encounter with the strangeness of other people's beliefs has been an instigation to cross-cultural study. Montaigne's 'On cannibals' (1958 [1578-80]) is an early *locus classicus* of relativistic argument based on such encounters.[1] And the Pitt-Rivers museum, that wonderful Victorian curiosity cabinet in Oxford, is a trove of voodoo dolls, amulets, hex signs, shrunken heads, sacrificial offerings, that have been brought together primarily because they seem to be the material traces of what were obviously (for its European visitors) strange beliefs.

Indeed, the problem of strange beliefs was one motive for formulating the very idea of 'culture' in its anthropological sense. When anthropologists attempted to explain shamanism, witchcraft, or human sacrifice, they seemed to need an idea like culture, for strange beliefs might turn out not to be so strange if viewed in the context of a background constellation of meanings more or less tacitly accepted by those people who were then held to share that culture. In that context, beliefs should not only make sense, they should also be evidence of the very existence of the culture that sustains them. But then the category of religion begins to slip – if we define it in terms of strange beliefs, then explain why, when properly understood, those beliefs are not strange, what remains of the category?[2] I shall return to this in a moment.

Other difficulties have presented themselves. One arises from the claim that there simply is not conceptual consistency or consensus across any given social group. The claim has become commonplace in portrayals of nation-states, diasporas, and so forth. But even in so-called 'small-scale societies', there can be non-trivial differences in what people know about the local ritual system. (As Knight and Astuti argue out in this volume, internal differences are only one problem raised by anthropological practices of belief ascription.) In the ritual system of the Baktaman of Papua New Guinea famously described by Frederik Barth (1975), women are largely excluded from the cult, about which, it seems, they may be quite dubious or indifferent. Men are inducted into its secrets by stages. With each new stage, the previous revelation is exposed as deceptive. So what one knows and what one accepts depend directly on one's gender and how far into the series one is at any moment – the majority of men, perhaps, never quite make it to the end of the series. Such a ritual system not only produces highly unevenly distributed knowledge, it also, according to Barth, is likely to foster considerable scepticism about any given understanding of the cult, since one never knows what might be exposed next.

The problem of unevenly distributed knowledge is vastly compounded in larger and more diverse groups. Claims about uniform or cohesive cultural systems turn in part on how far into the tacit background the analyst needs to go before finding a shared conceptual or moral framework. On the one hand, some arguments against strong views that culture is shared are superficial: from today's perspective, for example, the very ability of the English Victorians to debate the truth of religion depended on a host of shared assumptions. Similarly, it is commonly observed by outsiders that the American insistence on individual uniqueness is something a very large percentage of Americans seem to share. On the other hand, the more you have to appeal to deep background assumptions in order to defend the claim that culture is shared, the more you risk circularity. So what exactly is the background in terms of which any particular cultural phenomenon is to be explained? Or, put another way, what is the proper context for a context-sensitive analysis of the phenomenon? What would the entity to be explained count as evidence *for*?

Another difficulty concerns the concept of culture itself. When most social and cultural anthropologists were concerned with supposedly small, traditional societies, it was fairly easy to identify a religion with a culture, treated as an entity, and both the religion and the culture in turn could be located within a social group. In my own fieldwork on Sumba, in eastern Indonesia (Keane 1997a), with people whose rituals are addressed to specific clan ancestors, I heard a version of a home-grown relativism in the face of universal truth-claims. After patiently listening to the missionary's sermon, the people tell him, 'Your god is good for you, our gods are good for us'. Among other things, such a statement seems to depend upon a close identification of religion with social group. Similar stories have been reported from across the ethnographic spectrum. But those religions that most dominate our view today are a very different matter. Proselytizing religions such as Christianity, Islam, and Buddhism are predicated on at least one shared assumption: since their truth-claims are universal, it follows that, at least in principle, all humans are potential converts. Unlike local cults and ancestral rituals, these religions are highly portable: their scriptures and liturgies, creeds and modes of pedagogy are constructed to circulate (see Keane 2007, chap. 1). Their forms make them relatively easy to extract from and re-insert into almost any possible context. The 'local knowledge' model of religion is not well suited to cope with this (on Christianity, see Cannell 2006; Robbins 2004; Whitehouse 2006).

And yet another difficulty is a more general analytical problem of which the previous one is, in a sense, the empirical manifestation. Is the very category of 'religion' itself coherent across cases? This question is one version of the more general disciplinary difficulty that has been troubling anthropology since the 1970s, if not longer, the tension between its particularist and comparative projects (Keane 2003a). For some time now, anthropologists have been energetically casting doubt on the categories by which their comparisons had been made: tribe, kinship, culture, society, have by turns been rendered suspect. The general line of argument can be summarized this way: conceptual categories take their meanings from their place within larger constellations of concepts. The category cannot make sense independent of that context. This is, of course, one common definition of culture. To the extent that anthropologists have assumed that context forms a pattern, as Engelke observes in this volume, the evidentiary claims for their observations typically depend on showing their fit to that pattern. Such constellations are historically and socially specific formations. Since any conceptual world we want to understand involves its own such constellation of assumptions, any concept taken from one such context cannot be applied to others without doing violence to their internal coherence. (And, as the argument frequently continues, this epistemic violence is often coupled with the other forms of violence perpetrated by empires, states, and other political forces.) At the very least, the categories that were supposed to make comparison possible turn out to be irredeemably ethnocentric.

One response, famously articulated by Clifford Geertz (1983) has been to insist that what anthropologists do best is to grasp 'local knowledge'. And some have taken this assertion to mean that we should abandon explicit comparison in favour of rich, complex, highly particularized ethnographic descriptions. There are a number of well-known problems with this solution. One concerns the incoherence of any claim to be working *only* at the level of particulars, for even the most modest attempts at description are surely in some sense translations across conceptual schemes and thus incorrigibly comparative. If that is the case, then the disclaimers amount to a refusal to take responsibility for the conceptual apparatus that makes the translation possible. With this in mind, I want to turn to the problem of studying religion across cases.

Can there be an anthropology of religion? (I) The cognitive approach

There are two things anthropologists have usually claimed they can do well. One is to expand our empirical range *across contexts* in order to counteract a natural propensity to provincialism. The second is to situate empirical findings *within contexts*, an ambition at least once talked about in terms of understanding 'the native point of view'. The effort to do both at once seems to invite paradox, and most anthropologists have tended towards one or the other side. A glance at two recent discussions about 'religion' will illustrate the problem.

One recent attempt to develop a theory of religion as a universal phenomenon is that of Pascal Boyer (2001). Boyer makes the interesting (if hard to substantiate) claim that out of all possible ideas about the supernatural, only a relatively limited number actually appear on the ethnographic record, and many of these ideas seem to have been reinvented in unrelated societies. Applying the ideas of Dan Sperber (1996), he explains this by asserting that although people may come up with any number of ideas about the supernatural, only some of them will be interesting and memorable enough to circulate from person to person, and to be perpetuated over time. These will be ideas that are based on certain cognitive templates (such as the category of the 'PERSON') that are violated, but only in limited ways (a god is not visible and not mortal, but is like a person in every other way). This allows people to draw inferences that are not explicit in anything they have been taught about the supernatural.

I find two aspects of this theory useful. First, although Boyer tends towards func-tionalistic explanation in his particulars, he wisely avoids the pitfall of most universal theories of religion and does not claim that religion has any one purpose overall. Second, by giving an important place to inferences, the explanation frees up cultural phenomena from an excessive dependence on something like rote transmission from generation to generation.

In this one respect, at least, Boyer is in accord with other tendencies in cultural anthropology, for if there is anything anthropologists have come to stress in recent years, it is that cultures are creative projects as much as they are conservative traditions. Indeed, one of the more useful ways to think of culture is not in terms of sharing or persistence, but rather in terms of a capacity for innovation. Let us take the example of possible inferences in a society in which people tend to think of themselves as highly conservative. People in Anakalang, on the eastern Indonesian island of Sumba, perform rituals directed towards ancestral spirits. Most Sumbanese, including Christians, accept that those rituals were transmitted without any subsequent additions from the time of the earliest ancestors. But most Sumbanese have only the dimmest ideas about those spirits. Where they are located, what they are up to when you're not making offerings to them, how they actually carry out acts like making it rain, are simply not of interest. But because ancestor spirits are quasi-persons, it is possible to speculate beyond what tradition tells you, and every once in a while, someone like the man whom I will call Umbu Haingu, will do so. He was very happy to stay up all night with me, huddled around the hearth, pursuing the most arcane philosophical questions. The rest of the family tended to snicker at us: this was a harmless enough occupation, as long as it did not interfere in his ability to get the harvest in on time. But speculations like Umbu Haingu's just might eventually add something new to the cultural materials available to Sumbanese more widely. Indeed, as I will show below, there is clear evidence of inno-vation in Sumbanese ritual: nothing about ritual *per se* or even ritualists' assertions of their own conservatism rules out this possibility.

There are, however, at least two limitations to the usefulness of the sort of cognitive explanation Boyer lays out. One is the role of universal properties of the mind in explaining cultural phenomena; the other has to do with the category 'religion'. It is perhaps unremarkable to say, as Boyer and Sperber do, that culture depends on the properties of human cognition. How could it be otherwise? But then we might also say that marching, mountain-climbing, football, and dancing depend on bipedalism. They impose constraints on what is possible, but we might not be satisfied that we now have an explanation. Let me suggest a couple of things that the analysis of cultural phenomena, including religions, should attempt to deal with. One is their publicness, another concerns their historical character. Consider first the public character of cultural phenomena. William James (1902) famously attempted to derive religion from certain universally available subjective experiences. Suppose one day I am strolling home from the office and I encounter the Virgin Mary, or at night I dream I have been granted powers by a jaguar spirit, or suddenly start to speak fluently in a voice and a language that are not my own. Certainly people have such experiences, and we may even grant that each involves identifiable cognitive processes. But what makes these respectively a vision, a prophetic experience, and a case of spirit possession rather than, say, fantasies, dreams, psychotic episodes, the effects of drugs, or a sudden head injury? They are instances of categories that are recognizable *to other people*. This is not an automatic business: even in places where shamanism or spirit possession are well accepted, *in any given instance* local communities have to decide whether they now have a case of possession or, say, madness, fraud, or error. Ethnographers who have seen this decision-making in progress tell us it is not at all a foregone conclusion how the decisions will go (Irvine 1982; Wolf 1990). Cognition may provide some raw materials, but the socially relevant outcome results from the irreducible conjunction of a potentially open-ended set of things such as micro-politics, recent precedents, kinship ties, currently available concepts, and so forth. And these outcomes become the context within which subsequent actions and decisions are made.

Beyond this matter of social dynamics, the issue gets to the very nature of social categories themselves. Even unique cases such as, say, the star over Bethlehem or Saul's conversion on the road to Damascus must become recognizable as instances of something that is potentially repeatable (if only in the discursive form of a report) if they are to count as religious, or, more generally, if they are to have a potential for social existence. In order to be recognizable as instances of something knowable, they must take semiotic form. They must, that is, have some material manifestation that makes them available to, interpretable by, and, in most cases, replicable by other people: bodily actions, speech, the treatment of objects, and so forth. This is not simply an issue for remarkable events or the experiences of virtuosi. A similar point holds for spontaneous and commonplace cognitive phenomena, such as the child's invisible friends, or, say, the overwhelming urge to avoid stepping on sidewalk cracks lest irreparable harm befall one's maternal parent. It is apparent that what circulate are not ideas or experiences but rather semiotic forms. I do not have access to your ideas except insofar as they are mediated by signs such as words or movements. Signs have forms and material properties (see Urban 1996). They are also repeatable, but there is nothing to guarantee that they will produce identical interpretations or experiences across time or between persons.

Semiotic forms are public entities. That is, they are available as objects for the senses and not confined to inner or subjective experience.[3] As such, they have distinctive temporal dimensions. Because they are repeatable, they have the potential to persist over time and across social contexts. One result is they can enter into projects that people work on. Semiotic forms accumulate new features over time, contributed by different people, with different projects, in different contexts. The speculations of Umbu Haingu start from certain publicly available givens; most authoritatively, what in his youth he saw and heard the old men do when they were communicating with spirits. One of the things they do is make offerings of metal. A century ago, these were small pieces of metal. As money entered into the economy, over the last fifty years, it has become common to use a small denomination coin for this purpose. But if you do not have a coin, you can substitute paper money. Notice the quiet innovation, shifting the categorical identity of the offering from its physical properties (there is comparative evidence in this region that metal has long been associated with strengthening spiritual boundaries) to its association with value. That is, the relative salience or relevance of coexisting properties of the offering (a phenomenon I call *bundling*; see Keane 2003*b*) has been altered, but not the public identity of the offering itself. More generally, the work people put into cultural phenomena draws not just on ideas but on the properties of the semiotic forms. These properties characteristically form clusters with those of other phenomena: rituals develop multiple parts, scriptures acquire liturgies, gods acquire apotheoses, sacrifices acquire temples. Thus they are historical in character. One aspect of this historical character is simply path dependency: for instance, no writing, no scriptures. However much any *particular* component of the phenomenon may rest on some universal feature of human minds, the *assemblage* is the outcome of contingent factors of historical context.

Can there be an anthropology of religion? (II) The very category itself

Boyer never defines religion, or addresses the important criticisms that have been made of the category (e.g. Asad 1993; Saler 1993; J.Z. Smith 1982; see also Masuzawa 2005), but treats it as intuitively obvious. He assumes that religion forms a naturally existing category centred on beliefs in the supernatural. But can you define supernatural in a non-circular way? Recall the problem I posed at the beginning. What are strange beliefs? Beliefs you do not claim yourself. But if viewed in the context of other people's beliefs, then they should not appear strange. It is a truism (as Boyer himself acknowledges) that if you live in a world in which everyone accepts the existence of witches, witches will seem natural. And can people have a category of the supernatural if they have no category of the natural? One way is to say the supernatural is not subject to experience and is counterintuitive. But nothing in my experience warrants my belief in subatomic particles, and the fact that the earth revolves around the sun is counterintuitive; critics of String Theory say its assertions lie far beyond even the specialized empirical verification available to physics. So how does science, or any other expert knowledge, differ from religion? They differ in many ways, certainly, but not in the presence or absence of strange and counterintuitive beliefs. In sum, there are two difficulties here: defining religion in terms of belief, and defining the relevant beliefs through the category of the supernatural.

This criticism can be merely corrosive if it does no more than lead us back to hyper-particularism. But we might take it in another, more fruitful, direction, away from beliefs and towards practices as the unifying focus of analysis. To start in this direction, I first want to discuss an alternative, markedly historicist, approach to an anthropology of religion. Talal Asad (1993; see also 2003) has criticized efforts to define religion as a transhistorical and transcultural phenomenon in the first place. His argument has two distinct aspects, which I think can be treated separately. The first is that there cannot be a universal definition of religion because any such definition is itself a historical and parochial product. More specifically, the effort to define religion as a universal arises, he says, from certain problems within *Christianity*. Faced with competing creeds and the rise of natural science, the goal of such universal definitions was to find an underlying common essence that could be abstracted from concrete but divergent practices. According to Asad, the first efforts to produce a universal definition of religion appeared in the seventeenth century, after the fragmentation of Reformation, the wars of religion, and the first serious encounters with Asian religions. Taking Lord Herbert's account of Natural Religion as paradigmatic, he says its 'emphasis on beliefs meant that henceforth religion could be conceived as a set of propositions to which believers gave assent' (1993: 41).

The criticism of the category 'religion' as having a parochial origin is in itself problematic if we take it only to mean that we cannot make use of analytic categories, since they necessarily arise out of particular contexts. One approach is to claim we can find 'natural kinds'; another is to grant ourselves the heuristic device of ideal types. But Asad has something more specific in mind. This has to do with the way universalizing definitions of religion have tended to privilege *belief* as a cognitive and ultimately private or subjective phenomenon. Many familiar objections and alternatives have been posed against this privileging of belief (within anthropology, see, e.g., Douglas 1982; Needham 1972; Rappaport 1999; W.R. Smith 1969 [1927]). Asad raises two challenges in particular. The first is that the emphasis on belief had tended to fold into a further claim that those beliefs concern ultimate meanings – what is the purpose of life, what happens after death, how did it all begin, what are the foundations of morality? But by those terms, many of the things people do that we might want to count as religious – including Umbu Haingu's ancestral rituals – are simply ruled out of court. The apparently neutral description turns out, on examination, to be normative. For the Victorians, those who lack religion as understood in these terms occupy a low place on the evolutionary scale. Those whose religion is merely ritualistic or instrumental are only slightly higher (here the Victorians show themselves to be heirs of the anti-ritualism characteristic of the Protestant Reformation). More recently, for evangelists and, in places like contemporary Indonesia, the state, people who lack 'religion' under such definitions *require* missionization.

Taking practices to be primarily the evidence of inner states (or their lack) can, in some circumstances, reproduce the authority of those who would judge the condition of others. The demand for evidence, after all, is hardly confined to the sciences (a point elaborated from different angles by both Good and Pinney in this volume). In the courtroom and religious gathering, the demand for evidence can be the prerogative of power. Asad's argument, arising in the context of religious politics in the contemporary world, bears a sharp political edge.

In addition, any definition of religion that privileges particular subjective experiences or beliefs risks being circular. To avoid this, the category of religion must be capable of including not just the ardently faithful but the bored schoolboy who has memorized a credo which he recites by rote. To say the latter is not really 'religious' is to make the definition of religion, as a matter of genuine, wholehearted faith, self-confirming. I would argue that we need that schoolboy.[4] With the possible exception of divine revelation unmediated by any prior practices, institutions, or discourses (but even then, it must take semiotic form if it is to go further), belief ontogenically follows on practice.[5] The child learns a prayer, or listens to scripture in a foreign language like Latin or Arabic, or sees her grandmother go into trance, or helps the priest by holding a sacrificial chicken. She may develop beliefs as a result, but in most cases, at least, they depend on the prior existence of the practices.[6] This does not mean that beliefs are *determined* by practices. Quite the contrary, as the bored schoolboy should tell us. But even the most spiritualized of scriptural religions teach doctrines through concrete activities, such as catechisms, sermons, scripture-reading, exegesis. Even Saul's conversion experience on the road to Damascus had to become communicable in some form that made it recognizable to others.

Asad's second objection to universal definitions of religion in terms of propositions and meanings is this: if we ignore the processes by which meanings are constructed, then we separate religion from the domain of power. Yet even within Christianity, the power of disciplines to construct dispositions to believe was a central concern for, say, Saint Augustine. It is only with the rise of modern science and states, and the privatization of religion, Asad argues, that it makes sense to see religion as a state of *mind* rather than as practical knowledge of institutions and rules that orientates effective *activity*. It is a historically peculiar matter to see religion as a sphere quite apart from where the action is at.

There are therefore several reasons to start with material practices and not beliefs. One is that many religious traditions have little interest in either individual belief or public statements of doctrine. They may accept differences of interpretation as long as practices themselves remain consistent. What *is* of recurring significance is the question 'What can or must we do?' Moreover, even religions that *do* stress belief may still object to the subordination of material practices to inner states. For instance, Blaise Pascal insisted,

> The external must be joined to the internal to obtain anything from God, that is to say, we must kneel to pray with the lips, etc., in order that proud man, who would not submit himself to God, may be now subject to the creature ... [To] refuse to join [externals] to the internal is pride (1958 [1669]: 250).

The very existence of a practice may be the basis for moral judgement (see Rappaport 1999), and its semiotic form a component of its morality (Keane 2008; see Hirschkind 2006; Mahmood 2005).

Towards a comparative category: 'religious language'

Can we define religion in a way that takes seriously the perspective of its practitioners and can still guide research across contexts without inviting paradox? Can we do so in a way that respects the historicity of the phenomena, without returning to full-fledged particularism? It might be more productive to start not with 'religion' as a totality but with more limited domains of activity, bearing in mind the heterogeneous character of any particular conjunction of such domains. Here I will focus on linguistic activity. Although this is a selective focus, it is not arbitrary. For one thing, religions very often focus on language as a source of difficulty or of power – Quaker silence, Pentecostal speaking in tongues, Hindu and Buddhist mantras, Sumbanese couplets, and the use of opaque liturgical languages such as Arabic in Indonesia and Latin in colonial Africa can all be seen as responses to the properties of language (Keane 1997b).[7] Linguistic practices are especially interesting in the context of questions of belief, of course, because they so often seem to point us in the direction of thoughts. But this is a conclusion about which we should be very cautious. Instead, an examination of religious language may be more useful as a guide to how we might understand religious practices more generally, attending to their forms, pragmatics, and the semiotic ideologies they presuppose.

Let me start with a rather unorganized list. Reviewing ethnographic descriptions of ritual speech, the linguist John Du Bois (1986) identified some recurrent features:

- archaistic elements;
- use of a special register;
- elements borrowed from other languages;
- euphemism and metaphor;
- semantic opacity;
- semantic-grammatical parallelism;
- marked voice quality;
- stylized and restricted intonation contours;
- unusual fluency of speech;
- gestalt knowledge;
- personal volition disclaimers;
- avoidance of first- and second-person pronouns;
- speech style attributed to ancestors;
- use of mediating speakers.

This is a rather heterogeneous collection. As a first step towards organizing this list, we might observe that some of these items seem to be mutually determined. Fluent speaking style and gestalt knowledge, for instance, can both result from learning entire texts as seamless, and sometimes semantically opaque, wholes. Overall, however, these features must be understood as bearing family resemblances, insofar as they do not constitute necessary and sufficient conditions for membership in a set, but form linked clusters such that no single member of the family need possess every feature. But viewing this cluster in terms of pragmatic functions and semiotic characteristics may offer a way of widening our scope from ritual speech to religious language practices more generally.

These features seem to impose on ritual speech some markedness relative to other ways of speaking, a sense of being unusual. Moreover, to the practitioners, they seem either to involve some sort of difficulty of achievement or, simply, to make language itself the object of some kind of work. Ritual speech – in fact, religious language more generally – may demand extra control or aim to release language from control, to become more spontaneous; it may aim to make language more elaborate, or to simplify it. So, as an initial minimalist definition, let us suggest that 'religious language' concerns linguistic practices that are taken *by practitioners themselves* to be marked or unusual in some respect.

The background against which they are marked, however, is not necessarily a universal set of conversational norms. It may be nothing more than the assumptions of more specific ideologies of language. Language ideology refers to the ways in which language uses are always mediated by some prevailing local assumptions about what language is and how it functions (see Kroskrity 2000). Is the prototypical speech-act referring to objects and the making of predications about them, or is it a promise between two individuals, or a command between two hierarchical statuses? Is language a set of arbitrary signs established by social convention or is it a divine emanation expressing the true, if hidden, essence of the world? How you use words will depend in part on such assumptions.

The definition of religious language I have offered cannot claim to cover all activities that have been called religious. Nor, of course, are all marked forms of language taken by their users to be 'religious'. Languages of law, science, and poetry, for instance, may share many of these features. So this definition can only be a starting-point. But it does aim to satisfy the two opposed demands on the anthropologist: *to take practitioners' own perceptions as a guide, without foreclosing the possibility of comparison and generalization.* This approach presupposes that people have some intuitions, or language ideologies, about distinctions of markedness among different linguistic forms and practices. Since religious language practices may involve people's heightened awareness of language (among other things), they offer analysts insight into that awareness and its linguistic and, by extension, conceptual and social consequences. The intuitions or experiences to which I refer, however, are not the source of these practices so much as possible consequences. Beliefs can be understood as parasitic on activities, rather than activities as expressing – or as evidence for – prior beliefs.

Making strange interaction presupposable

Is there something that motivates the recurrence across the ethnographic spectrum of those features of ritual speech identified by Du Bois? The first obvious point to make is that these are instances of the framing function that can, in principle, be achieved by any linguistic property, such as esoteric vocabulary or unusual intonation that marks off a stretch of discourse from its surround. As such, a frame is indexical, that is, it points out something in the immediate context – indicating, for instance, 'this, now' is a ritual. But although indexes point, in themselves they do not furnish any information about what they are pointing to. Some further guidance is required. To the extent that what is being indexed is an instance of a publicly recognized speech genre, the frame is 'metapragmatic', that is, it says something about the kind of linguistic act being undertaken (see Silverstein 1993; 2003). As such, this specification is achieved by local language ideologies. But these can vary and change in partial independence of the linguistic forms they concern.

By emphasizing the formal properties of religious language, and their markedness, we can start to go beyond imputing the experiential effects of ritual to convention or belief. Rather, we can ask how those experiential effects derive from ritual forms as they unfold in real time. For example, Sumbanese rituals commonly display increasing depersonalization and decontextualization over the course of the event (Kuipers 1990). Indexes of the present time, place, or participants such as personal pronouns may be progressively eliminated; poetic formulae, prosodic regularity, and other regimentations of discourse becoming more stringent, such that the participants come increasingly to speak not as individuated, complex, politically interested, and temporally finite parties, but as more abstract, disinterested, and timeless elders or spirits. The outcome is due not wholly to convention or conscious intention but to subliminal effects of linguistic and pragmatic forms, regardless of any particular beliefs held by participants. This does not mean that belief plays no part in any given instance. But what those particular beliefs are and what role they play may vary enormously. It is likely to be the formal properties that remain consistent across contexts, a point to whose implications I return below.

I want to suggest that the semiotic properties of religious language commonly help make present what would otherwise, in the course of ordinary experience, be absent or imperceptible, or make that absence presupposable by virtue of the special means used to overcome it. In pragmatic terms, ritual often counteracts any assumption that one's interlocutors can see and hear one, that they share one's language, and that the relevant shared context and conversational goals are unproblematic. Ritual pragmatics, in effect, can provide intuitive evidence of the experiential absence they confront, that starting-point which is made explicit in the Berawan question I have already quoted, 'Where are you spirits?' As Holbraad suggests in this volume, evidence may be an offer less of truth than of a relationship.

The peculiar or marked forms and uses of language I am calling religious are constructed in such as way as to suggest, often in only the most implicit ways, that they involve entities or modes of agency which are considered by those practitioners to be consequentially distinct from more 'ordinary' experience or situated across some sort of ontological divide from something understood as a more everyday 'here and now'. By 'ontological divide' I mean that practitioners understand the difference to be a quali-tative one, as between kinds of things, rather than, say, simple spatial distance. The distinction is not, of course, always clear – the lines separating elders, ancestors, and deities, or otherworlds and distant places, may be quite blurred indeed. But there is another point to stress. We should not assume that the ontological divide is given in advance by belief. In some religious contexts, it may be precisely the function of language to raise questions like 'what's going on here?' and 'who's speaking now?' The practice is just as likely to provoke such questions, as it is merely to express or respond to them. There may be no particular answer.

Context and text

Forms that decontextualize discourse help create a perception that certain chunks of speech are self-contained, belong together, and could be reproduced in different con-texts without substantive consequences for the discourse itself. This results in what has been called a 'decentring of discourse' through what the linguistic anthropologists Michael Silverstein, Greg Urban (Silverstein & Urban 1996), and their colleagues have dubbed entextualization, the process of foregrounding the text-like and therefore context-independent properties of discourse. The words will seem to come from some source beyond the present situation in which they are being spoken and heard. Often the speakers seem to others or even themselves to have relatively little volition in producing their speech. They may be supposed, for instance, to be speaking exactly as the ancestors did, as the spirits who possess them dictate, or as has been written. Compelling examples of the dialectic of recontextualization are found in the use of scriptures among contemporary Christians. Certain parts of scripture, such as Christ's Sermon on the Mount or the Lord's Prayer, are taken by many believers to reproduce words that were originally spoken in a particular context. Circulating in textual form, the words are now available for broad dissemination. Indeed, some believers take a capacity for wide circulation, found, for example, in videotaped sermons, as evidence of the divinity of words even when they are not themselves sacred scripture (Coleman 2000).

Effects of linguistic form are likely to seem especially persuasive and realistic because they are not derived from explicit doctrines, which one might doubt or deny, but seem to come directly from experience. The decentring of discourse is one moment in a larger set of dialectical processes. These processes also include the centring or contex-tualizing of discourses which stress the relatively subjective experiences of language, such as the experience of inner speech and speaker's intentionality. The material properties of discourse, then, are relatively autonomous of anything they might be taken as evidence for. This permits them to function across contexts and to function independent of any particular evidentiary questions at all.

Since the experience of linguistic form is relatively independent of any particular intentions of or interpretations by language-users, people's responses to that experience will be historically variable. Suspicions of language in some religious traditions, such as Quakerism (Bauman 1983) or the Masowe apostolics (Engelke 2007), focus on the very same linguistic and pragmatic properties that other traditions may seek to exploit. To the extent that religious practices respond to or contribute to the perception of an ontological gap contrary to the assumptions of ordinary interaction, they may be prone to draw on the decentring and recentring possibilities of entextualization processes. For religions 'of the book', the very existence of a written scripture is often taken as evidence for claims to an authority that transcends any particular context, and provides semiotic grounds for their intuitive verification. But the same decontextualizing objectivity may become the target of reformers and critics who seek more direct access to divinity.

Voice and agency

Ways of reporting speech commonly express aspects of the relations among participants in a speech event or text (Vološinov 1973 [1930]). Responsibility for words can range from a sharp hierarchical distinction between what Erving Goffman (1981) called the author and the animator, to some degree of co-authorship or ambiguity. Differences in linguistic form can serve, under socially specified conditions, as evidence for differences in responsibility for what claims the words make, or actions they carry out (Hill & Irvine 1993). According to William Graham (1977; 1987), early Islam did not differentiate between the authority of words spoken by God and those spoken by the Prophet Muhammad. In the Qur'an, God's words appear as reported speech, and so are also the Prophet's words, as he is their animator. But Muhammad also animates prophetic speech of which he is the author – although its principal remains the divine source of his inspiration. Eventually, however, it became theologically important to distinguish prophetic speech from direct revelation, sharpening the boundary between reported speech and its frame, and thus between animator and author. This placed the original prophecy and its divine author at a greater remove from historical events, in order to accentuate the otherworldliness of the divinity and prevent the deification of the prophet.

One of the stakes in the precise distinction between author and animator is the degree of agency, authority, and responsibility a performer is willing or permitted to assume. Sumbanese ritualists insist that the most powerful words are those that come from absent authors. The forms of reported speech they deploy help make such distance (or its reverse) presupposable. In the US, evangelical Protestants often describe their conversion as a call to witness, testify, or preach to others (Harding 2000). Often this does not involve any particular change in *belief*, if we mean the doctrines to which they subscribe. Rather, in such cases, full conversion consists in becoming enabled to speak scriptural language with authority.

Such examples show imputed authorship to have creative effects, by making available to speakers an identity or a relationship to some special agent. This is an instance of the broader point, that one widespread effect of religious language is the creation or extension of agents and forms of agency beyond what is commonly available in unmarked interaction. Many of the effects of religious language can be better understood as expanding the presumptive speaker *above* the level of the individual (as I have argued is the case in Sumbanese ritual, see Keane 1997a). But the reverse may also occur, distinguishing among different voices *below* that level, emanating from a single body. As American folk preachers come to be 'filled with the spirit', their performances display emergent features such as highly rhythmical, repetitive utterances, marked vocabulary, gasping, and shouting (Titon 1988). These are taken to index the individual's loss of personal control in favour of a divine agent. More generally, spirit possession and glossolalia involve both a deity and human being using the same body but speaking in different voices, marked by contrasting prosodic and paralinguistic features, and sometimes distinct linguistic codes. The formal properties of highly ritualized performances often play down the agency of the living human participants in favour of powers ascribed to other entities. Conversely, modernist or reformist movements may place a great emphasis on cultivating sincere speaker intentionality, as in the demand that prayer be spontaneous.

The emphasis on sincere intentions usually manifests language ideology that privileges individual interiority. The encounter between this ideology and actual linguistic activities can have interesting consequences. For example, Swedish Evangelicals expect conscious individual intentions to be the source of human linguistic expressions. Therefore, when under stress they utter words they did not intend, they see the hand of divine agency (Stromberg 1993). Similarly, Catholic Charismatics tell rounds of stories that, like many group conversations, tend to develop a thematic unity over time. In light of their assumption that speech derives from individual volition, they find in the unplanned emergence of this collective unity evidence of God's intervention (Szuchewycz 1994). Language ideology is crucial to the interpretation of discursive forms. Religious language practices exploit a wide range of the ubiquitous formal and pragmatic features of everyday language in ways that help make available to experience and thought the very ontological divides to which they offer themselves as a response. These practices can assist the construction of forms of agency that are expanded, displaced, distributed, or otherwise different from – but clearly related to – what are already available.

Creed and belief

Creeds are part of a larger set of genres, including sermons, scripture-reading, and some kinds of prayer, that re-contextualize certain texts into liturgical and everyday practice. The creed, an explicit statement of religious tenets and norms for its verbal performance, is unique to the evangelizing, scripture-based religions (Christianity and Islam). The creed does a number of things that contribute to the global circulation of evangelical religion: it gives doctrine an explicit form; it places the primary locus of religion in the believer, not institutions; it dwells on differences among religions; and by taking textual form, it makes religion highly portable across contexts. The circulation of modular forms such as creeds works against the localizing forces on which anthropologists of global religions have tended to focus. This lack of location is part of their practical power.

A creed normally looks like a series of propositions about the world. But they are peculiar in certain respects. First, usually they are formulaic, condensing complex arguments about doctrine into a readily learned and reproduced form. Moreover, the propositions are attached to a performative of assent. The creed states an objective claim (it is the case that 'Jesus is the Son of God'). As such it appears to be merely a proposition. But it has performative force; the Nicene creed begins 'We believe'. It asserts the speaker's alignment with the claims ('Jesus is the Son of God' is true about the world, and I hold that it is true). Moreover, it publicly reports this alignment ('Jesus is the Son of God' is true about the world, and I hold that it is true, and I hereby state so – that is, I take responsibility for the match between my words and the world itself).

The creed takes the publicly circulating form of an assertion. It represents the speaker as taking responsibility for her own thoughts. To be sure, the schoolboy may memorize a creed as mere rote, and certainly many ritualized public recitations of the creed do not seem to demand much personal responsibility. But the persistent recurrence of religious reform movements suggests that the semiotic form of the creed entails a normative tilt towards taking responsibility for those words, making them one's own. Since they are supposed to be transparent to one's inner thoughts, this stance towards one's own words is a model for both sincerity and responsibility. The practice of speaking a creed helps convey a norm of being able to objectify thoughts as words, and, by avowing them in this way, taking responsibility for them. It thus encourages a distinction between the abstraction of thought and the materiality of its expressions, mediated by the norm of sincerity (see Keane 2007 for further discussion). The centrality of creeds to the conventional understanding of 'religion' in Western society reinforces the assumption that religions are, above all, about ideas.

Materiality, comparison, and history

There has been a strong divide between those who take history seriously and find that it makes comparison impossible, and those whose comparative projects lead them to treat the historicity of their object as inessential, mere noise. I have suggested that both positions at the extreme are untenable. By focusing on semiotic forms and the entailments of their materiality, we may start to develop an alternative to the particularist and universalizing extremes.

Innovators like Umbu Haingu tend to respond to the forms – the prayers, the procedures, the offerings – that experience has made available to them. That is, practices are not merely expressions or enactments of concepts, they are objects within experience to which people respond with intuitions and interpretations. They can thus become sources of new intuitions, habits, and concepts. An important element of the history of scriptural religions is the various struggles between correct dogma and practical deviations, purification and accretion. A recurrent theme in these struggles concerns the tension between abstract or immaterial entities and semiotic form, the indescribable god of the mystic or negative theologian and the physicality of the amulet, universal ethical norms and particular bodily habits, high doctrine and ritual sounds and smells. The Protestant Reformation is defined, in part, by the moment when the very same Roman Catholic liturgy that could have been experienced in terms of divine immanence becomes instead, in Martin Luther's words, so much 'babbling and bellowing' (quoted in Pelikan 2003: 165).

To the extent that semiotic form is an unavoidable component of any cultural phenomena, including those held to lie beyond representation, and involves an irreducibly public dimension, then reformist purifications cannot fully and permanently establish themselves. If religions continually produce material entities, those entities can never be reduced only to the status of evidence for something else, such as beliefs or other cognitive phenomena. As material things, they are enmeshed in causality, registered in and induced by their forms. As forms, they remain objects of experience. As objects, they persist across contexts and beyond any particular intentions and projects. To these objects, people may respond in new ways. To the extent that those responses become materialized in altered or new semiotic forms, those responses build on and are additive to responses of other people in other contexts. These materializations bear the marks of their temporality.

I have focused here on language, but the argument should hold for any semiotic form. Semiotic practices can therefore both furnish evidence of something that is not directly found in experience, and, as components of experience, give rise to new inferences and serve as evidence in new ways. But in their materiality, they are relatively autonomous of those inferences. Even the semiotic ideologies that mediate their place in social life respond to the prior existence of some material forms. One basis for anthropological comparison, then, might be to start by attending to the implications of the materiality of practices and objects, rather than those immaterial things we might take them as evidence for.

Religions may not always demand beliefs, but they will always involve material forms. It is in that materiality that they are part of experience and provoke responses, that they have public lives and enter into ongoing chains of causes and consequences. A few things follow from the relative autonomy of semiotic forms. First, material forms do not only permit new inferences, but, as objects that endure across time, they can, in principle, acquire features unrelated to the intentions of previous users or the inferences to which they have given rise in the past. This is in part because as material things they are prone to enter into new contexts. This is also the result of accumulation: the history of any set of cultural practices is in part a matter of accretion and of stripping away. To revelation is added commentary. Liturgies produce architectures; both require officers. Oral testimony comes to be inscribed; written texts can be kissed, enshrouded, worn about the neck as a talisman, rendered into ashes to be swallowed, inscribed as unreadable but gorgeous calligraphy, appreciated for their literary beauty. Offerings expect altars, altars support images, images enter art markets, art objects develop auras. Rituals provoke anti-ritualist purifiers. Purified religions develop heterodox rites. By virtue of their relative autonomy of particular uses and inferences, their capacity to circulate across social contexts, and their materially enduring character over time, practices are inherently prone to impurity and heterogeneity. Their very materiality gives them a historical character. In their materiality, they properly serve as evidence for something immaterial, such as beliefs, only under particular circumstances. To try to eliminate the materiality of religion by treating it as, above all, evidence for something immaterial, such as beliefs or prior experiences, risks denying the very conditions of sociality, and even time itself.

NOTES

This chapter began as a talk at the Center for Advanced Study in the Behavioral Sciences, Stanford, and was subsequently completed under a fellowship from the John Simon Guggenheim Foundation. The author gratefully acknowledges the generous fellowship support of the Center in 2003-4, and the stimulating discussion of his work by colleagues across a wide range of disciplines.

[1] Although Montaigne's essay concerns practices, one could argue that their strangeness lies in the beliefs (e.g. a lack of moral repugnance where it ought to be found) for which the practices can be taken as evidence.

[2] To be sure, some recent polemics, such as those of Richard Dawkins (2006) or Daniel Dennett (2006), define 'religion' by its very irrationality. But most observers would probably accept that not *all* elements of a

particular religion, for example an injunction against murder, are equally irrational. Conversely, not all forms of irrationality – passions for music, gambling, or sex, for example – necessarily fall within their definitions of 'religion'.

³ As Bloch points out in this volume, the particular modality by which these forms are made available to the senses can play a crucial role in how they are taken as evidence (in his example, 'seeing is believing'). I am not convinced, however, that these epistemic roles are universal. For instance, under certain conditions, hearing is believing, even in the face of worries about lying, a point I develop below. Whether one stresses the one or the other, or neither, is a matter of the particular semiotic ideologies that prevail in any given instance (see Keane 2007).

⁴ Even to understand religious systems that do privilege meaning requires attention to situations marked by the apparent absence of meaning (see Engelke & Tomlinson 2006).

⁵ This claim is different from William Robertson Smith's (1969) view that belief *historically* follows on practice, which has been taken to imply that creedal religions are more advanced than more ritualistic ones. Some such invidious comparison is consistent with Smith's assumption that early ritual was followed blindly, 'in the same unconscious way in which men fall into any habitual practice of the society in which they live' (1969 [1927]: 21). By contrast, as I argue below, one consequence of the materiality of practices is that people can respond to them in innovative ways.

⁶ As Charles Hirschkind (2006) and Saba Mahmood (2005) have argued, material disciplines are essential to the production of pious subjectivity in certain versions of Islam. What is crucial to observe in these accounts is that piety is not, in the end, something wholly internal or immaterial that can eventually be detached from material practices, such that the latter come to be extraneous to it.

⁷ Roy Rappaport goes so far as to say 'religion emerged with language' (1999: 16). Although I do not follow his strong evolutionary-functionalist approach, or his use of the category of 'the sacred', much of what follows here is, I think, consistent with his emphasis on the specific effects that language makes available, and on the formal properties of ritual practices more generally.

REFERENCES

ASAD, T. 1993. *Genealogies of religion: discipline and reasons of power in Christianity and Islam.* Baltimore: Johns Hopkins University Press.

———— 2003. *Formations of the secular: Christianity, Islam, modernity.* Stanford: University Press.

BARTH, F. 1975. *Ritual and knowledge among the Baktaman of New Guinea.* New Haven: Yale University Press.

BAUMAN, R. 1983. *Let your words be few: symbolism of speaking and silence among 17th-century Quakers.* Prospect Hill, Ill.: Waveland Press.

BOYER, P. 2001. *Religion explained: the evolutionary origins of religious thought.* New York: Basic Books.

CANNELL, F. 2006. Introduction: the anthropology of Christianity. In *The anthropology of Christianity* (ed.) F. Cannell, 1-50. Durham, N.C.: Duke University Press.

COLEMAN, S. 2000. *The globalisation of charismatic Christianity: spreading the gospel of prosperity.* Cambridge: University Press.

DAWKINS, R. 2006. *The god delusion.* Boston: Houghton Mifflin.

DENNETT, D.C. 2006. *Breaking the spell: religion as a natural phenomenon.* New York: Viking.

DOUGLAS, M. 1982. *Natural symbols: explorations in cosmology.* New York: Pantheon.

DU BOIS, J.W. 1986. Self-evidence and ritual speech. In *Evidentiality: the linguistic coding of epistemology* (eds.) W. Chafe & J. Nichols, 313-36. Norwood, N.J.: Ablex.

ENGELKE, M. 2007. *A problem of presence: beyond scripture in an African church.* Berkeley: University of California Press.

———— & M. TOMLINSON (eds) 2006. *The limits of meaning: case studies in the anthropology of Christianity.* New York: Berghahn.

GEERTZ, C. 1983. *Local knowledge: further essays in interpretive anthropology.* New York: Basic Books.

GOFFMAN, E. 1981. Footing. In *Forms of talk,* E. Goffman, 124-59. Philadelphia: University of Pennsylvania Press.

GRAHAM, W.A. 1977. *Divine word and prophetic word in early Islam: a reconsideration of the sources with special reference to the divine saying or Hadith Qudsi.* The Hague: Mouton.

———— 1987. *Beyond the written word: oral aspects of scripture in the history of religion.* Cambridge: University Press.

HARDING, S.F. 2000. *The book of Jerry Falwell: fundamentalist language and politics.* Princeton: University Press.

HILL, J.H. & J.T. IRVINE 1993. Introduction. In *Responsibility and evidence in oral discourse* (eds) J.H. Hill & J.T. Irvine, 1-23. Cambridge: University Press.

HIRSCHKIND, C. 2006. *The ethical soundscape: cassette sermons and Islamic counterpublics.* New York: Columbia University Press.

IRVINE, J.T. 1982. The creation of identity in spirit mediumship and possession. In *Semantic anthropology* (ed.) D. Parkin, 241-60. New York: Academic Press.

JAMES, W. 1902. *The varieties of religious experience: a study in human nature.* New York: Longman Green.

KEANE, W. 1997a. *Signs of recognition: powers and hazards of representation in an Indonesian society.* Berkeley: University of California Press.

——— 1997b. Religious language. *Annual Review of Anthropology* 26, 47-71.

——— 2003a. Self-interpretation, agency, and the objects of anthropology: reflections on a genealogy. *Comparative Studies in Society and History* 45, 222-48.

——— 2003b. Semiotics and the social analysis of material things. *Language and Communication* 23, 409-25.

——— 2007. *Christian moderns: freedom and fetish in the mission encounter.* Berkeley: University of California Press.

——— 2008. Market, materiality, and moral metalanguage. *Anthropological Theory* 8, 27-42.

KROSKRITY, P.V. (ed.) 2000. *Regimes of language: ideologies, polities, and identities.* Santa Fe: School of American Research Press.

KUIPERS, J.C. 1990. *Power in performance: the creation of textual authority in Weyewa prayer.* Philadelphia: University of Pennsylvania Press.

MAHMOOD, S. 2005. *The politics of piety: the Islamic revival and the feminist subject.* Princeton: University Press.

MASUZAWA, T. 2005. *The invention of world religions: or how European universalism was preserved in the language of pluralism.* Chicago: University Press.

METCALF, P. 1989. *Where are you spirits? Style and theme in Berawan prayer.* Washington, D.C.: Smithsonian Institution Press.

MONTAIGNE, M. de 1958 [1578-80]. Of cannibals. In *The complete essays of Montaigne* (trans. D.M. Frame), 150-9. Palo Alto, Calif.: Stanford University Press.

NEEDHAM, R. 1972. *Belief, language and experience.* Chicago: University Press.

PASCAL, B. 1958 [1669]. *Pascal's pensées* (trans. W.F. Trotter). New York: E.P. Dutton.

PELIKAN, J. 2003. *Credo: historical and theological guide to creeds and confessions of faith in the Western tradition.* New Haven: Yale University Press.

RAPPAPORT, R.A. 1999. *Ritual and religion in the making of humanity.* Cambridge: University Press.

ROBBINS, J. 2004. The globalization of Pentecostal and charismatic Christianity. *Annual Review of Anthropology* 33, 117-43.

SALER, B. 1993. *Conceptualizing religion: immanent anthropologists, transcendent natives, and unbounded categories.* Leiden: E. J. Brill.

SILVERSTEIN, M. 1993. Metapragmatic discourse and metapragmatic function. In *Reflexive language: reported speech and metapragmatics* (ed.) J. Lucy, 33-58. Cambridge: University Press.

——— 2003. Indexical order and the dialectics of sociolinguistic life. *Language and Communication* 23, 193-229.

——— & G. URBAN (eds) 1996. *Natural histories of discourse.* Chicago: University Press.

SMITH, J.Z. 1982. *Imagining religion: from Babylon to Jonestown.* Chicago: University Press.

SMITH, W.R. 1969 [1927]. *Lectures on the religion of the Semites: the fundamental institutions.* (Third edition). Jersey City, N.J.: KTAV Publishing House.

SPERBER, D. 1996. *Explaining culture: a naturalistic approach.* Oxford: Blackwell.

STROMBERG, P.G. 1993. *Language and self-transformation: a study of the Christian conversion narrative.* Cambridge: University Press.

SZUCHEWYCZ, B. 1994. Evidentiality in ritual discourse: the social construction of religious meaning. *Language in Society* 23, 389-410.

TITON, J.T. 1988. *Powerhouse for God: speech, chant, and song in an Appalachian Baptist church.* Austin: University of Texas Press.

URBAN, G. 1996. *Metaphysical community: the interplay of the senses and the intellect.* Austin: University of Texas Press.

VOLOŠINOV, V.N. 1973 [1930]. *Marxism and the philosophy of language* (trans. L. Matejka & I.R. Titinuk). New York: Seminar Press.

WHITEHOUSE, H. 2006. Appropriated and monolithic Christianity in Melanesia. In *The anthropology of Christianity* (ed.) F. Cannell, 295-307. Durham, N.C.: Duke University Press.

WOLF, M. 1990. The woman who didn't become a shaman. *American Ethnologist* 17, 419-30.

9

Linguistic and cultural variables in the psychology of numeracy

CHARLES STAFFORD *London School of Economics and Political Science*

It is sometimes said that anthropologists specialize in looking at human experience in very fine, even 'microscopic', detail. Perhaps this is true in some poetic sense or by comparison with, say, macroeconomists. Anthropologists do, of course, sometimes focus on the tiny details of rituals, language use, everyday life, and so on. But Alfred Gell once observed that the proper scale of anthropological analysis is the human life-cycle – which, if you think about it, is not exactly vanishingly small (Gell 1998: 10-11).

When I started reading the literature on numerical cognition a few years ago (as background for a project on numeracy and economic agency in China), it struck me that experimental psychologists are the ones who *really* do fine-grained research. For instance, an article by Starkey, Spelke, and Gelman entitled 'Numerical abstraction by human infants' (1990) rests largely on evidence about the reactions of 6- to 9-month old infants to displays of either two or three objects. The key question is whether or not their staring time – something measured by two independent observers, and taken as an indication of their level of interest in what they are being shown – will increase when the number of objects is changed from two to three, and back again. Would it ever occur to an anthropologist to consider *infant staring time* in such meticulous detail? Such things are surely well below our radar. (Note that when psychologists look at a 'small' aspect of human behaviour, such as infant staring time, they typically do so repeatedly – i.e. they seek a very large sample of it – whereas anthropologists often work with very restricted samples of (relatively) 'large' and multi-faceted human behaviours, such as 'the formation of Chinese identity'.)[1]

Needless to say, if experimental psychology seems fine-grained and rigorous by comparison with anthropology, it is partly because it is experimental. Unlike social and cultural anthropologists, psychologists spend much of their time and energy devising experimental protocols in order – eventually – to gather evidence related to tightly defined hypotheses (e.g. about the ability of human infants, at specific stages of cognitive development, to take in and process numerical information). This lends a precise and exacting nature to their work. But they are also prepared, more prosaically, to consider human life and thought in terms of manageable chunks. Instead of asking questions such as 'How do Chinese children learn to be good sons and daughters?' or 'What is the impact of globalization on Chinese conceptions of childhood?', they might ask questions such as 'How do Chinese children learn to count to three?' This scaling down (which does *not* mean that the questions at stake are any less important) makes it possible for them to be more precise about the evidence needed to sustain particular types of psychological claims; or perhaps one should say that the drive to sustain particular types of psychological claims is what leads, in the first place, to the scaling down. (My guess is that the two things go together.) Of course some anthropologists, for example linguistic anthropologists, also deal with the relatively micro, whereas some psychologists, for example educational psychologists, deal with the relatively macro. But as a general rule, psychologists seem quite happy – for better or worse – to eliminate variables and/or control them out of the analytical/experimental frame in order to have a manageable topic of research. Similarly, as Anthony Good notes (in this collection), legal practitioners typically seek to 'prune away "extraneous" details' (p. 47) in an attempt to get at underlying principles. By contrast, anthropologists seem preternaturally inclined – for better or worse – to try to take 'everything' into account.[2]

In spite of these marked differences in outlook and approach towards evidence and scale (which, of course, are far from the only differences between anthropologists and psychologists, cf. Knight & Astuti, this collection), there have been a growing number of calls in recent years for increased co-operation between the two disciplines (e.g. Astuti, Solomon & Carey 2004; Bloch 1998; Cole 1996; Hirschfeld 2000; Shore 1996). In simple terms, it has been suggested that psychologists can no longer ignore, or gently side-step, the historical and socio-cultural foundations of human knowledge, while anthropologists must surely now accept (*pace* Durkheim) that many of their most cherished topics of research – emotion, memory, identity, and so on – are intrinsically psychological in nature. Calls for co-operation are presumably a good thing, but will our basic orientations towards research scale and selectivity stand in the way? Are practitioners of either discipline actually going to cede methodological (as opposed to conceptual) ground in order to achieve a *rapprochement*? Will the kind of evidence routinely collected by anthropologists – our accounts of everything – ever *really* be of interest to psychologists, and vice versa?

Here I want to consider these questions with reference to work on human numeracy. This is an area of individual cognitive development in which, after all, the significance of cultural and linguistic variables is beyond doubt (cf. Butterworth 1999; Dehaene 1999). Lacking expertise in the variety of human cultures and languages, psychologists of numeracy might reasonably turn to anthropologists for help. But the psychology of numeracy is also a field of study in which, to a large extent, the most relevant data turn out to be very micro indeed, at least when seen from an anthropological perspective. In what follows, I will first discuss a recent case in which a psychologist went to the Amazon in search of 'ecologically valid' experimental evidence, collaborating along the way with a highly experienced field linguist – perhaps to his regret. Then I will turn to my own research in China, and to the question of the relationship between micro-features of Chinese language/culture and the numerical skills of people there. In both of these cases, I want to ask how much cultural evidence psychologists are prepared to take on board, and also to what extent anthropologists are prepared – or even able – to provide psychologists with the types of (stripped-down) evidence they want or need. My sense is that practitioners in both disciplines are committed, for the most part without even thinking about it, to their customary scales of research. In turn, this may make it difficult (good intentions notwithstanding) for them to engage seriously with evidence from the other side – which probably seems, respectively, either much too 'big' to be useful or much too 'small' to be interesting. I will suggest, however, that even relatively minor concessions in either direction can pay dividends.

* * *

In a fascinating article in *Science*, the psychologist Peter Gordon (2004) has recently discussed experiments he conducted amongst an Amazonian people, the Pirahã, who have an unusually limited vocabulary for numbers. To be more precise, they have terms which *can* be used to mean 'one' and 'two', but even these are not used very consistently by them. Beyond 'two', there is simply an expression for 'many'. From the point of view of a psychologist of numeracy like Gordon, the crucial (and very exciting) linguistic/cultural variable in this case is relatively circumscribed and (helpfully) can be stated negatively: the *lack* of Pirahã counting words above 'two'. (Note that from the point of view of most anthropologists, counting terms would likely seem a very micro feature of a whole way of life, the linguistic equivalent of infant staring time.) The key question that follows on from this relatively circumscribed variable also seems straightforward. In the absence of counting words, how well will these people perform on non-verbal numerical tasks, such as matching up sets of objects? In some respects, it is not very difficult to find out – although Gordon did have to spend a significant amount of time in Amazonia in order to do so. The results suggest, in brief, that the Pirahã are reasonably good at dealing with tasks involving very small numbers – one, two, sometimes three – whereas beyond this they lose the ability to be precise. However, if imprecision is allowed, they can also deal fairly well with larger quantities by drawing, Gordon claims, on the innate human ability to make 'analog magnitude representations' of a rather fuzzy kind. Language, he concludes, is what you need in order to represent large numerical values exactly (2004: 498).

However, Gordon's data are already being used to support very different theories about the role of language in the development of numeracy. Gelman and Butterworth cite the Pirahã case along with material from another Amazonian people, the Mundurukú, to support their claim (contra Gordon) that 'numerical concepts have an ontogenetic origin and a neural basis that are *independent of language*' (2005: 6, emphasis added; cf. Carey 2004; Gelman & Gallistel 2004; Pica, Lemer, Izard & Dehaene 2004). They stress that the peoples in question, in spite of having very restricted number vocabularies, are able to cope surprisingly well with large numerical approximations.

At stake in this debate, of course, are fundamental questions about the role of language and culture in human thought, and about our ability to think, if you like, without words. But in spite of these grand themes it might be noted – and this is not intended as a trivial observation – that the articles in question (specifically Gordon [2004] in *Science* and Gelman and Butterworth [2005] in *Trends in Cognitive Science*) are incredibly succinct by comparison with articles social scientists might find in, say, *Comparative Studies in Society and History*. For instance, both the crucial experimental evidence (e.g. 'The amazing result was that both groups succeeded on non-verbal number tasks that used displays representing values ... as large as 80') and the crucial descriptive evidence (e.g. 'The Pirahã do not even use the words for 1 and 2 consistently') are cited by Gelman and Butterworth in a bracingly stripped-down fashion that would rarely be encountered in reading anthropology (2005: 8-9). Of course, this is partly a matter of writing and publishing conventions – after all, how much can one say about language or culture in an article restricted to four or five pages, in which details of experimental protocols and results are meant to be the principal focus? But it is also surely a matter of intellectual priorities. At least on the surface, it seems that, for experimental psychologists, one does not need to know and/or say very much about Pirahã life – even about the bits of their life that relate directly to numeracy and numerical practices – in order to debate their numerical cognition. More specifically, although everyone (including Gordon, Gelman, and Butterworth) appears to be in no doubt that culture and language may sometimes matter a great deal, cultural and linguistic *evidence* typically enters these scientific debates in highly circumscribed form.

Of course, the existence of complex – perhaps hard to circumscribe – cultural variables does loom at the margins of the discussion. Gelman and Butterworth suggest, for example, that the lack of number words among the Pirahã and the Mundurukú might have 'a cultural basis'. In the course of their (succinct) consideration of this, they draw attention to the fact that

> Mundurukú culture differs from Western culture in innumerable ways, and it certainly uses numbers far less often than we do. It remains possible that one or more of these many differences were responsible for the differences in performance [on numerical tasks], and not just the lack of a counting vocabulary (2005: 9).

Gordon, for his part, provides brief descriptions of everyday numeracy practices among the Pirahã (such as their rather incompetent use of fingers as an enumeration aid), and his experiments were certainly intended to have ecological validity – that is, to take serious account of Pirahã culture and the flow of ordinary life amongst the people with whom he lived for some weeks.

But again: how much scope is there, within psychology, genuinely to incorporate evidence about the 'innumerable differences' between cultures, or indeed non-experimental evidence of any kind?[3] In an on-line discussion which followed the publication of his *Science* article, Gordon complains about the difficulty of doing precisely this. He says that his original manuscript contained some potentially very important information about Pirahã numeracy, more specifically about their ability/ inability to learn numbers in a *different* (i.e. non-Pirahã) language when presented with the opportunity. In brief, another scholar reported to him that a few years ago an attempt had been made to teach Portuguese numbers to Pirahã villagers. It seems that '[t]he adults had a horrible time with it, the children had no problems (but were later told not to continue [learning/using the numbers] by adults)'. Gordon points out that he had originally included this information in a footnote to his paper, but was 'rebuked by a reviewer who said that such anecdotal evidence does not belong in the pages of *Science*'.[4] (Note that what is rejected here is not 'macro' evidence, as such, but rather non-experimental evidence. However, as suggested above, the need to design plausible experiments may itself lead to a scaling down towards 'micro' features of human behaviour – the two things go together.)

Equally interesting is Gordon's tetchy response (in the same on-line discussion) to the suggestion that neighbouring tribes should have served as control groups for his experiments among the Pirahã. Here the costs of ecological validity come crashing in as a justification:

> I think we all need a lesson here in doing research in the jungle. You don't just walk into a tribe and start doing experiments ... If you want to contact a tribe as isolated as the Pirahã, you run a very high risk of being killed ... [T]o study like this isn't just a matter of holing up in a hotel and driving down to the village, but requires staying for weeks at a time in the tribe, sleeping outside with jaguars roaming around at night, tarantulas dropping onto your hammock, poisonous snakes ... The shameful secret of doing actual field research – as opposed to some idealized design that you concoct at your computer in your air-conditioned office at MIT – is that you take advantage of what is available and you try not to get yourself killed in the process.[5]

This appeal to the difficulty of 'being there', however overwrought, will have a familiar ring to most anthropologists.

However, given Gordon's reliance, in the end, on standard research protocols, does this background noise about cultural particularities, the perils of real life, and so forth, really make any difference? He certainly stresses that his conclusions are informed not only by the experiments but also by his direct experience of the Pirahã way of life. Significantly, they are further informed by the 'background of continuous and extensive immersion in the Pirahã culture' of the two scholars who made the project possible in the first place: Daniel and Keren Everett (Gordon 2004: 496). After all, Daniel Everett, a linguistic anthropologist, has been living and working with the tribe for over twenty years. Who better to give the imprimatur of holistic cultural understanding to Gordon's tightly focused experimental work?

But while Gordon must have anticipated criticisms from fellow psychologists, recent comments from Everett – the man who introduced him to the Pirahã – will perhaps have been more surprising.[6] Everett says that Gordon's very general conclusions about Pirahã numeracy are 'likely correct', but he also says, rather confusingly, that he disagrees with them – pointing out that Gordon's experimental design was culturally insensitive, making the Pirahã do precisely the kinds of things they hate to do.[7] Of course, Everett might have helped the psychologist (his friend and former colleague) avoid this pitfall, but he says that 'during the time that he was working on the experiments, I had my own priorities and offered little help'. He adds:

> Following the experiments, Gordon worked alone in interpreting the results, hampered by his lack of knowledge of the Pirahã language or culture, as well as by the fact that neither [Keren Everett] nor I were available to help him by discussing with him the plausibility of his results, or even the relevance of his experimental design to test numerosity in Pirahã.

So much for collaboration!

Perhaps psychologists who disagree with Gordon's linguistic determinism (i.e. with his view that language is a prerequisite of precise numeration) will take pleasure in Everett's comments. But I wonder what they will make of Everett's own recent, and strongly *cultural* determinist, discussion of the Pirahã in *Current Anthropology*? He claims not only that they lack number terms but also that, among other things, they lack colour terms, that they have 'the simplest pronoun inventory known', that they lack creation myths and fiction, that they have 'the simplest kinship system yet documented', that they have no 'individual or collective memory of more than two generations past', that they do not draw or produce art of any kind, and that they have 'one of the simplest material cultures documented' (Everett 2005: 621-34). These extremely surprising features of Pirahã life, Everett suggests, are all the product of one thing: a culture that makes Pirahã talk only about 'nonabstract subjects which fall within the immediate experience of interlocutors' (2005: 621). It is this – according to Everett – that constrains the development or adoption by them of linguistic or cultural features (such as telling stories about the past or using relative tenses) that are found in most human societies.

Now, even if Everett's claims about the facts of Pirahã life are true, his arguments about the relationship between their culture, language, and thought are certainly open to question (see the comments section at Everett 2005: 635-44). For one thing, a key plank of his argument is the fact that, in spite of over 200 years of contact with outsiders, the Pirahã have strenuously rejected the outside world. He says they ask questions about the outside 'largely for the entertainment value of the answers' (2005: 626). And yet he observes that they routinely trade with non-Pirahã, that they are very keen on buying whisky in particular, that Pirahã women have sexual relations with Brazilians (and sometimes have children by them), and that they specifically asked Everett and his wife to teach them how to count and how to read so that they could become better traders. At the very least, this suggests a degree of ambivalence towards the outside world rather than a total rejection of it – but to say so would weaken Everett's argument for the cultural determination of language.

In any case, I mention all of this because Everett has relied, along the way, on some classic anthropological arguments. Notably, he is a *linguistic* anthropologist and, as his *Current Anthropology* article shows, he is not averse to the micro scale of research typically found in psychology. But like a true anthropologist, he also says that language (including the language of number) must be studied in the context of its use; that one should be extremely cautious about 'testing' people through procedures which are alien to their way of life; and, perhaps most importantly, that human societies and human thought are highly synthetic – everything is embedded in, and connected to, everything else. He, like Gordon, is intrigued by the 'small' fact of the absence of counting words among the Pirahã. But if you really want to understand Pirahã numeracy, Everett seems to be saying to Gordon, you need to visit them over the course of twenty years and collect evidence about kinship, whisky-buying, trading, sexual relations, and so on: that is, you need to collect evidence about 'everything'. (Indeed, as Good notes in this collection, anthropologists often define both expertise and reliability of data precisely in relation to the investigator's 'extent of experience'.) By contrast, Gordon, of course, simply wanted to know if the Pirahã, lacking number words, could or could not do some simple non-verbal numerical tasks such as matching two objects to two objects. This is an empirical question, and Gordon (to his everlasting credit) went to a great deal of trouble to generate what is, in fact, a rather minimal and tightly focused data set in order to try to answer it. It is presumably this evidence which will be taken up and debated by other psychologists – not the fine details of Pirahã social life, and certainly not Everett's radical holism.

What does this case tell us? Gordon's search for experimental evidence is driven by existing debates in the psychology of numeracy which relate to language and culture but which are nevertheless mostly framed at a level below the anthropological radar. He travels to Amazonia and appears to have gone somewhat anthropological, in the sense that he ends up having to explain to his fellow psychologists how complicated things are out there – that is, the Pirahã way of life is complicated and doing 'real world' research is complicated too. In the end, however, his primary task is to show how Pirahã language does or does not influence numerical skills. Taking Gordon's conclusions about language and thought as a starting-point (some might say a straw man), Everett goes on to suggest that Pirahã culture shapes not only numerical skills, but also grammar, collective memory, kinship, art, material culture, and so on. His comprehensive knowledge of Pirahã language and life, the fruit of over twenty years' work, is presumably almost entirely wasted on his psychological colleagues, including (or so it seems) Gordon, for whom it must surely comprise too much information.

* * *

Now let me shift focus to a very different place and a very different context for studies of numerical cognition: China. Not only does the Chinese language – unlike the Pirahã language – have a full complement of counting words, the numeration system has the further advantage (shared by other East Asian languages) of being consistent with base-ten logic. This happens to make it much easier to master than, say, the English one. In English, a child learning to count to twenty starts by learning ten new words ('one', 'two', 'three', etc). Then she learns some *additional* new words – 'eleven' and 'twelve' – which do not, on their own, tell her that she has shifted into a second set of tens, or indeed that there is anything special about 'ten'. It is a confusing business. The Chinese system, by comparison, is a model of clarity, with everything based on combinations of the original ten words. Eleven is simply a combination of 'ten' (*shi*) and 'one' (*yi*): 'ten-one' (*shi-yi*). Twelve is 'ten-two', thirteen is 'ten-three', and so on. This (when taken in combination with other features of the system) makes it easier for very young children to grasp that eleven is ten plus one and that twelve is ten plus two – and, more importantly, that there is something special about 'ten'.

Now, this difference in counting words may seem a rather minor linguistic phenomenon, since children using either the Chinese or English system can perfectly well learn how to count. (And, like infant staring time, it is the kind of thing most anthropologists would scarcely notice.) Reviewing the evidence, however, Geary suggests that children who learn to count in Chinese (and associated East Asian languages) have some significant advantages over those who do not. They appear to 'make fewer counting errors; understand counting and number concepts at an earlier age; make fewer problem-solving errors in arithmetic; and understand basic arithmetical concepts, such as place value and trading, at a much younger age than their American and European peers' (Geary 1994: 244; cf. Geary, Bow-Thomas, Liu & Siegler 1996; for converging evidence from Korea and Japan, see Fuson & Kwon 1992; Miura 1987; Miura, Kim, Chang & Okamoto 1988; Miura, Okamoto, Kim, Steere & Fayol 1993).

Of course, by the time this happy outcome is achieved, a number of variables other than language – such as schooling and parental pressure – may have intervened, and these, too, are discussed in the literature. For this reason, it is instructive to compare the Chinese case with the Pirahã one outlined above. For the Pirahã, the relatively simple claim (as formulated by Gordon within the framework of developmental cognitive science) is that they do not have many number words, and this limits their ability to carry out numerical tasks beyond very small numbers. This is shown experimentally. In the Chinese case, the relatively complex claim (as formulated by Geary within the framework of developmental cognitive science *and* educational psychology) is that the system of number words contributes in positive ways to the development of children's numerical/arithmetical skills. The support for this claim has to be built up from separate bits of evidence (e.g. about children's counting error rates, or about their grasp of basic concepts at different ages, by comparison with non-Chinese children). Even then, because of the conflation of many factors in China which might produce the observed outcomes (ranging from schooling, to abacus training, to parental pressure), the educational psychology claim is undoubtedly harder to sustain – and perhaps in some ways more anthropological? – than the Amazonian one. It is a synthetic claim, based on the aggregation of different studies, and probably more open to refutation.

In any case, because Chinese counting terms (forgetting about schools, abacuses, parents, etc.) provide a powerful illustration of how linguistic/cultural variables shape numerical skills, they have been repeatedly cited and discussed in the psychological literature (e.g. in Butterworth 1999: 129-33; Dehaene 1999: 91-106; Fuson & Kwon 1992; Miller, Smith, Zhu & Zhang 1995). Here is proof that culture really *does* have an impact on numerical cognition. And I suspect that many psychologists, in their eagerness to use cultural illustrations of this kind, find it hard to resist a form of cultural butterfly collecting – which is not without its dangers.

In neuropsychology, for example, each 'cultural case' becomes – or so it seems to me – the equivalent of cases of patients with brain function impairments of various kinds, and in this sense the more exotic the better. This is for the good reason that highly unusual constraints (such as severe brain impairments following accidents, or highly atypical counting systems) may reveal a great deal about human thinking. (There is an irony here, given that many anthropologists are attracted to cognitive science precisely because it appears to offer an escape from the endless exoticism and circularity of cultural relativism.) In the index of *The number sense*, written by the neuropsychologist Stephan Dehaene (1999), there are entries for Aborigines, Arabs, Aztecs, Chinese, Dutch, Egyptians, French, Germans, Greeks, and so on. The index to Brian Butterworth's *The mathematical brain* (1999) – he is also a neuropsychologist – refers to Africans, Amazonians, Arabs, Babylonians, Basques, Chinese, Danish, and so on. Both of these books are fascinating and deeply impressive introductions to the psychology of numeracy. But one potential problem with the accumulation of examples (whether it is being done, as in these cases, for the purposes of illustration in books aimed at popular audiences, or in scholarly research papers) is that only an iconic detail or two about each culture is typically up for discussion (e.g. 'the Pirahã do not have counting words above two'), often by people who do not have direct experience of the language/culture in question. And as these iconic details – which are normally iconic for the good reason that *somebody is able to make evidence-based claims about them* – become the source material for a range of debates, their selective nature may be problematic.

For example, in the literature on numerical cognition, only two variables related to the Chinese *language* (as opposed to the Chinese education system, etc.) appear to have come up for serious discussion. The first, as I have just noted, is the system of counting words. The second is the speed at which these words can be pronounced. With respect to the latter, the basic argument is that because you can (apparently) say strings of Chinese numbers faster than, for example, strings of French numbers, Chinese-speakers find it easier than French-speakers to recall long number sequences. This, in turn, has an impact on their ability to do mental calculation (cf. Chen & Stevenson 1988; Dehaene 1999: 102-3; Geary, Bow-Thomas, Liu & Siegler 1993; Stigler, Lee & Stevenson 1986). As a research object for psychologists, this speed-of-pronunciation variable has the advantage of being micro and quantifiable (like infant staring time), thus making comparisons across languages possible.

But if you consider Chinese number skills with respect to the whole human life-cycle – to go back to that gigantic scale of anthropological analysis – both the number words set and the speed at which they are spoken look like being tiny blips on the radar. It is hard for me, as an anthropologist, to see how data about these two micro-variables can be *genuinely* integrated with the kind of ethnographic evidence I have collected about the flow of everyday life in Chinese villages, or vice versa. Obviously, children there embed number words in (sometimes long and rambling and incoherent) sentences, and even by the time they are 12 or 13 years old their 'numerical cognition' is rooted in complex social practices such as learning physics at school or haggling with old ladies when buying vegetables at the local market. Like Everett, I find myself suffering from holism, that is, from an overload of causal variables and a mountain of highly diffuse ethnographic evidence collected month after month in the Chinese countryside.

But let me return briefly to the question of the memory for numbers – which, as I have just said, the speed-of-pronunciation variable is meant to influence. As it happens, I can think of plenty of other things which might influence the ability of Chinese people to recall numbers, to hold them in mind. I shall restrict myself here, by way of illustration, to one 'small' candidate influence and one 'big' one.

The 'small' candidate influence is the tonality of the language. Along with other tonal languages, Chinese is effectively sung rather than spoken, and number sequences therefore always take on a (potentially memorable) melody. Assuming this *does* influence memory for numbers, my hunch is that for native speakers this would rarely be an explicit (conscious) phenomenon, but that it would still influence performance. It is interesting, by the way, to think what directions the general discussions of numerical cognition might have taken if tonality, a completely different type of variable, had been somewhere on the agenda. For one thing, tonality provides a kind of musical structure to language, and numeracy itself is, of course, closely connected to the apprehension of structure and pattern in experience (cf. Gallistel & Gelman 2005).

The 'big' candidate influence on number recall (by which I really mean that it is an aggregate of different variables) is the almost generic importance of numbers in China. (While this may not, at first glance, seem like a linguistic variable, I believe that it can be so construed.) In short, the relevance of numerical information – and here I am using 'relevance' in the sense intended by Sperber and Wilson (1995; 1997) – is redundantly *communicated* in China both through the direct use of language and through a wide range of communicative social practices (Stafford 2003). To give an obvious illustration: Chinese religion and cosmology are very numerical/mathematical in orientation. It is therefore widely assumed that numbers (and the manipulation of numbers) may reveal significant things about the fate of individuals in the flow of time. Following on from this, popular religious practice is often explicitly focused on numerical issues of various kinds (how many offerings to give, how many times to bow, how to read numerical divination signs, etc.). The importance of numbers is further heightened, in contemporary China and Taiwan, by their connection to the worlds of money and business – which, in the popular view, are also thought of as highly 'fateful' and therefore not unrelated to cosmology and religion. I could go on with a long list of illustrations, but the basic point is simple: numbers are crucially important and are explicitly seen to be so by ordinary people. This message of relevance is redundantly communicated to them by Chinese culture.

Now, the educational psychology literature *does*, in fact, make reference to this kind of thing. Geary and others have discussed, for instance, the high value attached to mathematics education in East Asia, and the possible impact of this on the educational achievement of children (Geary 1996; cf. Hatano 1990). But with reference to Japan, Miura says that although social factors such as parental expectations about mathematics achievement 'undoubtedly affect overall performance [in school], it is unlikely that they specifically influence the way in which a child mentally represents number' (1987: 82). It is not clear to me why this should be so, and my interest is precisely in the possibility that a generalized cultural valuation of number could itself have cognitive effects, by redundantly stressing the relevance of numerical information in cognitive environments.

These observations are likely, however, to raise a string of questions from sceptical psychologists – and sceptical anthropologists. What exactly do I mean by saying that in China numbers have an 'almost generic importance'? When does the influence of this variable kick in? During childhood? How does it interact with other variables (such as counting terms or schooling)? Given that the importance of numbers could be expected to vary over historical time in China, and even between different individuals at the same time, what are the risks of treating it as an aggregate, ahistorical variable? And if I want to disaggregate this variable, in order to make it more testable, where should I start? With the importance of numbers in religion, in business, or somewhere else? Finally, how could I prove that this cultural variable actually motivates attention to numbers?

When it comes to collaboration, my guess is that psychologists would appreciate it if anthropologists would come up with ideas like my 'small' candidate influence – tonality. Again, this is partly an issue of scale. It is a relatively restricted point, and one can imagine that it could be tested in some straightforward ways. And yet from an anthropological point of view it is an incredibly small bit of information about Chinese language/culture. How much could I say about it based on my long-term fieldwork in Chinese and Taiwanese villages? Almost nothing. By contrast, I could say a lot about my 'big' candidate influence (the generic importance of numbers in Chinese society and culture); this is the kind of topic that could easily fill an anthropological monograph. However, I suspect that for most experimental psychologists such a monograph would simply provide interesting background noise, awaiting clarification through a process of disembedding, scaling down, and experimentation. It would be like learning that the Pirahã have been trading with the Brazilians for a long time ...

* * *

My point in considering these two cases – the Pirahã one and the Chinese one – is not to highlight the fatal incompatibility of anthropological holism (taking everything into account) and psychological particularism (looking for repeated examples of *one small thing*). Nor do I want to suggest that psychologists, in spite of their interest in cultural/

linguistic variables, are never going to be able to cope with the complexities of culture in the real world. Instead, I would like to conclude this discussion by noting two rather common sins, as I see it, on the anthropological side – sins which relate very directly to the overarching topics of evidence and scale addressed in this collection. The first is the use of anthropological holism as an excuse for avoiding detail, and therefore avoiding saying anything falsifiable. By holding that all things are interconnected, we tend to make falsification of our claims (e.g. via experimentation) more or less impossible. The second is the romanticization of anthropological research, and more specifically the idea that it has an ecological validity unmatched by other disciplines – this in spite of the fact that fieldwork is, of course, a dramatic intervention in the lives of our informants. Would it really be such an unnatural imposition for anthropologists to examine the micro, as psychologists do, using experimental techniques?

Bearing this in mind, and inspired by my reading in (micro) cognitive psychology, during a recent period of fieldwork in rural Taiwan I carried out a pilot project in which I tried precisely to see whether or not I could quantify the 'big' variable I mentioned above – i.e. the 'generic importance attributed to numbers'. Very briefly: I showed subjects a drawing of a street scene in which certain types of information was embedded: colour (e.g. the colour of a girl's dress), written language (e.g. words on a street sign), explicit number (by which I mean numbers written out, e.g. numbers on a licence plate), and implicit number (by which I mean objects that could be counted, e.g. birds in the sky). Subjects were given fifteen seconds to look at the drawing, after which it was taken away and they were asked a series of questions about the content – such as 'What colour is the dog?', 'What is the number on the house?', 'How many trees are there?', and so on. A sample of respondents from the UK, approximately matched in terms of age and educational level, provided a control group for the research.

My hypothesis was that the Taiwanese subjects – having been enculturated into the Chinese way of thinking of numerical information as having an intrinsic relevance, regardless of context – would be more likely than UK subjects to notice and recall correctly the numbers embedded in the drawing. In fact, the results (based on this very limited pilot project) showed no such thing: the UK subjects were marginally more likely to get the numbers right. Of course, this outcome might be explained in many ways, including the possibility that my research design was completely wrong, or – just as likely – that my hypothesis was an implausible one to start with.

And yet, the simple fact of attempting to prove, through quantification, a general claim I was making about Chinese numeracy was extremely productive for me in a range of ways. One rather simple point is that the drawings proved to be a good prompt for general discussions. The task facing my friends in the village was a completely unexpected one, and it provoked them into saying interesting, sometimes very telling, things about numbers and numerical skills. As well as prompting interesting discussions, the experiment (well, the quasi-experiment) forced me to think – in ways which anthropologists are often *not* forced to think – about exactly what I was trying to say or claim about numbers in China. For instance, the task called on subjects to remember numbers, and from this I would infer whether or not they think that numerical information is, by default, important. But this raises the complex question of whether *remembering* something is the same thing as attributing *relevance* to it. Also, although my hypothesis was that numbers would be shown to have 'intrinsic relevance', a more likely scenario (as I suspected from the outset) is that numerical relevance is highly context-specific. This raises the question of which contextual effects would elicit more attention to numbers, and whether or not these effects, which are very hard to reproduce artificially, could be tested in an ecologically valid way.

In short, simply using the pilot project as a heuristic device had the effect of improving my thinking, as an anthropologist, about Chinese numerical culture and how it is learned and used. This involved scaling down – giving up a little bit on anthropological holism, and trying to be more precise about how my claims and observations could, or could not, be supported.

I have mentioned, in the course of this discussion, variables of the 'micro' kind around which psychologists sometimes focus their own research on numeracy: infant staring time, small sets of counting terms, the speed at which number words are pronounced. Although anthropologists claim to revel in the small details of everyday life – and so they often do – the fact is that many experimental psychologists look at human life in finer detail than we do. They do this not because they are miniaturists, but because they seek to make and support falsifiable claims about human thought and behaviour. The same standard of falsifiability does not apply in anthropology, and this arguably tends to push anthropologists in the opposite direction in terms of research scale. To be an expert in psychology (at least of the kind I have been discussing in this chapter) is convincingly to use evidence drawn from the tiny details of life in order to support claims related to very big themes (such as the relation of language to thought). To be an expert in social and cultural anthropology is, for the most part, to possess a kind of encyclopaedic store of evidence – historical, ethnographic, anecdotal – about a particular group of people. The risk for psychologists is that, caught up in the activity of eliminating variables and restricting scale, they might not see the forest for the trees. (For example, they might get obsessed with counting terms and then not see the full variety of ways in which Chinese language and language use influence numerical cognition.) The risk for anthropologists, caught up in the activity of accumulating variables and expanding scale, is that they might not understand any of the trees very well, and simply wander around the forest making claims that can never be falsified.

NOTES

[1] See also Stephan Ecks's comments, in this collection, about the contrast between evidence-based medicine, which depends on very large samples of patient behaviour, and medical anthropology, which, he says, 'usually insists on the soundness of small samples, which can sometimes consist of [evidence from] just one patient or healer' (p. 80).

[2] As Good observes (this collection), anthropologists 'treat ambiguity and complexity as immanent aspects of all real-life situations' (p. 47). They therefore tend to *include* complicating variables in their accounts.

[3] As Nicola Knight has rightly pointed out to me, the evidence used by Gordon would, in fact, be considered quasi-experimental by most scientists. But it is still of course *more* experimental (i.e. less descriptive, less anecdotal) than the evidence typically used by most anthropologists most of the time.

[4] Exchange between Daniel Casasanto and Peter Gordon at *http://listserv.linguistlist.org/cgi-bin/wa?A2=indo409&L=cogling&D=1&F=&S=&P=2114*, accessed 11 January 2008.

[5] Ibid.

[6] Interesting background information about the Everetts, and about their relationship with Gordon, can be found in the recent *New Yorker* piece by John Colapinto (2007), published after this article was written.

[7] All of the comments by Everett cited in this paragraph are found in Appendix C of the on-line material accompanying Everett (2005), which can be found at *http://www.journals.uchicago.edu/doi/abs/10.1086/431525* (last accessed 11 January 2008).

REFERENCES

ASTUTI, R., G. SOLOMON & S. CAREY 2004. *Constraints on conceptual development: a case study of the acquisition of folkbiological and folksociological knowledge in Madagascar.* (Monographs of the Society for Research in Child Development **69: 3**, vii-135).

BLOCH, M. 1998. *How we think they think*. Boulder, Colo.: Westview Press.

BUTTERWORTH, B. 1999. *The mathematical brain*. London: Macmillan.

CAREY, S. 2004. Bootstrapping and the origin of concepts. *Daedalus*, Winter, 59-68.

CHEN, C. & H. STEVENSON 1988. Cross-linguistic differences in digit span of preschool children. *Journal of Experimental Child Psychology* **46**, 150-8.

COLAPINTO, J. 2007. The interpreter: the puzzling language of an Amazonian tribe. *The New Yorker*, 16 Apr., 118-37.

COLE, M. 1996. *Cultural psychology: a once and future discipline*. Cambridge, Mass.: Harvard University Press.

DEHAENE, S. 1999. *The number sense: how the mind creates mathematics*. London: Penguin.

EVERETT, D.L. 2005. Cultural constraints on grammar and cognition in Pirahã. *Current Anthropology* **46**, 621-46.

FUSON, K. & Y. KWON 1992. Learning addition and subtraction: effects of number words and other cultural tools. In *Pathways to number: children's developing numerical abilities* (eds) J. Bideaud, J. Fischer, C. Greenbaum & C. Meljac, 283-306. Hillsdale, N.J.: Lawrence Erlbaum.

GALLISTEL, C. & R. GELMAN 2005. Mathematical cognition. In *The Cambridge handbook of thinking and reasoning* (eds) K. Holyoak & R. Morrison, 559-88. Cambridge: University Press.

GEARY, D. 1994. *Children's mathematical development*. Washington, D.C.: American Psychological Association.

——— 1996. International differences in mathematical achievement: their nature, causes, and consequences. *Current Directions in Psychological Science* **5**, 133-7.

———, C. BOW-THOMAS, F. LIU & R. SIEGLER 1993. Even before formal instruction, Chinese children outperform American children in mental arithmetic. *Cognitive Development* **8**, 517-29.

———, ———, ——— & ——— 1996. Development of arithmetical competencies in Chinese and American children: influence of age, language and schooling. *Child Development* **67**, 2022-44.

GELL, A. 1998. *Art and agency: an anthropological theory*. Oxford: University Press.

GELMAN, R. & B. BUTTERWORTH 2005. Number and language: how are they related? *Trends in Cognitive Science* **9**, 6-10.

——— & C.R. GALLISTEL 2004. Language and the origin of numerical concepts. *Science* **306**, 441-3.

GORDON, P. 2004. Numerical cognition without words: evidence from Amazonia. *Science* **306**, 496-9.

HATANO, G. 1990. Toward the cultural psychology of mathematical cognition. Commentary on H.W. Stevensen *et al.*, *Contexts of achievement: a study of American, Chinese and Japanese children*. (Monographs of the Society for Research in Child Development **55**: 1-2, 108-15).

HIRSCHFELD, L. 2000. The inside story. *American Anthropologist* **102**, 620-9.

MILLER, K., C. SMITH, J. ZHU & H. ZHANG 1995. Preschool origins of cross-national differences in mathematical competence: the role of number-naming systems. *Psychological Science* **6**, 56-60.

MIURA, I. 1987. Mathematics achievement as a function of language. *Journal of Educational Psychology* **79**, 79-82.

———, C. KIM, C. CHANG & Y. OKAMOTO 1988. Effects of language characteristics on children's cognitive representation of number: cross-national comparisons. *Child Development* **59**, 1445-50.

———, Y. OKAMOTO, C. KIM, M. STEERE & M. FAYOL 1993. First graders' cognitive representation of number and understanding of place value: cross-national comparisons – France, Japan, Korea, Sweden, and the United States. *Journal of Educational Psychology* **85**: 1, 24-30.

PICA, P., C. LEMER, V. IZARD & S. DEHAENE 2004. Exact and approximate arithmetic in an Amazonian indigene group. *Science* **306**, 499-503.

SHORE, B. 1996. *Culture in mind*. New York: Oxford University Press.

SPERBER, D. & D. WILSON 1995. *Relevance: communication and cognition*. (Second edition). Oxford: Blackwell.

——— & ——— 1997. Remarks on relevance theory and the social sciences. *Multilingua* **16**, 145-51.

STAFFORD, C. 2003. Langage et apprentissage des nombres en Chine et à Taïwan. *Terrain* **40**, 65-80.

STARKEY, P., E. SPELKE & R. GELMAN 1990. Numerical abstraction by human infants. *Cognition* **36**, 97-127.

STIGLER, J., S. LEE & H. STEVENSON 1986. Digit memory in Chinese and English: evidence for a temporally limited store. *Cognition* **23**, 1-20.

10

Some problems with property ascription

NICOLA KNIGHT *University of Michigan/London School of Economics and Political Science*
RITA ASTUTI *London School of Economics and Political Science*

Ascription in general

Through fieldwork, anthropologists acquire knowledge about what individuals in a social group tend to do and say. They also progressively become able to make accurate inferences about the desires, beliefs, preferences, and so on, of some individuals in that group. In writing ethnography, anthropologists routinely ascribe such behavioural and mental properties to some or all individuals in their chosen population. In this chapter, we look at some troublesome aspects of the practice of ascription in anthropology. To begin, we need to specify what we mean by ascription.

Ascription refers to the practice of attributing a property to an individual or a group. There are several kinds of ascription, dealing with different aspects of the individual or group in which one is interested. Most individual physical properties can be ascribed after a single observation (e.g. '*x has blue eyes*'). In contrast, behavioural properties, while observable, require at least repeated observation to be accurate. For example, imagine that an observer wishes to state that a certain individual wears hats – clearly, a single observation of hat-wearing behaviour is not sufficient. Of course, this is not to say that individual behavioural properties cannot be ascribed at all. Someone need only observe a consistent pattern over a period of time and report it; if the person in question wears a hat significantly more frequently than others in his social group,[1] then the ascription is warranted. This is not to say that it is an error-proof endeavour: for example, once a working hypothesis has been established (in this case, that someone wears hats), the observer can unwittingly assign more weight to instances that confirm, rather than disconfirm, the hypothesis.[2] Luckily, biases of this sort can easily be controlled by simple statistical means.

In many cases anthropologists are interested in going beyond simple behavioural observations to describe mental activity – beliefs, desires, preferences, emotions, and so on. This endeavour still requires the anthropologist to rely on the observation of behaviour, and to infer the existence and characteristics of mental activity from those observations.[3] This process of inference is more error-prone than that involved in the ascription of readily observable properties, such as behavioural or physical traits, because an inferential step is added in order to understand the non-observable cognitive processes believed to be the cause of behaviour (Jones 2000). The complexity of this inferential process is also compounded by the fact that we do not yet fully comprehend the nature of thought.

To appreciate the extra layer of complexity that this problem generates, consider the following comparison. Celestial bodies that are too remote to be visible from earth, while not observable, can still be perceived in many cases. The discovery of their existence (and the estimation of their location and mass) often derives from the observation of unexpected movements in the trajectory of other, visible objects. Thus astrophysicists, like anthropologists, have to rely on the observation of the perceivable in order to make inferences about the non-perceivable. But anthropologists encounter an additional problem. The visible and invisible objects in which astrophysicists are interested are fundamentally homogeneous. This has resulted in the establishment of standard procedures for locating non-visible objects in space. Thought, on the other hand, is quite different from behaviour. Thinking ultimately takes the form of electrical activity in the brain. Beyond that, there is no agreed-upon description of the form of mental activity except that it consists in some sort of computation. That is problematic, because the neural level is not necessarily the most valuable level of description of all cognitive processes.

Psychology, and the cognitive sciences in general, have not yet reached a stage of development where they can produce laws of mental activity comparable to those of astrophysics. Because there exist no universally applicable formal principles to guide belief ascription, social scientists often use an intuitive process. This, a component of the human 'mindreading' system (Harris 1992; Nichols & Stich 2003; Perner 1993; Wellman 1990; Wellman, Cross & Watson 2001), is remarkably efficient in guiding our everyday interactions with other human beings (and some animals, some imaginary entities, and perhaps even some inanimate objects), and as such it is routinely exploited by anthropologists in the field, even without their awareness. Lienhardt (1961), while describing an instance of Dinka sacrifice, invokes the notion of 'collective concentration' of attention on a single action, and postulates that this is a defining characteristic of such ritual activity. He does not operationalize this notion or speculate on its psychological nature; and yet, as inferred by Carrithers (1992), he is able to perceive that collective concentration is taking place from a variety of cues such as eye gaze, body orientation, and changes in activity. The nature of many intuitive cognitive systems devoted to the understanding of social dynamics is such that they are often employed by anthropologists in the field before becoming the object of psychological research. Indeed, psychological arguments for the existence and importance of the joint attention mechanism as a building block of the human capacity for culture have only recently been made by Tomasello, Carpenter, Call, Behne, and Moll (2005).

The capacity of anthropologists to use intuitive, informal attribution has the distinct advantage of allowing them to understand the people they study with reasonably high success and reasonably little effort, and to pass on this knowledge to others. At the same time, the unreflective use of ascription can lead to inaccurate or misleading descriptions. By way of example, let us consider a typical anthropological ascription: 'The Dobuans are bad sailors, *hugging the reef and disembarking every night*' (Benedict 1989

[1934]: 157, our emphasis). The italicized claim is a behavioural ascription, based on Reo Fortune's observations during his fieldwork in Dobu, and is entirely justifiable – assuming that it is supported by easily obtainable and verifiable evidence. We can guess that Fortune accurately observed that Dobuans did not stray far from the reef, nor did they show any willingness to sail overnight (in sharp contrast with the members of other Melanesian societies). But note that the quote also carries an implicit ascription of a mental property, captured by the evaluative expression 'bad sailors'. In this case, it is clear that by the use of the word 'bad', Fortune intends to emphasize that the Dobuans' tendency to hug the reef does not derive from, say, a religious rule prohibiting high-seas navigation, but rather from the fact that the Dobuans, lacking any special necessity to engage in demanding sailing activities, devote little effort to the improvement of their nautical skills.

It would be surprising if a competent anthropologist such as Fortune had completely failed to grasp the reason for the Dobuans' lack of sailing proficiency; readers are aware of that and so, when reading the above statement, are immediately able to understand what it entails. But not all forms of ascription are as useful as this one; and the ease with which anthropologists produce ascriptions, and readers understand them, means that some misleading ones may well go unnoticed.

There are many ways in which ascription can be misleading. We will focus on what we see as the most common and problematic cases, namely those where:

1.   a property is ascribed to a collective entity, but it is unevenly distributed among social sub-groupings;
2.   an ascribed mental property is alleged to cause an individual's behaviour, but its existence is empirically unsupported;
3.   a belief is ascribed to an individual, although another belief that effectively contradicts the first one is also entertained by the same individual.

The first sort of problem has been recognized by anthropologists and has been, in our opinion, successfully dealt with. The other two, which deal with anthropological claims about cognition, will need to be rethought in the light of what we now know about the operating principles of the mind.

Collective ascription and social variability

Collective ascription refers to the practice of attributing properties to groups rather than to individuals. This is in many ways unavoidable, in that the aim of most anthropologists is to present culturally distributed patterns of action and belief, rather than idiosyncratic ones. However, when a property is unevenly distributed among the members of a society, and its distribution happens to map onto some social sub-groupings, ascribing that property to the entire society is unwarranted.

A number of anthropologists, starting more formally with the establishment of the 'ethnoscience' approach in the 1960s, have tried to show how collective ascription has the potential to mask the diversity present in even the smallest society (Bernard *et al.* 1986; Pelto & Pelto 1975; Rodseth 1998; Vayda 1994). While these anthropologists did not dispute the usefulness of generalized abstraction, they also believe that it should not be the discipline's single aim or sole form of presentation of evidence. Vayda (1994) and Pelto and Pelto (1975) went further by saying that the study of variation is potentially even more revealing than the study of shared properties. This approach takes as its starting-point empirical observations of intra-cultural differences in knowledge or belief and tries to map them onto grouping variables such as age, urbanization, and gender. These grouping variables are implicitly assumed to be (at least in part) causally responsible for the existence of differences. A number of empirical studies demonstrate the existence of, and propose explanations for, intra-cultural differences in a variety of domains, including: preference for delayed economic gratification in Uganda, across the rural/urban axis (Thompson 1975); medical knowledge in a Tarascan community, across age and expertise levels (Garro 1986); botanical knowledge among the Aguaruna, across expertise levels (Boster 1986); and beliefs about the role and significance of breastfeeding among the Navajo, across age and degree of bilingualism (Wright, Bauer, Clark, Morgan & Begishe 1993). It has now become impossible for anthropologists to ignore the uneven distribution of cultural content across adults in any society.

More recently, some anthropologists have proposed that differences between children and adults are also very relevant. In particular, Toren (1993) and Hirschfeld (2002) have noted how, since anthropology is primarily concerned with culture, and since much of culture is believed to be socially transmitted, interactions between older and younger generations are presumably responsible for the reproduction of a large amount of cultural knowledge. In spite of these crucial implications for the study of culture, and of the availability of several ethnographies dealing with childrearing practices, child health and nutrition, and other related matters, no strong anthropological interest in development has emerged. Conversely, the psychological study of cognitive development has generated an impressive number of findings relating to the development of the understanding of the biological world, other people's beliefs and desires, number and mathematics, physics, and social groupings, which are all but ignored by anthropologists, regardless of how relevant they may be to their concerns. The use of collective ascription (perhaps a reflection of this neglect) can obscure the highly important processes whereby culture is acquired, and misleadingly present an image of society where a 7-year-old, an adolescent, an adult, and an elderly person perceive and think about the world in just the same way.

The theoretical stance of these ethnoscientists and developmental anthropologists, regardless of their differences, contrasts sharply with old and new defenders of the particularist approach, particularly of the postmodern variety (e.g. Crapanzano 1980; Price 1998), who, while anti-essentialist in orientation, are not concerned with the *explanation* of variability. The non-postmodern approach to intra-cultural variability, we might say, is concerned with variability that is not random with respect to the socio-cultural environment (Malley & Knight 2008). Many postmodern anthropologists, instead, are in general interested in variability *per se*. Variability, in this latter sense, is perceived as being irreducible to social or cultural categories – or at least such reduction is judged to be uninteresting.

Ascription of empirically under-supported mental properties

The type of collective ascription criticized above fails because social variability is not taken into account. If a property is temporary or in flux, or if not all members of a social group can be shown to possess a certain property to a similar extent, unqualified collective ascription is not an adequate means of description. Other problems with ascription are neither as obvious to see nor as easy to correct. In some cases, anthropologists explicitly state that the property they ascribe to a group is meant to be possessed by all of its members; the degree of intra-cultural variability is presumed to be minimal.[4] There is nothing psychologically unsound about this approach; but if the ascribed property proves to be empirically unsupported, the ascription is unwarranted. Here, we look at two examples: the ascription of 'structuring' and 'irrational' beliefs.

The ascription of 'structuring' beliefs

Naming one of his influences as Freudian psychoanalysis, Lévi-Strauss is well known for ascribing unconscious motives to people that cause their thoughts to be structured in certain cross-culturally recurring ways. Defenders of the structuralist approach postulate the existence of a level of cognition which is inaccessible to conscious thought, but which none the less informs it. Lévi-Strauss, like Freud, insisted (quite rightly, as it turns out) that people are often unaware of what drives them to action. The Lévi-Straussian unconscious, however, differs in significant respects from the Freudian one, most importantly in that the former is not thought to originate in the affective bonds of the family and society (Hénaff 1998). In a sense, Lévi-Strauss adds to claims about the psychic unity of humanity a multi-layered view of the mind, in which primacy is given to the structuring unconscious (the mind that causes) over the conscious (the mind that thinks). But besides the now dated characterization of psychological processes as either fully accessible or fully inaccessible to consciousness, the problem with structuralism and similar psychoanalytic theories is that most of the explanatory work is done by mental structures whose nature and workings are extremely vague. As a result, while they can be invoked to produce plausible *a posteriori* explanations of certain phenomena, it is very difficult to produce a test that can give evidence for the phenomena being the product of these structures, or of some quite different structures or processes.

For example, Lévi-Strauss proposes that all humans are endowed with a 'dualistic' or 'binary' mind. A direct consequence of this is that all sorts of cultural phenomena – ranging from social organization patterns to categorization to myth – are dually structured, one part standing in opposition to the other in various ways. While it is true that many cultural products are indeed dually structured, we should not immediately subscribe to Lévi-Strauss's conclusion that they are so structured because they are a product of a dualistic mind. Indeed, almost everything we know about cognition today suggests that the brain is a collection of specialized mechanisms dedicated to handle specific input (see, e.g., the papers in Hirschfeld & Gelman 1994). Lévi-Strauss's theory can account for the patterns we observe, but it is neither strongly predictive (because all sorts of cultural objects can stand in all sorts of binary, ternary, quaternary, etc., opposing relations to almost anything else), nor does it converge with other evidence about mental processes.

Other symbolic approaches run into similar problems. Jones classifies structuralist ascriptions of cognitive properties as a type within the category of ascription of unconscious symbolic beliefs, which he defines as '[beliefs] in which, without being aware of it, one categorizes things as having attributes far different from the ones that appear on the surface' (2000: 132). Jones observes that the cognitively naïve theory of the unconscious that characterizes such kinds of ascription makes it impossible to decide which thoughts are being processed beyond what can be directly perceived from the environment. This impossibility renders arbitrary the choice of one thought over others as a means of explanation. Jones defends the idea that there are empirically sound ways to constrain the range of possible thoughts taking place in someone's mind at a specific time. Psychological theory, unlike structuralist and psychoanalytic theories, allows one to place such constraints by postulating that the mind is organized in such a way that only a restricted number of related thoughts can become available at any one time. The associative structure of semantic memory is an example of a mechanism that could serve this purpose, at least in some cases.

The ascription of 'irrational' beliefs

'The Bororo ... boast that they are red Araras [Macaws].' That does not simply mean that after their death they become Araras, nor that the Araras are Bororo metamorphosed, and must be treated as such. It means another thing altogether. 'The Bororo,' states von den Steinen, who did not want to believe them, but had to give in to their formal statements, 'quite clearly state that they *actually are* Araras, exactly as if a caterpillar stated that it is a butterfly.' This is not a name that they are giving themselves; this is not a parentage that they are proclaiming. What they want to mean is a relationship of fundamental identity.

Lévy-Bruhl 1910: part I, chap. 2, quoting von den Steinen 1894 (authors' translation)

This is a well-known account of lowland South American Indians recorded by von den Steinen and used by Lévy-Bruhl as one of the main pieces of evidence for his theory of primitive mentality. This sort of ascription carries with it the implication that some fundamental cognitive properties displayed by the traditional subjects of anthropological inquiry differ dramatically from those of Westerners. Debates about the rationality of 'primitives' have a long history in philosophy and the social sciences and focus on many different aspects (Hollis & Lukes 1982; Wilson 1970). Here, we will focus on 'irrational' beliefs of the sort reported by von den Steinen and briefly sketch the two most popular positions taken in this debate – intellectualism and symbolism – and one possible solution to the disagreements, and then relate these three positions to the practice of ascription.

Many anthropologists of the late nineteenth and early twentieth centuries were concerned with showing how 'irrational' beliefs such as those relating to magic were in fact fully rational, given the limited or erroneous knowledge available to people in the specific group in which such beliefs obtained. This approach, championed by J.G. Frazer (Frazer 1976 [1890]) among others, has become known as 'intellectualism'. In contrast, defendants of the symbolist approach like Mary Douglas, Victor Turner, and Lévi-Strauss propose that the language used to express apparently irrational beliefs is not to be interpreted literally. Such beliefs are simply an indirect expression of other domains, ranging from cosmology to social structure to ways of classifying the world and its contents. Therefore, apparently irrational beliefs are unproblematic – for the same reason that metaphors are not irrational. For example, a more recent ethnographer reinterpreted the Bororo assertion reported by von den Steinen in terms of social relations:

It turns out that (1) only men say 'we are red macaws;' (2) red macaws are owned as pets by Bororo women; (3) because of matrilineal descent and uxorilocal residence, men are in important ways dependent on women; (4) both men and macaws are thought to reach beyond the women's sphere through their contacts with spirits (Crocker, cited in Sperber 1982: 152).

Symbolist interpretations of apparently irrational beliefs thus appear to be quite plausible; yet when attempting to interpret other 'irrational' beliefs in the same way, one soon finds out that not all such beliefs can be so reduced to other rational meanings. For example, the Bororo also state that they can have real contact with spirits, and are quite adamant about the literal truth of such statements. Sperber (1982) has proposed an explanation that is neither intellectualist nor symbolist, but rationalist and universalist. He noted that propositions by themselves cannot be rational or irrational; it is what one does with propositions that determines their rationality. It is possible that these 'apparently irrational beliefs' are unlike other beliefs; in particular, that people have a conscious appreciation of an epistemological difference between them and purely factual beliefs. Apparently irrational beliefs are believed, but are believed in a different sense from such things as 'water wets the skin when applied to it'.[5] Sperber, in other words, introduces the notion that commonly used terms used in ascription, such as *thought* and *belief*, may refer to a suite of related, but different, phenomena. The possibility that different forms of beliefs might exist should not be ignored. Anthropologists are understandably drawn to unusual, surprising, or counterintuitive utterances; but when they assert that these reflect a speaker's *beliefs*, they risk producing unwarranted ascriptions. Over the years, statements like 'we are red macaws' have caused observers to ascribe to the speakers the properties of irrationality, of limited understanding of the natural world and causality, and of symbolic/associative thinking. None of these strategies provides strong evidence that the property being ascribed is what is causing the 'irrational' utterance to be produced. In contrast, an approach like Sperber's is more psychologically plausible and open to empirical confirmation. For example, when people reason about apparently irrational beliefs, we should expect that their inferential processes be impaired, producing fewer and shallower chains of inference; that the products of such inferences be less readily agreed upon; and that the holders of these beliefs refer to authority more often.

Intra-individual variability, context effects, and the ascription of belief

In this section, we argue that ascription can fail because of another way in which the common usage of the category of *belief* is misleading. We start by reviewing empirical work that suggests that incompatible representations of a single concept[6] may exist in the mind and be accessed in different contexts, and we will suggest that to ascribe one form of belief when one has evidence of incompatible representations is deceptive.[7] In the following discussion, we take it for granted that there is value in studying aspects of culture in relative isolation. We recognize that this is not an uncontroversial claim. Stafford (this volume) argues that the uneasy relationship between anthropologists and psychologists originates in this very issue, and rightly points out that there is much to be learned by looking at many aspects of a culture at once. Here, as in the rest of this chapter, we have no intention to dismiss anthropological methods altogether, but wish to suggest that the problems that we illustrate in this section can in most cases be circumvented through careful use of methods derived from psychology.

Evidence for the existence of incompatible representations
'Virgin birth' among the Australians and Melanesians
Starting in the late 1800s, ethnographic reports started appearing which purported to show that people in some Australian and Melanesian societies lacked knowledge of the link between sexual intercourse and procreation (or, in other interpretations, of the

sperm and egg fertilization process, and in others still, of physiological paternity). These reports provoked widespread discussion in anthropological circles. In an early review, Ashley-Montagu stated that 'by far the largest number of field-workers assert that the Australians are ignorant of the relationship between intercourse and childbirth' (1937: 176). He also noted how contemporary critics either believed that Australians never possessed this knowledge, or that they had, but then lost it through the acquisition of new and incompatible spiritual beliefs.

Several decades later, Leach (1961; 1966) reignited the debate, partly in response to the continued claims of some anthropologists (notably Spiro 1968) about lack of knowledge of physiological paternity among Australians. Leach, in his typically impassioned style, presents several strands of evidence for his conviction that Australians and Trobrianders are not ignorant of such facts. First, he notes how Roth, the author of the late eighteenth-century ethnography of the Tully River Blacks that started the controversy, reports that his informants freely stated that the cause of pregnancy in animals other than humans is indeed copulation. Secondly, Leach refers to more recent ethnography by Meggitt, which suggests that context may make a difference to how Walbiri talk about conception: '[I]n ritual contexts, men speak of the action of the *guruwari* (spirit entities) as the significant factor; in secular contexts they nominate both the *guruwari* and sexual intercourse. The women, having few ritual attitudes, generally emphasise copulation' (Meggitt 1962, cited in Leach 1966: 40). Lastly, Leach suggests that Roth's and other anthropologists' tendency to attribute implausible beliefs to non-Western people is simply a reflection of their beliefs in the irrationality of primitive peoples. After all, Westerners also have beliefs about virgin birth, but these are imbued with religious significance, and play an insignificant role in everyday life; therefore, these 'untrue' beliefs about procreation should be interpreted in structural terms, as key elements of a cross-culturally recurrent pattern of ideas.

Unfortunately, the evidence is insufficient to allow us to settle the question of what Australians and Melanesians actually knew about reproduction.[8] But it is possible that they had incompatible representations of reproduction in which one version of the concepts was used in everyday contexts (e.g. when talking about non-human animals, and possibly in some instances even when talking about humans), while the other, akin to religious dogma, was reserved for the ritual context and for answering direct questions about the process of social reproduction. Leach seems to intuit this possibility, but he is unable to articulate this in psychological terms because of his reliance on the old anthropological notion of belief that Sperber criticizes. We will return to the question of belief and rationality at the end of this section, after giving further examples of incompatible representations from the anthropological and psychological literature.

Understandings of biological inheritance among the Vezo
During her fieldwork in Madagascar, Astuti noted that Vezo adults invoke a variety of social mechanisms to account for the physiognomy of their young infants. For example, a child might be said to look like someone his mother used to dislike when she was pregnant or like someone in whose company she used to spend a lot of time; the infant's appearance might suddenly change because of a spirit's unwelcome visitation; the birth of a baby with a misshapen foot might be explained by the fact that the mother, when still a child, used to make fun of a person with a similar handicap; and

so on. What is striking about these causal accounts is that they all establish the resemblance of infants with people who are *not* biologically related to them. Therefore, based on what they say about their children, one could conclude that Vezo adults do not distinguish between social and biological causality, as they seemingly ignore the role that procreation plays in the transmission of bodily properties from parents to offspring. This conclusion has great theoretical relevance for anthropology, because it appears to support the culturalist orientation in kinship studies, which claims that people in different cultural traditions have radically different understandings of the process of birth and of biological kinship, often emphasizing social aspects at the expense of biological ones.

Yet Vezo adults are also able to articulate a different view of the processes that give babies their looks. When asked to reason about the hypothetical adoption of a child whose birth parents had died soon after the birth of their son, Vezo adults overwhelmingly judged that the adopted child would grow up to have the same bodily properties of his birth parents, while sharing the beliefs, skills and customs of his adoptive parents (see Astuti, Solomon & Carey 2004 and Bloch, Solomon & Carey 2001 for further details). Vezo informants thus articulated different representations of the process of procreation and reproduction and of the link that exists between parents and their offspring. Crucially, the biological representation is articulated when people reason inferentially about fictional kinship relations. In contrast, when people are engaged in social life, they tend to articulate the non-biological view. By claiming that infants resemble those who are not biologically related to them, people manage to extend and stretch kinship relations well beyond the boundaries of biological kinship.

Understandings of non-human life forms among the Ma' Betisék

Karim (1981) reports that the Ma' Betisék of Malaysia hold a belief system about plants and non-human animals and their relation to humans that contains two irreconcilable views. The first, expressed by the concept of *tulah* (curse), refers to the idea that plants and animals, having been cursed by the ancestors, are fit for human consumption. The second, expressed by the concept of *kemali'* (tabooed object), refers to the idea that 'acts involving the killing and destruction of plants and animals bring humans misfortune and death because both plant and animal life are derived from, and are essentially similar to, human life' (Karim 1981: 1). As in the Vezo case, *tulah* and *kemali'* ideas are often relegated to specific contexts – the former appearing more frequently when people engage in economic activities, the latter when they do so in ritual ones.

Understanding of God among US students

Barrett and Keil (1996) found a discrepancy between the way US college students thought about God when asked directly and while engaged in recall tasks. As the authors expected, participants explicitly represented God as possessing a number of non-anthropomorphic properties such as omnipotence, omnipresence, infinity, non-materiality – in accordance with current theological principles. However, when asked to recall and paraphrase stories, they attributed more anthropomorphic traits to God: for example, they tended to imagine God as moving very swiftly from place to place rather than being everywhere at the same time. This example suggests that the non-anthropomorphic properties that people learn and explicitly maintain to be characteristic of God are not easily accessible when performing moderately taxing cognitive tasks.

Self-construal among Westerners

Psychologists Hazel Markus and Shinobu Kitayama (1991) have argued for a cultural tendency to construe and perceive the self as more or less interdependent, or connected to other members of one's group. They have also suggested that different patterns of self-construal prevail regionally, and in particular that the Japanese and other East Asians rate high on the interdependence scale, while Americans of European descent rate low. More recently, a large number of studies have shown that forms of self-construal appear to affect other aspects of cognition, such as categorization, inductive reasoning, and so on (Knight & Nisbett 2007; Nisbett 2003; Nisbett, Peng, Choi & Norenzayan 2001). Yet, regardless of their broad cultural patterning and wide cognitive impact, these conceptions of the self have also been found not to be fully stable within cultures. Gardner, Gabriel, and Lee (1999) showed that it is possible to make European-Americans answer questions about social values in a more interdependent manner if they are subtly primed beforehand by having to circle plural (rather than singular) pronouns in a text, as part of an unrelated reading task. The effect found by Gardner *et al.*, while not invalidating the findings of Markus and Kitayama (1991), shows that the cross-cultural differences may be best explained by the culturally influenced preferential adoption of a cognitive style. This hypothesis is both plausible, because it does not require radically different cognitive endowment at birth, and interesting for anthropologists, because it offers a way of explaining cultural variability. More to the point, it shows once again that people can hold contrasting and incompatible representations of the same concept – in this case, the self – and deploy them in different contexts.

Theories of incompatible representations and their relation to ascription

In the above examples, the context in which a concept is deployed was shown to have an effect on the way it was represented. It is trivially true that all of cognition takes place within a context. It is equally self-evident for anthropologists that different contexts elicit different behaviours. The role of context in shaping behaviour is a popular topic in psychology (see, e.g., Darley & Batson 1973; Ross & Nisbett 1991), but the possibility of concepts being represented and deployed in radically different ways according to context is relatively understudied. This possibility significantly impacts the practice of ascription. Statements to the effect that:

- Australians and Melanesians believe that there is no link between sexual intercourse and procreation;
- the Vezo believe that bodily properties are socially transmitted;
- the Ma' Betisék believe that animals and plants are human-like and therefore unfit for human consumption;
- European-Americans believe God to be omnipresent and the self to be an independent and bounded entity

are not erroneous. However, they are incomplete, because they fail to mention that virtually opposite forms of these beliefs are held by the same individuals and deployed in certain contexts.

It is true that anthropological terms such as 'contested' and 'negotiated', routinely used to qualify the nature of ascribed meanings and beliefs, are evidence of an intuitive appreciation of the problems of belief ascription. However, such terms rarely carry with them the precision necessary to do justice to this particular phenomenon. The need for a change in language is clear, but exactly what sort of change is needed depends on a full understanding of the cognitive underpinnings of incompatible representations.

While we are still far from such an understanding, contemporary theories of concepts offer some clues. It has often been assumed that concepts are represented by linguistic (or language-like) lists or networks of features. These feature lists are thought to be instantiated in a non-linguistic, amodal form in the brain. A closely related and widely accepted assumption is that concepts are context-independent – the representation of the concept of *chair*, for instance, includes features such as *has legs*, *is used to sit on*, and so forth, but excludes such information as where a chair is usually found. Some psychologists, however, disagree. Lawrence Barsalou and his colleagues (Barsalou 1982; 2002; Barsalou *et al.* 1993; Yeh & Barsalou 2006) have argued that concepts are mentally represented by a combination of generic and episodic information. Furthermore, they have challenged a fundamental assumption of category learning, that the cognitive system collects shared features of concepts while discarding information about the situations in which one is likely to encounter the concepts. According to Barsalou, background information of this sort is stored along with feature information, and influences performance on a variety of cognitive tasks. The information that is relevant for a concept varies depending on the goal of the situation. For example, Barclay, Bransford, Franks, McCarrell, and Nitsch (1974) presented participants with a series of sentences containing the same word (e.g. *piano*) in different contexts. Some of the sentences stressed one feature of the target word (e.g. *The man lifted the piano*) and some another (e.g. *The man tuned the piano*). After studying the sentences, participants were asked to recall them, and were given cue words to help recall. Sentence recall was significantly better when cues were related to the situation-specific concept of the target word (e.g. *heavy*, for the first example) than when they were related to the target word but not to the situation (e.g. *has a nice sound*, for the first example).

Barsalou and colleagues' proposal offers a very general explanation for the sort of phenomena we are describing. However, the situated cognition model needs some modifications if it is to be used to explain our examples of incompatible representations. Whereas the features of the piano evoked in different contexts in Barclay *et al.*'s experiment are not contradictory (it is easy to state that a piano is both heavy and sounds nice in the same sentence), the features of the cases we describe above are always so (it is harder to state that sexual intercourse does and does not play a role in procreation at the same time). In other words, while it is true that a certain situation may cause participants to be more attentive to certain features at the expense of others, in the examples we outlined above situations seem to cause participants to attribute to concepts certain features in one situation and their opposites in another. By analogy, we should be able to devise a situation in which people readily attributed the feature of lightness to a piano – that, however, does not seem plausible.

This issue should not induce us to believe that incompatible representation is not explainable within the framework of situated cognition. It is possible that the set of incompatible representations we looked at form a subset of all instances of situated cognition, characterized by this peculiar context-dependent denial or affirmation of features. We give two arguments to support this suggestion, one psychological and proximate, the other anthropological and ultimate.

First, current psychological models of semantic memory can provide a simple implementation of the process of incompatible representation. Network theories of semantic memory suggest that incompatible representations may not require special- ized psychological machinery. Memorized concepts are generally believed to be roughly instantiated in network form, with a central node and several associated properties instantiated as links to other nodes. Each of the links that connects central and peripheral nodes is weighted: that is, it is more or less strongly associated with the concept. The number and weight of links attached to each concept vary according to social, cultural, and individual factors. Some concepts are linked to a number of attributes in complex ways: different contexts may cause the weights to alter so that some properties become more strongly activated and others less so. If we think of concepts as network representations with a weighted set of properties, it becomes possible to sketch a basic psychological model of how incompatible representations may be processed in the brain. The properties of concepts with incompatible repre- sentations could be grouped into two (or more) mutually exclusive subsets. When a certain context causes a significant number of the members of the first subset to fire, members of the other subset stop firing and become inhibited, and vice versa. The difference between incompatible and normal representation could, therefore, be merely quantitative.

But this account of process is insufficient; we also need to ask why incompatible representations should exist at all, where ordinary cognitive tasks can be tackled with little effort by the situated cognition model. Maurice Bloch (1989a; 1989b) has suggested that anthropologists' fascination with rituals and the ritual context has often obscured their understanding of other, more mundane ways of conceptualizing the world that take place outside of that context and in many ways contradict it. Non-ritual ways of thinking about the world are based in humans' (evolved) cognitive capacities interact- ing with, and developing in, a varied social and ecological environment. Yet anthro- pologists have been singularly reluctant to talk about non-ritual cognition, perhaps because it is less obviously variable across cultures (and thus less 'visible'), or perhaps because of a vested disciplinary interest in emphasizing difference. Bloch (1989b) has suggested that several anthropological claims about ways of experiencing and under- standing the world presented as being peculiar to certain societies (such as the non- durational concept of time that Geertz ascribes to the Balinese) are indeed incomplete. What they show is not the existence of radically different ways of conceptualizing the world, but rather the fact that people in different cultures will use in the ritual context versions of some everyday concepts, ideas, and so on, that are incompatible with their everyday use. In another paper, Bloch (1989a) has also proposed that the products of cognition in the ritual context be termed 'ideology'. Cognition in the ritual context is only explainable with reference to the process of political domination. The practice of ritual creates images of society that contradict everyday understandings of it; these images are endorsed by those who hold the power, and serve both to legitimate power and to 'mystify, invert and hide the real conditions of existence' (Bloch 1989a: 130).

The everyday/ritual distinction seems to provide a *prima facie* explanation for most of the cases of incompatible representation we outlined above. It is also psychologically plausible, in that it underscores the role of cognitive effort in dealing with certain concepts or, more accurately, with certain ways of representing concepts. Cognition in the ritual context seems to be more expensive – affording fewer and shallower infer- ences, and so on. This is not surprising; after all, Bloch's argument is an evolutionary one, suggesting that the mechanisms used in non-ritual contexts are better suited for the majority of mental activity, which happens to take place in the everyday, non-ritual context.

However, it appears that not all cases of incompatible representation can be mapped on an everyday/ritual context shift. Take, for example, the shift between independent and interdependent views of the self that Gardner *et al.* (1999) demonstrated. This phenomenon does not appear to be dependent on ideology and the ritual context. Both views of the self are equally ontologically plausible and philosophically defensible; both are emphasized in US culture. This suggests two alternative interpretations. On the one hand, it may be that what we are calling incompatible representations are a psychologically unitary phenomenon, which in some (or even in most) cases can be explained in terms of Bloch's theory. Cases such as the representations of the self could simply be less typical exemplars. On the other hand, it may be that incompatible representations are only superficially similar phenomena with different psychological underpinnings. From the few instances of context-dependent incompatible representations that have been described by anthropologists and psychologists, it is difficult to choose between these two alternatives.

Conclusions

In the course of this chapter, we have noted several problems with ascription as it has been practised in anthropology. We would like to emphasize once again that ascription is a given of anthropological writing, in many ways unavoidable, and in a large number of cases even beneficial to understanding. Collective ascription that is justified and well supported is an excellent way to present data in a compact and easily interpretable way. Therefore, we have chosen to focus on cases where the common language of ascription is an inappropriate way of presenting evidence. Some of these cases have been successfully addressed by anthropologists. With the knowledge we now have about how ideas, beliefs, skills, expertise, and so forth, are unevenly distributed within social groups, careless claims – common only a few decades ago – that the *x* do or believe *y* (Jones 2005) have become harder to defend, and fallen out of favour among anthropologists (although they remain popular in everyday language). But the ascription of cognitive properties without sufficient justification is still practised in anthropology. The discipline's ambitious (though not universally shared) aim to be a science of humankind means that practitioners of other, more strictly bounded and epistemologically uniform disciplines will often take issue with the methodology, theoretical orientation, or form of evidence presentation of anthropologists – this much is unavoidable, and should not necessarily discourage anthropologists from attempting to answer big questions. Yet to make strong claims about cognition without engaging with psychologists and other cognitive scientists is not defensible, and ultimately counterproductive, as parts of anthropology become liable to be taken over by related fields.

A different problem arises from our description of recent findings that suggest that concepts may be deployed in context-specific, incompatible forms. This is a more difficult issue, since there is no consensus in psychology and allied disciplines as to the cognitive underpinnings of these phenomena. Until a mapping of their domain and explanation of their psychological nature are available, anthropologists would be well advised to consider contextual effects on representation, and to temper strong ascriptions of belief in the light of the cross-cultural evidence reviewed here.

NOTES

We thank Maurice Bloch, Matthew Engelke, Jonathan Parry, Charles Stafford, and the participants of the 'Objects of evidence' workshop at the London School of Economics and Political Science for helpful comments.

[1] Just how much of the time one needs to be wearing a hat to have that property ascribed depends on one's assumptions and objectives. For example, imagine we want to contrast the behaviour of an individual – call him Paul – with some people who never wear hats. If we want to ascribe to Paul the behavioural property of hat-wearing, we might be satisfied if he wears a hat only infrequently. In contrast, if our aim is to compare Paul to a group of people who often wear hats, the proportion of time when Paul wears a hat needs to be significantly higher if the ascription is to be more than trivial. This, of course, is also true if we substitute groups for individuals.

[2] Comprehensive descriptions of the psychological characteristics of this and other biases are available in many textbooks and collections, including those edited by Gilovich, Griffin & Kahneman (2002) and Kahneman & Tversky (2000).

[3] Not all mental activity is inaccessible to the same degree. For example, it is argued that physiological markers of some emotions, such as fear or embarrassment, can be directly measured without necessarily having to look at measures of mental activity. Similarly, behavioural economists are able to elicit preferences by having people make choices in experimental situations, rather than stating their preferences outright. The advantage of these techniques is that they allow the investigator to circumvent problems inherent in self-report described by Nisbett & Wilson (1977).

[4] In the previous section, we encountered cases where the property shows variability, and where this variability can be shown to map onto social sub-groupings. Now we are going to deal with cases where the property is supposed not to show variability, and therefore to be equally distributed among social sub-groupings. There is, of course, another possibility: that the property shows variability, and that the variability does not map onto social sub-groupings. An example of such a property is blood type; properties of this kind are not interesting to anthropologists, because their presence and distribution in a population are not attributable to socio-cultural processes.

[5] Sperber further suggests that many apparently irrational beliefs – which can take the form of statements such as 'God is everywhere' – do not refer to single, well-understood propositions. He uses the term *semi-propositional* to refer to those representations that can be plausibly interpreted in different ways within or across individuals.

[6] Here we deal with the simplest case, in which two representations are clearly dissociable. However, we cannot exclude that in some instances, even including several of the cases we describe, further representations may exist.

[7] It could be argued that the examples we review can be explained in terms of Sperber's theory, outlined in the previous subsection. That is, the Bororo could have a dual incompatible representation of the self – one as humans, the other as red macaws. While this is indeed possible – and even likely – we treat the cases we look at in this section separately, because they do not all focus on claims of irrationality.

[8] Helpful evidence would include a simple experiment that required people to reason about human procreation in unfamiliar contexts. Several of the following illustrations rely on such experiments to argue for the existence of incompatible representations.

REFERENCES

ASHLEY-MONTAGU, M.F. 1937. Physiological paternity in Australia. *American Anthropologist* **39**, 175-83.

ASTUTI, R., G.E.A. SOLOMON & S. CAREY 2004. *Constraints on conceptual development: a case study of the acquisition of folkbiological and folksociological knowledge in Madagascar.* (Monographs of the Society for Research in Child Development 277: **69/3**). Oxford: Blackwell.

BARCLAY, J.R., J.D. BRANSFORD, J.J. FRANKS, N.S. MCCARRELL & K. NITSCH 1974. Comprehension and semantic flexibility. *Journal of Verbal Learning and Behavior* **13**, 471-81.

BARRETT, J.L. & F.C. KEIL 1996. Conceptualizing a non-natural entity: anthropomorphism in God concepts. *Cognitive Psychology* **31**, 219-47.

BARSALOU, L.W. 1982. Context-independent and context-dependent information in concepts. *Memory and Cognition* **10**, 82-93.

———— 2002. Being there conceptually: simulating categories in preparation for situated action. In *Representation, memory, and development: essays in honor of Jean Mandler* (eds) N.L. Stein, P.J. Bauer & M. Rabinowitz, 1-16. Mahwah, NJ: Erlbaum.

————, W. YEH, B.J. LUKA, K.L. OLSETH, K.S. MIX & L.-L. WU 1993. Concepts and meaning. In *Chicago Linguistics Society 29: papers from the parasession on conceptual representations* (eds) K. Beals, G. Cooke, D. Kathman, K.E. McCullough, S. Kita & D. Testen, 23-61. Chicago: University Press.

BENEDICT, R. 1989 [1934]. *Patterns of culture*. Boston: Houghton Mifflin.

BERNARD, H.R., P.J. PELTO, O. WERNER, J. BOSTER, A.K. ROMNEY, A. JOHNSON, C.R. EMBER & A. KASAKOFF 1986. The construction of primary data in cultural anthropology. *Current Anthropology* **4**, 382-96.

BLOCH, M. 1989a. From cognition to ideology. In *Ritual, history, and power: selected papers in anthropology*, M. Bloch, 106-36. London: Athlone Press.

———— 1989b. The past and the present in the present. In *Ritual, history, and power: selected papers in anthropology*, M. Bloch, 1-18. London: Athlone Press.

————, G.E.A. SOLOMON & S. CAREY 2001. Zafimaniry: an understanding of what is passed on from parents to children: a cross cultural investigation. *Journal of Cognition and Culture* **1**, 43-68.

BOSTER, J.S. 1986. Exchange of varieties and information between Aguaruna manioc cultivators. *American Anthropologist* **88**, 428-36.

CARRITHERS, M. 1992. *Why humans have cultures: explaining anthropology and social diversity*. Oxford: University Press.

CRAPANZANO, V. 1980. *Tuhami: portrait of a Moroccan*. Chicago: University Press.

DARLEY, J.M. & C.D. BATSON 1973. 'From Jerusalem to Jericho': a study of situational and dispositional variables in helping behavior. *Journal of Personality and Social Psychology* **27**, 100-8.

FRAZER, J.G. 1976 [1890]. *The golden bough*. London: Macmillan.

GARDNER, W.L., S. GABRIEL & A.Y. LEE 1999. 'I' value freedom, but 'we' value relationships: self-construal priming mirrors cultural differences in judgment. *Psychological Science* **10**, 321-6.

GARRO, L.C. 1986. Intracultural variation in folk medical knowledge: a comparison between curers and noncurers. *American Anthropologist* **88**, 351-70.

GILOVICH, T., D. GRIFFIN & D. KAHNEMAN (eds) 2002. *Heuristics and biases: the psychology of intuitive judgment*. Cambridge: University Press.

HARRIS, P. 1992. From simulation to folk psychology: the case for development. *Mind and Language* **7**, 120-44.

HÉNAFF, M. 1998. *Claude Lévi-Strauss and the making of structural anthropology* (trans. M. Baker). Minneapolis: University of Minnesota Press.

HIRSCHFELD, L.A. 2002. Why don't anthropologists like children? *American Anthropologist* **104**, 611-27.

———— & S.A. GELMAN (eds) 1994. *Mapping the mind: domain specificity in cognition and culture*. Cambridge: University Press.

HOLLIS, M. & S. LUKES (eds) 1982. *Rationality and relativism*. Oxford: Blackwell.

JONES, T.E. 2000. Ethnography, belief ascription, and epistemological barriers. *Human Relations* **53**, 117-52.

———— 2005. How many New Yorkers need to like bagels before you can say 'New Yorkers like bagels?' Understanding collective ascription. *The Philosophical Forum* **36**, 279-306.

KAHNEMAN, D. & A. TVERSKY (eds) 2000. *Choices, values, and frames*. Cambridge: University Press.

KARIM, W.-J.B. 1981. *Ma' Betisék concepts of living things*. London: Athlone Press.

KNIGHT, N. & R.E. NISBETT 2007. Culture, class and cognition: evidence from Italy. *Journal of Cognition and Culture* **7**, 283-91.

LEACH, E.R. 1961. Golden bough or gilded twig? *Dædalus*, Spring, 371-87.

———— 1966. Virgin birth. *Proceedings of the Royal Anthropological Institute*, 39-49.

LÉVY-BRUHL, L. 1910. Les fonctions mentales dans les sociétés inférieures (available on-line: *http://www.uqac.ca/class/classiques/levy_bruhl/fonctions_mentales/fonctions_mentales.html*, accessed 5 January 2008).

LIENHARDT, R.G. 1961. *Divinity and experience: the religion of the Dinka*. Oxford: Clarendon Press.

MALLEY, B.E. & N. KNIGHT 2008. Some cognitive origins of cultural order. *Journal of Cognition and Culture* **8/1-2**, 49-69.

MARKUS, H.R. & S. KITAYAMA 1991. Culture and the self: implications for cognition, emotion, and motivation. *Psychological Review* **98**, 224-53.

MEGGITT, M.J. 1962. *Desert people*. Sydney: Angus & Robertson.

NICHOLS, S. & S. STICH 2003. *Mindreading: an integrated account of pretence, self-awareness, and understanding other minds*. Oxford: University Press.

NISBETT, R.E. 2003. *The geography of thought: how Asians and Westerners think differently ... and why*. New York: Free Press.

————, K. PENG, I. CHOI & A. NORENZAYAN 2001. Culture and systems of thought: holistic versus analytic cognition. *Psychological Review* **108**, 291-310.

————— & T.D. WILSON 1977. Telling more than we can know: verbal reports on mental processes. *Psychological Review* **83**, 231-59.

PELTO, P.J. & G.H. PELTO 1975. Intra-cultural diversity: some theoretical issues. *American Ethnologist* **2**, 1-18.

PERNER, J. 1993. *Understanding the representational mind*. Cambridge, Mass.: MIT Press.

PRICE, R. 1998. *The convict and the colonel: a story of colonialism and resistance in the Caribbean*. Boston: Beacon Press.

RODSETH, L. 1998. Distributive models of culture: a Sapirian alternative to essentialism. *American Anthropologist* **100**, 55-69.

ROSS, L. & R.E. NISBETT 1991. Introduction. In *The person and the situation: perspectives of social psychology*. Philadelphia: Temple University Press.

SPERBER, D. 1982. Apparently irrational beliefs. In *Rationality and relativism* (eds) M. Hollis & S. Lukes, 149-80. Oxford: Basil Blackwell.

SPIRO, M.E. 1968. Virgin birth, parthenogenesis and physiological paternity: an essay in cultural interpretation. *Man* (N.S.) **3**, 242-61.

THOMPSON, R.W. 1975. Gratification patterns in Buganda: an exploration of intra-cultural diversity. *American Ethnologist* **2**, 193-206.

TOMASELLO, M., M. CARPENTER, J. CALL, T. BEHNE & H. MOLL 2005. Understanding and sharing intentions: the origins of cultural cognition. *Behavioral and Brain Sciences* **28**, 675-735.

TOREN, C. 1993. Making history: the significance of childhood cognition for a comparative anthropology of mind. *Man* (N.S.) **28**, 461-78.

VAYDA, A.P. 1994. Actions, variations, and change: the emerging anti-essentialist view in anthropology. In *Assessing cultural anthropology* (ed.) R. Borofsky, 320-30. New York: McGraw-Hill.

VON DEN STEINEN, K. 1894. *Unter den Naturvölkern Zentralbrasiliens*. Berlin: Dietrich Reimer Verlag.

WELLMAN, H.M. 1990. *The child's theory of mind*. Cambridge, Mass.: MIT Press.

—————, D. CROSS & J. WATSON 2001. Meta-analysis of theory-of-mind development: the truth about false belief. *Child Development* **62**, 655-84.

WILSON, B.R. (ed.) 1970. *Rationality*. New York: Harper & Row.

WRIGHT, A.L., M. BAUER, C. CLARK, F. MORGAN & K. BEGISHE 1993. Cultural interpretations and intracultural variability in Navajo beliefs about breastfeeding. *American Ethnologist* **20**, 781-96.

YEH, W. & L.W. BARSALOU 2006. The situated nature of concepts. *American Journal of Psychology* **119**, 349-84.

Index

38930589R00097

Made in the USA
Lexington, KY
01 February 2015